D1256541

THE CATHOLIC CHURCH
IN AUSTRALIA

THE CATHOLIC CHURCH
IN AUSTRALIA

A Short History: 1788-1967

PATRICK O'FARRELL, M.A., Ph.D.

GEOFFREY CHAPMAN
LONDON DUBLIN MELBOURNE 1969

GEOFFREY CHAPMAN LTD
18 High Street, Wimbledon, London SW 19

GEOFFREY CHAPMAN (IRELAND) LTD
5—7 Main Street, Blackrock, County Dublin

GEOFFREY CHAPMAN PTY LTD
44 Latrobe Street, Melbourne, Vic 3000, Australia

First published, Nelsons Australian Paperbacks, 1968
© Copyright, 1968, Thomas Nelson (Australia) Ltd
Library edition, first published by Geoffrey Chapman, 1969

Printed in Great Britain
by Compton Printing Ltd.,
London & Aylesbury

Acknowledgements

We should like to thank the following for giving permission
for the use of material:

The *Daily Telegraph,* Sydney, for the cartoon 'The Bargain-
ers'; the *Sydney Morning Herald* for the photograph of
Cardinal Gilroy; the archives of St Mary's Cathedral,
Sydney, and the Good Samaritan archives, St Scholastica's,
Glebe Point, for other illustrations.

Contents

Illustrations

Preface

The aim of this book is to provide, in reasonably brief form, a historical survey of the Catholic church in Australia from its beginnings to the present. Such a survey demands a selective emphasis. Here, it is on the attempt to distil and delineate the essence of the major phases of the church's history, and to give something of their distinctive flavour. Stress has been placed not on the mere accumulation of facts, but on the attempt to discover and discuss their meaning and significance. Inevitably, the demands of brevity and of the need to give some detailed attention to the most important issues have meant that much that is interesting and worthwhile has had to be sacrificed. Those interested mainly in church architecture, art or liturgy—to mention a few of the lacunae—will find, I regret, small sustenance in what is primarily a history of the character and policies of the church. Similarly, attention has been concentrated on the prominent persons, and on the places where major developments occurred. It has not been possible to deal with the many fascinating persons and developments of more local importance.

The education question is one of the main themes in this book. However, on this subject I refer the reader in search of greater detail to the comprehensive work of Brother Ronald Fogarty, particularly in regard to the many religious orders whose histories are part of the history of Catholic education. I cannot offer any similar source which might remedy the deficiencies of my treatment of the laity, both *en masse* and of individual laymen. It could be argued, I believe, that the balance of my consideration of the laity reflects, to some extent and in some vital ways, the actual importance of their role in the church during much of its history; and one could also remark on the relative paucity of sources, as the ordinary people were the least of all accustomed to writing things down, to leaving records of what they thought and felt. But at a time when the laity are becoming rapidly more conscious of an expanding role, such suggestions may appear as excuses. It would be more to the point to make clear that a detailed analysis of the history of the laity is one of the many things that are inadequately pursued in this book. I hope that others will not only correct the faults that appear here, but remedy my deficiencies and fill the many gaps that have been left.

The particular approach followed in this book, and its considerable use of direct quotation from the participants in the story, derive, to some extent, from the way the book came about. For the last several years I have been collecting material for two related studies, on revolutionary nationalism in Ireland in the nineteenth and twentieth centuries, and on Irish nationalism in Australia, 1915-25. The search for sources in Australia, Ireland and Rome, on subjects strongly politico-religious, took me into a variety of archives, many of them ecclesiastical. In these ecclesiastical archives, I was constantly confronted by material which threw new light on the history of the Catholic church in Australia, as well as that relating directly to my main purpose. Such was the obvious Australian historical value of this illuminating and hitherto unpublished material in Ireland and Rome, that its collection became an adjunct to and a by-product of my major research projects. The collection of these particular documents interacted with previous research work on this subject, and a long-standing interest, to produce the decision to write this book.

It follows that what is presented here is set in the general context of my continuing research projects in Irish and Irish-Australian history. I would like to hope that this book has benefited from the wider context of those studies, particularly when they come into close relationship and impinge on each other, as in the background and setting of the chapter entitled 'Dr Mannix 1911-1925'. For this reason it is appropriate to acknowledge my indebtedness, in this broader context, to the University of New South Wales and to University College, Dublin, whose assistance made possible my research work in Ireland and Rome; also to acknowledge the support of the Australian Research Grants Committee towards the collection of material relevant to my studies in revolution in Ireland, and Irish nationalism in Australia.

Specifically, in direct relation to the subject, my debts are numerous and large. Particularly are they great to His

Eminence Cardinal Gilroy, whose generous co-operation and assistance did not stop with ready permission to consult the archives of St Mary's Cathedral, but extended, through his wide contacts, to substantially facilitating my work in Rome and Ireland. My debt to Right Reverend Monsignor C. J. Duffy, Sydney Archdiocesan Archivist and President of the Australian Catholic Historical Society, is also very great. His extensive knowledge of Catholic history and of St Mary's archives was always at my disposal, and in practical terms my research work has been greatly assisted by his kindness. I am also happily obliged to Reverend Dr C. Tierney, Librarian of St Patrick's College, Manly, for his substantial practical help.

The obligations I incurred in Ireland and Rome are similarly considerable and extensive, too numerous to detail in full. However, I cannot neglect to acknowledge, specifically, the hospitality and generous help I received from Cardinal Conway, Archbishop of Armagh; Very Reverend Monsignor D. Conway, Rector of the Irish College in Rome; Very Reverend Father T. Fagan and Father K. Condon of All Hallows College, Dublin; His Grace Archbishop McQuaid and Very Reverend Dr G. Sheehy of Dublin; Most Reverend H. Murphy and Father P. J. O'Callaghan of Limerick; and Very Reverend Professor Patrick J. Corish, President of St Patrick's College, Maynooth. I am also generally indebted to members of the History Department of University College, Dublin.

Of course, none of the churchmen from whom I have received help are necessarily in agreement with the views presented in this history: the responsibility for these is my own.

Several people have read some or all of the drafts for this book. Again, I am obliged to Monsignor Duffy, who added to his practical assistance his knowledge and keen perceptive judgement of religious history. Mr A. E. Cahill, of the History Department of the University of Sydney, has given me the benefit of his deep erudition in this field, his wide knowledge of the sources, and a profound historical understanding. My brother, of Blackfriars Priory, Canberra, made valuable comments on the work as it progressed.

Needless to say, I have been greatly assisted by their

corrections of fact, and by their informed advice, but what remains, by way of sins of omission and commission, remains my own. Or rather perhaps, to some extent, mine and my wife's: some of what appears hereafter is the direct outcome of our long discussions about the meaning and significance of what happened, and why.

There are two points of acknowledgement of a bibliographical kind. A substantial section of Chapter 5 is based on an address 'Dr Mannix and Conscription', which I gave under the auspices of the Mannix Centre at Ballarat on 5 May 1967. Some sections towards the end of the last chapter are closely related to my article 'The Church in Australia', which appeared in the *Dublin Review,* Summer 1966.

One final acknowledgement remains to be made—to the subject itself and to those who have peopled it. Even among those who would reject the divine origin and supernatural character of the Catholic church, it is hard to believe that many would not be moved, humbled even, in simple human terms, by the procession that herein passes the eye. To make a judgement of that procession—perhaps one of the greater feats of modern Catholicism (contrast it with the decline of the church in nineteenth century Europe)—may seem, to some few of traditionally pious mind, to savour of presumption. But the fact is that precisely this task of judging and interpreting, has been enjoined upon historians as a duty, 'the condition and source of any real success, of any solid progress in Catholic science', by the papacy itself, notably Pius XII, and by the Decrees of the Second Vatican Council. It was Pius XII's hope, as expressed to the Tenth International Congress of Historical Sciences, that historians would 'make past history a lesson for the present and the future'. Nothing of historical worth is to be learnt from sanctimonious self-praise, pious inventions, edifying fables or comfortable forgetfulness—or from blind partisanship. I hope that none of these faults, whatever others, have crept in here.

PATRICK O'FARRELL

School of History
University of New South Wales
May 1968

1

Foundations 1788-1835

William Ullathorne came to Australia as its first Catholic Vicar-General in 1833. He summed up that penal colony as he found it. 'We have taken a vast portion of God's earth and made it a cesspool, . . . we have poured down scum upon scum and dregs upon dregs of the offscourings of mankind and we are building up with them a nation . . . to be . . . a curse and a plague.' Australian Catholicism was born in this prison. Its inheritance is expressed neatly in the circumstances of the first recorded Mass, which was celebrated for a congregation of prisoners in Sydney in May 1803, under strict regulations drafted by Governor King, and with police surveillance, by an Irish convict priest, transported— by mistake, it seems—for alleged complicity in the 1798 Irish rebellion. The Governor's regulations stressed that the Catholics, so favoured by this 'extension of liberal toleration', must show 'becoming gratitude'; that assembly for Mass must never be the occasion of 'seditious conversation'; that the priest, Reverend Mr Dixon, was fully responsible for his congregation and must exert himself to detect and report any sign of disturbance or disaffection. This toleration of Catholic worship had come fifteen years after the colony's foundation. It was withdrawn in a year, and, although Father Dixon, and after him Father Harold, exercised their ministry in a private capacity, it was another sixteen years, not until 1820, that Mass could be celebrated publicly again.

In the British Isles, penal laws, originating in the Reformation, still oppressed Catholics and their religion. Emancipation did not begin until 1829. In Europe, Catholicism—the very papacy itself—was reeling under the blows of the French Revolution and its Napoleonic aftermath. At the beginning of the nineteenth century, Catholicism was everywhere at a disadvantage, fighting for its life. But only in New South Wales and Van Diemen's Land did Catholicism

1

exist, almost entirely, as a religion of men degraded, deserted
and physically imprisoned—criminals to the world.

Who were Australia's first Catholics? Convicts, almost
exclusively Irish. Of all convicts transported to Australia (up
to 1868), about a quarter, 30,000 men and 9,000 women,
came directly from Ireland. Of these, a large group were not
ordinary criminals. Even in their felony, the Irish tended to
stand apart. Whereas the English and the Scots were mostly
thieves, nearly a third of the 2,086 offenders transported
from Ireland between 1791 and 1803 had been convicted
for riot and sedition. That is, among the Irish convicts there
was a large number whose personal characters were often
the reverse of evil, men of dedication, principle, spirit and
integrity whose crime was some form of rebellion against
British rule. The interpretation of the early history of
Catholicism in Australia has been deeply coloured by the
popular conception of unfortunate convicts, manly and independent victims of injustice and persecution, more sinned
against than sinning. If, as Archbishop Kelly claimed in
1922, echoing Dr Eris O'Brien, 'the large majority were
merely political offenders, and in their personal character,
high-minded, industrious and progressive', and that 'These
were the men who formed the nucleus of the Catholic
Church in Australia in the early days', then the foundations
of Australian Catholicism were indeed well laid, and on firm
ground.

In statistical fact, this rosy picture is only a section—albeit
an important one—of a much grimmer, more repulsive
canvas; it was criminals 'proper', thieves and men of violence
and cunning, who made up the great majority of Irish trans-
portees. Only about one-fifth of all Irish convicts can be
described as nationalists, or social rebels, victims of political
oppression. Descendants are prone to believe, in gratitude
if not in complacency, that their forefathers must have built
well, without major fault or shortcoming. In truth, those
founders, like all men, established imperfectly, or worse.
Australia, as a whole, has little reason to be proud of her
origins as a prison, an outpost of exported crime. And
Australian Catholicism shared those origins in considerable
part, but it had less taint in that more of the adherents of
that religion, earlier one-third and overall one-fifth, were

not common criminals. And it had more hope. Bishop Polding saw in Australia a unique mission; the sufferings of the convicts would open their hearts to Divine Grace.

Irish and Catholic were virtually synonymous. Whereas the English and Scots convicts were nearly all Protestants, the Irish were nearly all Catholics. Most of the Irish were peasants, most of the English came from towns. Many of the Irish did not speak English, but Gaelic. The Irish were a minority. Every circumstance, save their common servitude, conspired to mark Catholics off, as a group, from the rest of Australia's convict population.

The deepest chasm that existed within penal Australia was more specific than that between gaoler and prisoner; it was the bitter gulf between those who held power and authority, and Irish Catholic convicts. To the Protestant ascendancy of penal Australia—comprising the governors, the officers, the administrators, the leading churchmen and citizens—there were two essential conditions of civilisation: the Protestant religion and British political and social institutions. On both of these counts the Irish were barbarians. Irish history offered the British ample evidence of this. Since the sixteenth century, Ireland had offered constant resistance to British rule, resistance met with repression. From the misery and ignorance of eighteenth century Ireland, burdened with penal laws, sprang brutality, drunkenness, irresponsibility, malevolence—and, in 1798, a bloody rebellion. The righteous English Protestant regarded the Irish with dark suspicion and short contempt. And fear. English rule in Ireland bred rebellions, and enshrined the power of the priesthood as leaders of discontent. Popery and priestcraft, expressed in resistance to English rule, were seen as a sinister menace to that higher order of civilisation which the English so passionately believed they represented. As in Ireland, so in Australia: there, planted with the colony itself, grew an exacerbated form of the Irish social relationship of prejudice, fear and hatred. This obsessive antagonism between English Protestant ascendancy and Irish convict Catholicism, established with the foundation of Australia, has been a central and persistent theme in the history of Catholicism's relations with its Australian environment. Its influence has been tragically corrosive.

The early years of the colony were haunted by the fear of Irish Catholic sedition. Gaolers commonly lived in fear of their prisoners, and, particularly after the 1798 rebellion, Australia's rulers were ridden by the nagging anxiety that they might be engulfed by an Irish Catholic eruption, and the land laid waste by the poverty, ignorance, superstition and tyranny which Catholicism represented. At the end of 1800, unnerved by rumours of impending rebellion by Irish convicts, Governor King issued orders for handling any such emergency. By May 1802, as Irish political prisoners continued to arrive in the wake of the 1798 rebellion, Governor Hunter was praying the home government to send no more Irishmen, and in any case 'as few as possible of those convicted of sedition and republican practices, otherwise in a very short time the whole colony would be imbued with the same seditious spirit.' His fears were confirmed in March 1804 when William Johnston, an Irishman transported for his part in the 1798 rebellion, assembled over three hundred men at Castle Hill, intent on armed rebellion to take vengeance on their English gaolers. The rebellion was quickly and bloodily repressed, the affair ending in executions, floggings and sentences to Norfolk Island. King was convinced, as was the whole panic-stricken Protestant establishment, that Father Dixon had been in some way implicated, and that, obscurely, the rebellion was the outcome of Catholic teachings. Dixon's privileges of public ministry were withdrawn.

Dixon was one of three Irish priests transported for alleged complicity in the 1798 rebellion. First to arrive was James Harold in January 1800, but he was soon sent to Norfolk Island on suspicion of being engaged in seditious activity. Later he was transferred to Tasmania, and returned to Ireland in 1810. Dixon also arrived in January 1800. Governor King judged him, in May 1803, sufficiently quiet—and stupid—to be allowed, under strict regulation, to minister to Catholics. News of this reached Rome where Dixon was constituted by the Holy See, Prefect Apostolic of New Holland. But the Castle Hill rebellion killed Dixon's ministry. He returned to Ireland in 1808. Father Harold replaced him briefly in Sydney until 1810, but when he left the settlement was without any priest for eight years. The other convict priest was Peter O'Neil who arrived in 1801, returning to Ireland after being pardoned in 1803.

Except for Father Dixon's brief ministry, none of these priests was allowed to act as such. They were convicts and their religion was not recognised. Catholics were forced to attend Protestant services, a compulsion that lingered in Van Diemen's Land into the 1840s. This compulsion, accepted passively by some Catholics and bitterly resented by others, was not so much exerted in any spirit of encouragement of true belief, but rather, flowing as it did from civil authority, was directed towards social order. The colonial rulers' attitude towards religion was determined by their estimate of its social utility. Claims based on rights of conscience met deaf ears: such a petition from five free and emancipist Catholics was presented to Governor Phillip in 1792. In 1796, when there were about 800 Catholics in New South Wales, another petition was couched in language readily understandable to the administration; the petitioners' main argument was that the appointment of Catholic priests would result in an improvement in convict conduct. Thereafter this very practical argument kept recurring in Catholic claims, and it seems to have influenced King in his decision to allow Dixon to minister in 1803. Essentially, the matter of some toleration for Catholics was seen as a practical political question. Would their own priests and religious practices encourage tranquillity among Irish convicts? Or would priests foment rebellion, and the Catholic religion divide and eventually disintegrate the infant colony?

The Reverend Samuel Marsden, Anglican chaplain in New South Wales, concerned himself with this question in 1806-7. He identified Catholicism with rebellion. As an obsession which prevailed in some Protestant quarters into the twentieth century, this merits some investigation. Marsden believed that the 1804 rebellion had shown that toleration of the Catholic Mass had proved nearly fatal to the colony. He predicted: 'It is more than probable that if the Catholic Religion was once allowed to be celebrated by Authority, that the colony would be lost to the British Empire in less than one year.' His supporting argument ran thus. The number of Catholic convicts was very great; most of them were Irish of the lowest class, 'wild, ignorant and savage . . .

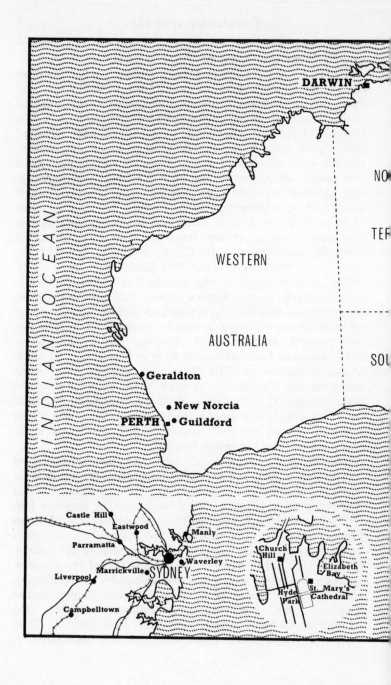

men that have been familiar with Robberies, Murders and every Horrid Crime from their infancy.' To Marsden, they seemed 'destitute of every Principle of Religion & Morality . . . governed entirely by the impulse of Passion, and always alive to Rebellion.' Were the Mass allowed, it would become the occasion of seditious assemblies which would issue in assassination, arson and destruction, and the overthrow of the government; for not only was there the 'natural ferocity' of the Catholic Irish, but they would infect other convicts with their turbulence, and that horror of the colony's rulers, a mass convict mutiny, would surely occur. Marsden's remedy was simple: continue the monopoly of Protestantism, particularly in the education of children, and in a few years there would be no Catholics. He stressed the practical benefits of this. A single religion would stabilise the state and eliminate internal divisions, and it would lessen public expense because it would make the Irish contented and productive, instead of factious and truculent. It is significant that Marsden did not refer to the question of religious truth, as such. He had no need to—his readers shared his assumption that popery was spurious.

> On the other hand if the Catholic Religion is in the least tolerated, the Influence of the Priests [on] the depraved turbulent dispositions of the Catholics who are in this Colony together with their extreme Superstition will keep the Settlement in perpetual Alarm, prevent all Reformation, check the operations of Agriculture, and endanger his Majesty's Government.

Viewpoints akin to Marsden's were dominant into the 1820s and continued to be influential. So prevalent were they, that they dictated the terms of the Catholic argument for toleration. Catholics were forced to plead for recognition not on religious principles, but on liberal principles and the crudest practical grounds. In asserting the rights of religious conscience in 1825, Father Therry, then Catholic chaplain, called on the Governor as 'a friend to religious and civil liberty, inimical to tyranny, oppression', and claimed that freedom of religious belief and practice furthered public order and induced submissiveness. Catholics were forced to occupy the peculiar position of claiming a social liberty on the understanding that they would use it for merely personal

purposes. They undertook, implicitly and perhaps uncon-
sciously, to conform their religion as a social force to the
Anglican concept of subsidiarity to the state. Catholicism
was slowly recognised, but toleration was extended not to the
principles of religion, or to conscientious difference, but, as
a political device, to the practice of religion. In this lay the
seeds of future conflict, for Catholicism refused to play the
role the state had laid down for it.

How true was Marsden's picture of the Catholics? It was
not without its unfortunate realities, though Governor
Brisbane exaggerated when he recorded in the early 1820s:

> . . . every Murder or diabolical Crime, which has been com-
> mitted in the Colony since my arrival has been perpetrated by
> Roman Catholics. And this I ascribe entirely to their bar-
> barous ignorance and total want of education, the invariable
> companions of bigotry and cruelty, as well as the parent of
> crime . . . They are benighted and bereft of every advantage
> that can adorn the mind of Man . . .

Brisbane's was a terrible indictment—of British rule in
Ireland, and of the penal system; and he neglected to allow
for the remarkable number of convicts who embraced
Catholicism for the first time as they prepared for death.
Nevertheless, similar testimony came from the Irish themselves. John O'Sullivan, a free settler, wrote to the
Archbishop of Dublin in 1830: '. . . some of our unfortunate
and wretched countrymen are foremost in perpetrating the
shocking crimes that mark this colony . . . I did not think
the Irish character capable of performing the villainous
deeds that are daily blazoned forth.' Even at its best, the
Catholicism which had come with the Irish to Australia
was a Catholicism of poverty and the peasantry, violent,
crude and ignorant, with a priesthood largely sharing its
passions and prejudices. Its heart was bitter against the
English oppressor, its religious temper narrow, unlovely,
belligerent. These things Protestants saw, adding them to
their obsession that Catholicism was a gigantic conspiracy
to enslave men and destroy all that was free and good in
civilisation. They were blind to, or would not accept, the
qualities which contradicted their estimate—the intensity
and otherworldliness of Irish faith, its charm, nobility,

humanity and astonishing perseverance. And Irish Catholics, in their rejection of Protestant England, rejected too its cultivation of refinement, learning, urbanity, the arts and pleasures of a liberal civilisation—rejected, and at the same time coveted. If this was true of the better Catholics, what of the worse? The Australian prison was a Devil's Island, contaminating and warping all those who went there, gaolers and prisoners alike. No one could deny that the moral tone of the settlement was appallingly low; every kind of immorality thrived. And there was much truth in Marsden's observation that 'When men became Convicts, a difference of religious opinions is hardly discoverable amongst them.' Catholics were brutalised and depraved with the rest. They lived together unmarried, their children unbaptised, some because they would not submit to having religious services performed for them by Protestant clergymen, but others because they had abandoned not only their own faith, but all Christian belief and morality.

Although Australian society generally, and Australian Catholicism, were eventually to emerge from the horror of their origins, those origins left deep and disfiguring scars. What is most remarkable about Catholicism in the first thirty years of settlement is that, priestless and persecuted in the midst of corruption, it endured at all. That it did is partly attributable to the fact that the cause of Catholicism was entangled with the cause of Ireland. Practically, these causes became but two aspects of the one ancient grievance, a development fostered by the appointment of Protestant clerics as magistrates. Such clerics, invariably anti-Catholic, fixed punishments in accordance with England's laws. Where Catholicism faltered in the morass of convict depravity, stern Irishism came to its aid. But Irishism alone cannot explain why Catholicism survived. The roots of faith and hope went deep indeed, though charity had been shrivelled, in part, by hatred of the oppressor, the gaoler, the bigot.

How strong that faith, resilient that hope (and bitter that hatred) may be inferred, in retrospect, from the legends that accumulated around the next incident in Australian Catholic pre-history, the affair of the Reverend Jeremiah Francis O'Flynn.

One of those transported in connection with the 1798

Irish rebellion, and soon emancipated, was Michael Hayes. Hayes conducted a considerable correspondence with his brother Richard, a Franciscan in Rome, who, in 1816, took up with the Sacred Congregation of Propaganda the problem of the religious destitution of Australian Catholics, who by then had been six years without a priest. This long neglect reflects the grave weakness and disorganisation of Catholicism in Europe and the British Isles at the time. From 1809 to 1814 the Pope was Napoleon's prisoner in France, and the centre of Church authority was in disorder. As a British colony, Australia was the ecclesiastical responsibility of the Vicar-Apostolic of London, Dr Poynter; but the English Catholic church was a tiny minority fighting for toleration, without sufficient priests, and treading warily lest any sign of aggression—expansive missionary ambitions, for instance —should prejudice the chances of its securing emancipation. The Irish church, from which nearly all the Catholics in Australia had come, was enmeshed in problems arising out of the penal laws, the aftermath of the 1798 rebellion, the political union with Britain in 1800, and, especially, the prolonged Veto conflict. This conflict arose from British insistence that the English government should have control over the appointment of Irish bishops. In 1814 the papacy sided with England, but the Irish bishops refused to accept this and the question was not finally settled in Ireland's favour until 1829. Compared with these enormous local problems of survival and religious integrity, the condition of a few thousand Catholics at the other side of the world was a very minor matter.

At the time of Richard Hayes's approach to Propaganda in 1816, there was in Rome an Irish Cistercian priest, Jeremiah O'Flynn. After his ordination in 1813, O'Flynn had spent an energetic but flagrantly insubordinate three years in the French West Indian mission, years full of disputes with ecclesiastical authority. He had come to Rome to fight his case. In the English language, at least, he was only semi-literate; he was also deficient in theological knowledge. With that impulsiveness and effrontery which distinguished his whole career, O'Flynn volunteered for the Australian mission, was absolved from all censure, secularised, and appointed Prefect Apostolic of New Holland.

The circumstances are obscure, but it seems that Hayes arranged O'Flynn's appointment through an anti-English Cardinal as a manoeuvre against the English Vicar Apostolic, with whom he was in conflict over the Veto question. Certainly O'Flynn was appointed without the English church being consulted, and he was the kind of man to whom the independence and title of Prefect Apostolic appealed.

Armed with a Roman recommendation to the Irish (but not the English) bishops, O'Flynn went to Ireland, then London. There he sought official authorisation from the British government to minister to Australia's Catholic convicts. His letters convinced the Colonial Secretary, Lord Bathurst, that O'Flynn was ill-educated, not a man of sober learning or respectable position, and thus unfit for a chaplaincy. Bathurst was willing to accept a well-recommended clergyman of respectable character, but O'Flynn did not appear to meet these requirements. He consulted the English Vicar Apostolic; Dr Poynter did not condemn O'Flynn, but neither could he make a positive recommendation. The Colonial Secretary refused to authorise O'Flynn's mission. Despite this, O'Flynn left for Sydney and arrived there in November 1817.

Calling on Governor Macquarie to request his permission to minister to the 6,000 or so Catholics in the colony, O'Flynn gave Macquarie to understand that credentials from the Colonial Office would be coming on the next ship. Macquarie was suspicious. He regarded priests as troublemakers and was reluctant to believe that the government had any intention of appointing a Catholic chaplain. However, impressed by the title 'Prefect Apostolic', he allowed O'Flynn to remain in the colony until the situation clarified, but only on condition that he did not minister publicly. No authorisation from the Colonial Office arrived, and meanwhile O'Flynn had begun an active public ministry, saying Masses at which Catholics assembled, with or without leave from their overseers. When the Governor ordered him to leave the colony, O'Flynn went into hiding. He was deported under arrest in May 1818, the Colonial Office fully supporting Macquarie's action.

O'Flynn's character and actions have been obscured by pious remembrance. A man who knew him in Sydney wrote, in 1866, 'He was a meek and holy priest, whose only delight, when not engaged in spiritual matters or the advancement of his people, scattered throughout the colony, was in lowly singing "Sweet are the nails and sweet the wood", etc., or some other favourite hymn.' Certainly his ministry, after long years without a priest, went deep into the spiritual lives of Sydney Catholics. Seventy-six soldiers of the New South Wales Corps petitioned the Governor, on behalf of two hundred Catholic soldiers, to allow O'Flynn to remain, and free Catholic settlers were no less grateful for his coming. Some of his reputation for piety seems to have arisen from his fluency in the Irish language, an attribute which made his priesthood even more immediate and wonderful. O'Flynn's public activities, however, convey the strong impression of a silly, aggressive man blundering unknowingly through the intricacies of delicate situations. His biographer, Dr O'Brien, refers to his 'unbalanced character and lack of practical sense . . . He lacked discretion and humility, though he had an abundance of faith, hope and charity . . . he had never sought advice and could not bear restraint.' His earlier life suggests this. So do his activities after he left Australia—more disputes, more grave episcopal charges of indiscipline, and involvement with American Catholic schismatic movements. Yet O'Flynn became an Australian Catholic hero, and this for two reasons: he was deported from the colony, and, when he went, he left the Blessed Sacrament behind.

O'Flynn's deportation was interpreted by Catholics as religious persecution—his zeal and piety had incensed the anti-Catholic party; the fact that he came to the colony without permission was a mere pretext for getting rid of him; he had been forced to conceal himself from the hunting of bigots. The facts are open to less dramatic interpretation. Macquarie was afraid that any priest might become the centre for disturbance in the colony. O'Flynn arrived unannounced, without authorisation or even recommendation. He showed little education, told misleading tales, and then openly, and in breach of his promise, disobeyed the Governor's explicit instructions. When ordered to leave, he hid. It is not surprising that he was deported. Macquarie was no lover of Catholics, but it was the principle of civil authority which he considered was endangered. As the Governor urged on the Colonial Office, 'If it should at any time be advisable to sanction the Ministry of Popish Priests in New South Wales, I would beg to suggest that they should be Englishmen of liberal Education and Sound constitutional principles.' It was not O'Flynn the priest that Macquarie deported, but O'Flynn the 'muddling, ignorant, dangerous character'. But the fact that O'Flynn was a priest blinded Catholic eyes to all other considerations, and made him, and those left bereft of his ministry, martyrs to bigotry. If martyrdom this was, it was martyrdom brought about largely by O'Flynn's aggressive and self-centred imprudence.

More basic still to O'Flynn's reputation is the tradition that, by accident or design (in breach of canon law), he left the Blessed Sacrament behind in Sydney. The sacred particle remained, in the house of William Davis near the site of the present St Patrick's, Church Hill, constantly venerated. So strong was this tradition that it impressed Pope Pius XI to authorise the holding of the Twenty-fourth International Eucharistic Congress in Sydney in 1928. There is no contemporary historical evidence to substantiate this story: many of its ramifications are pious or dramatic inventions, even to the extent of the suggestion of miracles. The strong probabilities are as follows. The Blessed Sacrament was indeed left by O'Flynn, but in the Kent Street house of James Dempsey, who, like Davis, had been transported for his part in the 1798 rebellion and had since been emancipated. There, the Sacrament was the object of the constant devotion of a small confraternity of five or six old men, and became the centre of what Catholic life existed in Sydney. That community was small in numbers. One of Dempsey's rooms was the chapel and, on Sundays, worshippers overflowed to the verandah, sometimes onto the street, to the amusement of scoffers. Descriptions give the impression of a congregation of perhaps a hundred people, perhaps less. However, Dempsey's house had more than local importance: it was a meeting place for Catholics from other settlements, such as Parramatta, Liverpool and Campbelltown, where Catholics had formed themselves into committees for prayer and society. In November 1819 the Sacrament was consumed by the chaplain of a visiting

French ship. All else, Father O'Flynn's motives, miracles and so forth, however edifying, lies (unless further evidence is forthcoming) outside the realms of historical proof.

So does Dr O'Brien's claim that 'It is abundantly evident that in the Australian part of his [O'Flynn's] career he was the weak and uncomprehending agent of an extraordinary plan by which Divine Providence had determined to establish the Catholic Church in the penal settlement, despite the opposition of government and the absence of missionaries.' This refers to the consequences of O'Flynn's deportation. It led to a political rumpus in England, to which the government responded with the provision of salaries for two Catholic chaplains—£100 per annum each, in contrast with the £250 minimum for Protestant chaplains. Thus, in Cardinal Moran's judgement,

> In the ways of Providence . . . the very failure of Father Flynn's mission led to the triumph of the missionary cause which was so dear to him. The Government could no longer conceal the fact that there were thousands of Catholics in Australia, devoted to their faith, who, nevertheless, were most barbarously debarred from the possibility of fulfilling its duties.

In placing all blame for the deprivations of Australian Catholicism on the British government, this comment ignores the remarkable tardiness of Catholics to take advantage of the Colonial Secretary's willingness to accept a suitable Catholic chaplain. This delay sprang from the circumstances of Catholic authorities in Rome, London and Dublin, their preoccupation with their own problems, their hostility towards each other, and their lack of liaison or communication —all of which was apparent before O'Flynn returned to England, indeed before his initial appointment. Without doubt, O'Flynn's escapade drew the attention of the Catholic authorities to Australia's needs. In English politics his case became another stick with which liberals and radicals could belabour the government. In New South Wales, where Macquarie's rule was facing increasing criticism, it was cited as another illustration of the Governor's arrogation of dictatorial powers, and O'Flynn achieved the status of martyrdom on that count, even among some Protestants. By the time of

O'Flynn's removal, the authoritarian regime characteristic of the colony's early days was under severe censure. A more liberal, tolerant spirit had grown. Administrative opinion was swinging away from the belief that to give Australia Catholic priests would risk rebellion. The opposite proposition seemed more valid: priests would quieten the Catholic populace. The context was, however, the same—fear of Catholic sedition and subversion. It is not without significance that while the salaries of Protestant chaplains were paid from the Treasury proper, the salaries of the first Catholic priests were paid from the Police Fund.

The first two Catholic chaplains arrived in Sydney in May 1820, thirty years after the arrival of the first Catholic convicts. A continuous history had begun, but these beginnings had no triumphal ring. The ship on which the two priests travelled was made the subject of a judicial enquiry; Father Therry testified to the crew's wholesale prostitution of the female convicts. It was a harsh but fitting introduction to what was far less a mission than a prison chaplaincy, to a society whose cohesion rested mainly on vice. Worse, soon after their arrival the two priests, both Irish, quarrelled and parted. One, Therry, for all his Christian love and generosity, was to follow a life stunted and half wasted in faction and dispute. The other, Conolly, proceeded to the relative neglect of his mission, to drunkenness perhaps, at least to strange oddities of manner, and to a tombstone engraved in sorrow: 'My days have declined like a shadow, and I am withered like grass.'

The British had taken the Cape of Good Hope in 1806 and the island of Mauritius in 1810. England demanded for these conquests priests who were British subjects, so Rome gave this mission to the English Benedictines. In June 1818 Edward Slater was appointed Vicar Apostolic of the Cape, Mauritius, Madagascar and New Holland (that is, Australasia). To administer the Australasian section of his vast responsibility, Slater appointed Philip Conolly senior chaplain; in Ireland, Conolly began fund raising, issuing testimonials from Protestants as to his loyalty and peaceful character. Slater then selected John Joseph Therry, a young priest of outstanding zeal, integrity and honesty, who as a student had decided on missionary work. Therry was keenly aware of his own deficiencies. He told Slater that, because of family difficulties, he had been ordained prematurely, before his theological knowledge was sufficient. His intellectual equipment was on a par with O'Flynn's; he did not disguise this: 'I am to confess, if not absolutely ignorant, at least, very deficient, in the knowledge which any ordinary missioner ought to possess. Besides, I am utterly destitute of any acquaintance with the Irish language.' Nevertheless, Slater was delighted to have him, for he had heard of Therry's qualities of spirituality and heart. His choices made, Slater virtually left Australia in their hands; it was but a tiny part of his new care, embracing as it did Southern Africa. He had problems enough, overwhelming problems, there.

When Conolly and Therry reached Sydney, they promptly arranged a meeting to organise a subscription to build a Catholic chapel. It was attended by 'all the respectable Catholics of the settlement, and also some Protestant gentlemen of sentiments friendly to the design.' The tone of this 'respectable' gathering verged on the obsequious, in sharp contrast to the spirit of vigorous protest against deprivation usually imputed to the Catholicism of this time.

> . . . we deem it a primary and most pleasing duty not to lose this opportunity to express our esteem and veneration for His Majesty's Government in England, and our gratitude to the enlightened and benevolent Minister who presides over the Colonial Department, whose anxious care has afforded us the object of our solicitations, in selecting and sending to us ministers of the Roman Catholic Church, to administer to us the long-looked-for rites of our holy religion.

The meeting went on to express 'confidence in, and gratitude to' Governor Macquarie, and to record that sympathetic Protestants merited 'lasting esteem and gratitude'. Here, openly, for the first time in Australian Catholic history, appears one of its major themes: the careful pursuit of acceptance in a hostile society. If one reaction to hostility and oppression was aggressive rebellion—carried to the point of violence in 1804 at Castle Hill—another was the attempt to quietly conform, as far as was possible. The individual's reaction usually depended on his economic and social position, what he had to lose. Few among the Catholics had much to lose, and those who did, walked quietly. They walked quietly in more ways than one, for by the 1820s some Catholic emancipists had grown successful, as property owners and in commerce, a few to the point of considerable wealth. Little of this wealth found its way to the assistance of the church. It would be a distorted picture of the Catholic laity which overlooked that minority of rich Catholics whose close attachment to their wealth remained a resistant strand in Australian Catholicism, impervious to the complaints and denunciations of Bishop Polding and, later, Cardinal Moran. But the rich were very few. The great majority had nothing, or next to nothing, and many had been crushed into apathy and indifference. But between those who had not and Father Therry sprang up a fierce sympathy, for he saw the world through their excluded, resentful eyes.

At first, all went smoothly. Conolly and Therry consulted Macquarie as to how they should act as pastors. Given the preconceptions of that time, the Governor's reply was friendly and liberal: the priests were free to minister to all Catholics, but to them alone, and they were expected to follow the administrative procedures, hours for services, register-keeping, notifications and the like, followed by the Church of England. Macquarie made two strong prohibitions: on no account whatever were the priests to celebrate marriages between Protestants, or between a Catholic and a Protestant. In this, the Governor's main concern seems to have been not the interests of the Protestant religion, but social harmony and particularly the fact that such prohibited marriages would raise, in law, questions of legitimacy, property and inheritance. He also prohibited any interference with the religious education of orphans in the government's charitable institutions. These were an Anglican preserve. The Governor also included two warnings—that the priests should endeavour not to make converts, as this would cause trouble, and that they be especially careful that no disaffection or sedition arose in relation to their ministry. The priests voiced no immediate protest against Macquarie's instructions. They were by now at odds, and early in 1821 Conolly departed for Tasmania, leaving Therry doubly buried in pastoral demands and in what was rapidly becoming an obsession, the building of a church. He had been granted by the government the site of the present St Mary's Cathedral in uncleared bushland close to the convict quarter, not the site on Church Hill for which he had applied.

When, on 29 October 1821, Governor Macquarie laid the foundation stone of St Mary's, it seemed that a new era of constructive cordiality had begun in the religious affairs of the colony. In laying that stone, Macquarie set it firmly into British earth, and expressed the hope that the government's supplying of Catholic clergymen 'will be the means of strengthening and augmenting (if that be possible) the attachment of the Catholics of New South Wales to the British Government, and will prove an inducement to them to continue, as I have ever found them to be, loyal and faithful subjects of the Crown.' Macquarie's conception of religion was political, narrow and earth-bound; religion, like all things, had its proper place. Therry, to whom religion was life, and all life, could accept no such limitations.

Between 1820 and 1833 Therry dominated the small world of Australian Catholicism, impressing on it—with remarkable permanency—many of the extraordinary characteristics of his contradictory personality. When he came to the colony in 1820, Therry was thirty, a young man whose direct eyes, firm mouth and jutting jaw suggested strong will and temper. He was a dynamo of apostolic energy, energy which often ran wild with ambitious dreams of a noble religious future. Slater, his Bishop, discerned some of this when he cautioned, in October 1822, 'you must remember that an ardent head will always form plans more rapidly than the most active hand can execute them, particularly when the kindly affections of the heart, elevated to the rank of Christian charities, are in union with the wishes of the head.' None who knew Therry well could see him as other than one eaten up with missionary zeal and burning love of souls. Nevertheless, in applying that zeal and love to Australian society Therry attracted not only the affection of his flock, but also a procession of conflicts and disputes which seriously weakened his ministry.

Some of Therry's problems were of his own making, others lay in the nature of his parish. When he arrived, there were about 6,000 Catholics in the colony. According to the 1828 Census there were 11,236 Catholics in a total population of 36,598. By 1833 there were, perhaps, 18,000. Through most of this period Therry was the only priest: comment on the enormity of his task is superfluous. Moreover, the traditional picture of a pious 'Church of the Catacombs' at this time is quite unreal. In fact, Therry, as he admitted himself, could make little headway in that uncharted sea of vice and irreligion. The sheer inadequacy of his efforts constantly troubled the lonely priest. He wrote in 1822:

> It requires at least seven priests to discharge in a proper and regular manner the duties which devolve on me, but which I perform in a very irregular and superficial manner . . . Many persons die at the distant settlements without benefit of the Sacraments. Even here, in consequence of the confessional not being regularly attended, we have scarcely any communicants.

Therry's was a ministry of sickbed, suffering, death and burial, not of vigorous sacramental life, though, through the long years, he said his daily Mass without fail and prepared his sermons thoughtfully.

In Sydney, the gaol dominated his life. From there welled up the ceaseless cry of anguished illiterate men and women, in fear of death and judgement. 'For Christ's sake he loved them with an intense, devoted love, and the fiercest and worst of them soon began to return his affection.' Elsewhere, his pastoral world was one of alarms and excursions, constant travelling, long rides on horseback through heat and flood. This facet of Therry's life is summed up in the story which begins: 'Word was brought to Father Therry that a convict, sentenced to execution, desired to see him for confession. Many miles had to be traversed in haste . . .'. Therry, pulled on a rope through a torrent, mounting another horse, drenched, yet arriving in time with the consolations of religion. Such was the pattern of his priestly life, for such were the necessities of his mission. It was a mission which demanded a hero, and, for all his faults, Therry filled that demand. It was also a mission which reduced religion to the search for morality. Every pioneering circumstance of the colony, and the evangelical flavour of that religious age, dictated an emphasis on practical morality devoid of intellectual roots—more than anything, the depraved moral climate of colonial Australia enforced it; the redemption of men's behaviour was a first task. A religious man was a man who observed the big moral rules.

Therry's energetic pastoral work, his display (he loved liturgical processions and singing) and his aggressive disposition soon led to direct conflict with the colonial administration. If this, perhaps, was not his intention, he certainly accepted a policy of direct confrontation willingly. From his own viewpoint, two alternative attitudes to the existing situation were possible—acceptance or protest. He chose protest. The choice was logical, given his character and his understanding of the existing situation. What was that situation? For the previous thirty years the settlement's life had been dominated by officials and settlers to whom Catholicism was anathema. If Catholicism, cowed and diminished, its strength sapped by its continuing subjection, was to survive, Therry saw only one possible course—to stand up and fight. His objective? To wrest the control of Catholic lives from 'the establishment' and capture that control for the church, in the person of himself; for there was no one else. In this contest he made what allies he could, playing politics to gain the support he needed, and thus becoming a nuisance and troublemaker in the eyes of the established order.

Soon, under the pressure of his duties and the urgent demands of individual situations, he was breaking Macquarie's regulations. For him, the interests of religion, of souls, was paramount: for officials, the law had to be enforced. From 1825 onwards, officialdom took on an anti-Catholic complexion. This was the year of the Church and Schools Estates Corporation Charter, whereby one-seventh of colonial land grants was to be set aside for the maintenance of the Anglican church. It was the year of the arrival of Archdeacon Scott, dedicated to securing the official establishment of the Anglican religion; and of the coming of Governor Darling who was intolerant of Catholicism.

Therry had early appreciated the key place of education in the religious future. He had, it seems, established a school in Parramatta in 1820, and one in Sydney in 1822, with no great success; the Parramatta school was forced to close in 1823. In 1824 he was urging on the Colonial Secretary the establishment of a seminary, stressing its practical advantages, that it 'would have a general and most salutary influence on the morals of the rising generations . . . [who would be] kept at a distance from the contagion of bad example so peculiarly and universally prevalent in this colony.' Among Macquarie's regulations, the one which incensed Therry most was that reserving the Orphan Schools to the Anglican religion. Therry regarded this as naked proselytism, so familiar in his Irish experience, designed to rob Catholic children of their faith. The tone of his protests may be gauged from a letter which he wrote to the Colonial Secretary in July 1826:

> The lambs are allured abroad, and forcibly prevented from returning to the fold of the only Good Shepherd, Christ Jesus, Our Lord, and must His Humble watchman hold his peace? Is he to be silent? Is he to be worse than a dumb dog? Is he, by consulting his personal interests, or his personal safety, to betray his precious trust, purchased as it has been by his Divine Master's most sacred blood?

This language jarred on official ears, and in any case Governor Darling was not inclined to sympathy. He summed up the outspoken cleric with evident distaste:

> Mr Therry is a man of strong feelings and not much discretion. He is evidently disposed to be troublesome, and, constituted as this community is, might be dangerous . . . He is indefatigable in his endeavours to preserve his influence among his countrymen, and is constantly going from place to place with this view. From the similarity of character, he can hardly fail to succeed . . .

Darling's venomous appraisal was made after Therry's dismissal as chaplain. On 14 June 1825 Therry published in the *Sydney Gazette* his proposal to establish a Catholic Education Society. This was his plan to resolve the choice placed before the Catholic poor—either to allow their children an education in the Orphan Schools at the expense of their religion, or deprive their children completely of the benefits of education. He expressed, in referring to Protestant clergymen, his 'unqualified respect', but a printer's error altered it to 'qualified respect'. This was the occasion for a vigorous demand, led by Archdeacon Scott, for Therry's removal. Despite a correction and apology from the *Gazette,* Therry was dismissed as chaplain and his salary stopped. He was given to understand that £300 was available from the government for his return passage to England. He refused to go.

Therry's dismissal—he was not reinstated until 1837—increased his popular reputation. His criticism of the government became more intense, his ego more assertive. His pen had an acid touch which annoyed the administration; his words ran away with him into clever, stinging taunts. 'I have not been, I can safely affirm, an unprofitable Servant to his Majesty', he informed the Executive Council.

> I consider myself to have been much more profitable, I shall take the liberty to add, than many who are better paid for their services [the reference was to Protestant clergymen who received triple his salary]; but, as the utility of a Catholic clergyman consists principally in the prevention and not the discovery and punishment of crime [a reference to the fact that Protestant clergymen were often magistrates], his services, however important, are often either unnoticed or undervalued.

Now deprived of official status, Therry's problems and difficulties multiplied. His difficulties in raising money for St Mary's church had been considerable from the beginning, for Catholics were the poorest section of the community. Moreover he had no knowledge of keeping accounts, and despite his efforts to raise funds by farming and stock-breeding, confusion and debt marked his financial affairs. Promised government assistance for the church had not been forthcoming, and by 1827 work had come to a halt, with only the walls standing. The government had decided, as had some of the Catholics, that Therry's plans for a large cathedral were too ambitious, 'disproportionate to the Class of Communicants'. Governor Darling was hostile to it.

There were other problems too. The previous governor, Brisbane, had recognised the rights of military and convicts to full liberty of conscience. Nevertheless, Therry had to fight constantly to extort this against the obstruction of officials and private citizens. Foremost in arousing Therry's ire was his exclusion, as without official status, from attendance on convicts and soldiers who sought his ministry. His most frequent and vehement attacks were on those who thwarted him in the care of souls, particularly the Medical Superintendent of Sydney hospital who would not admit him to dying Catholics. Therry used every device to gain his point. He could at one and the same time advance the most elevated conservative principles—'The Altar and the Throne are never respectively so secure, as when reciprocally assisted and mutually supported by each other'—and use force, with the support of the government's opponents: on W. C. Wentworth's advice he broke down the door of the Court House, which he had used for Mass, but which was closed against him when he lost his official chaplaincy.

Father Therry's determined and persistent assertion of the fundamental rights of religion places him squarely at the beginnings of one of the continuing themes of Australian Catholic history. Although he was not interested in reform or freedom as such, he has been justly credited with a more than incidentally important place in the history of civil liberties. Where government regulations or attitudes conflicted with what he saw as the law of God, he stood firm for that law and its rights. But whereas, in other men who were to follow, a firm stand in controversy brought dignity and greatness of spirit, controversy entered into Father Therry like a parasite, devouring him and becoming the habit of his life. It was bad enough, in a land crying for succour, that much of his time should be taken up in controversy; tragically worse that his attacking fury and restless personal manoeuvres were not restricted to confronting the government, but extended to all—even brother priests —who crossed him or seemed likely to curb his urge to dominate and have his way. 'Remember,' Slater cautioned him about his dispute with Father Conolly, 'that charity, soft, indulgent, forbearing charity, is the spirit which animates a faithful servant of Christ . . .'

After Therry's dismissal, the government set about replacing him. Father Daniel Power, another Irishman, arrived in Sydney in January 1827 as official chaplain. Therry, whose hold over Catholics had been greatly strengthened by his dismissal, began to undermine and frustrate Power's ministry. Power, a man afflicted by ill-health and ill-temper, was soon in an impossible position. Perhaps it is true that Governor Darling deliberately attempted to play him off against Therry. Yet, it is a fact that Power was official chaplain, and this, reasonably, necessitated co-operation. But, by Therry's followers at least, Power was branded a creature of a persecuting government, and soon the Sydney situation was tending towards two rival congregations. It seems likely that Therry spent some of the money collected for St Mary's on a chapel of his own, to preserve his own influence in Sydney independent of the official chaplain. Power fought back with vigorous criticisms of Therry's supporters. These counterattacks had limited success. He told the people of Goulburn that Christmas dues were to be paid to him, as the recognised chaplain; they sent the dues to Therry. Without doubt, Therry was the aggressor in this conflict. How serious it was is shown by his action in striking Power during a dispute which flared up between them when they were both in attendance at an execution. Power believed that by this violence Therry had excommunicated himself. Basic to Therry's flaming sense of grievance was the fact that Power's presence allowed the government to persist in its refusal to recognise Therry's ministry, even to the extent of declaring his marriages invalid.

Power died in March 1830, to be succeeded by a young Irish Dominican, Christopher Dowling, who arrived in Sydney in September 1831. The dissensions among the Catholic body intensified. The gaunt and hollow shell of St Mary's stood as mouldering testimony to Therry's holy ambition. Some of the laity, out of patience with Therry, wanted the construction entrusted to Dowling. Therry would have none of this, nor would he accept Dowling as in any way his clerical superior. As with Power, he regarded the other priest as an intruder on his personal preserves, and the same situation of rivalry developed. Dowling's temperament—'a man of fervid popular eloquence and heated imagination'— had much in common with Therry's. Their clash was violent and bitter, centering on Therry's determination to retain full control of the St Mary's project. Two discreditable incidents were recorded by Ullathorne. 'Mr Dowling in a sermon on fraternal charity made strong allusions to Mr Therry, who in the heat of momentary excitement dragged Mr Dowling from the altar, but immediately afterwards went down on his knees and begged his pardon.' Therry was in the habit of going down after Mass in his vestments to the church door with the collection box. He would praise loudly those who put in most. One Sunday Dowling decided to challenge this, attempting to seize the collection box. A tug of war between the two vestmented priests took place in front of the retiring congregation.

Dowling left Sydney and went to Newcastle. Therry had made impossible any ministry other than his own. His removal from the chaplaincy—construed as persecution—identified him with all those Catholics, mainly convicts, who felt themselves victims of the injustices of authority: they saw in Therry themselves. Therry was able to turn this sympathy into antagonism to the official chaplains, whom he identified with the government and thus discredited.

However, by 1830 the environment of religion was changing rapidly. The British Act of 1829, which emancipated Catholics, allowed them to hold government appointments. The first such Australian appointment was of the Irishman, Roger Therry, as Commissioner of the Court of Requests. Roger Therry, who arrived late in 1829, soon became a champion of Catholic causes, and went on to a distinguished career on the bench in Victoria and N.S.W. On his arrival, he found the Catholics almost entirely Irish, and almost without exception poor. Of the 6,000 or so Catholics in Sydney, only perhaps fifty were free emigrants (a considerable underestimate by Therry—there were perhaps 250). When he and his wife attended their first Mass in the colony, Mrs Therry's bonnet created a sensation: it was the first which had appeared in the congregation. There were some Catholics in the administration, but, for fear of dismissal, they avoided the public practice of their religion. The next high official appointment was that of John Plunkett, another Irishman, as Solicitor-General in 1832. Before he came, Plunkett obtained from the government the appointment of an additional Catholic chaplain, who travelled with him to Australia. This was John McEncroe, an Irish priest of con-

siderable missionary experience, who had eventually reached
the level of Vicar-General in America. When he arrived he
was thirty-seven; Ullathorne was to find him a 'grave,
experienced man' of intense dedication. He had the somewhat rare ability of being able to get on with Father Therry.
Or, more precisely, he was able to maintain friendly relations
with him: he could do nothing to change any of Therry's
entrenched ways. In fact, the situation in which Therry was
the central figure had become much worse. The arrival of
Governor Bourke in 1830 had marked a revolution in the
attitude of authority—both of Governor and Colonial Office
—towards Catholics. In 1832 a grant of £500 was made
towards the construction of St Mary's. However, by that
time Therry was in dispute with the government over the
title to the land on which the partially completed church
stood. He had no formal deeds, and his impression of its
extent differed from the government's; when a group of
workmen came to erect a boundary fence, he picked up a
stake and threatened to knock down any man who encroach-
ed on what he regarded as his land—and it was his land in
a very personal sense, for he refused to vest it in trustees.

This episode, coming after years of trouble with Therry,
prompted the colonial government to seek the appointment
of a Catholic ecclesiastical authority with whom it could
treat. William Morris, who had succeeded Bishop Slater in
Mauritius, appointed William Ullathorne his Australian
Vicar-General. The government provided a salary of £200
a year and an allowance of £1 a day when travelling. Ullathorne was a newly ordained English Benedictine priest,
only twenty-seven when he arrived in the colony. He was a
student of Dr Polding, who had inspired him with missionary
zeal. A slight, youthful figure, intellectual, introspective,
with a self-confessed 'fondness for reading pursued to excess',
Ullathorne nevertheless possessed remarkable poise, firmness and self-confidence. His friends remarked on his
calmness, indifference even, in the face of setting out to the
furthest extremity of the world. He told them that having
God with him, the authority of the Church, and a great
vocation before him, he felt that he was in the right place
and had nothing else to care for. However, he took five
hundred books, chiefly ecclesiastical but also some of the

choicest classics. Ullathorne was a man with few self-doubts, not without a sense of his own superiority and rectitude which went, perhaps, beyond the limits of fair self-regard. It was typical of him that later, when he wrote a book on the virtue of humility, he was very proud of it: his reputation was to suffer from the very human resentment aroused by a man conscious (his critics would say boastful) of his considerable gifts.

Before leaving England, Ullathorne had been given 'a sad account' of Catholic affairs in Australia. His reactions were to be coloured by the process of finding what he had expected to see. When he arrived in Tasmania early in 1833, he beheld what he took to be the wreckage of Father Conolly's ministry, the neglect of the primitive church building, its filth and disorder, pastoral work untended, the sacraments seldom approached, the laity alienated, the priest himself strange, usually absent, occasionally affected by drink. Ullathorne had seen in Capetown the effects of loneliness on a brother Benedictine; a priest destined for insanity, constantly grinding his teeth. Conolly's difficulties in Tasmania were immense. He was bedevilled by poverty and by an obstructive, self-willed laity. He had not seen another priest for thirteen years, and, in the charitable words of a priest who knew him later, 'had become rather antiquated in his manners, on account of being so long by himself'. He had tried to attend to his duties, but circumstances, obstruction by civil authorities and by his own laity, had proved too much for him: he had been defeated. Ullathorne, young, with little tolerance, and unfamiliar with the problems of this difficult mission, judged Conolly's performance promptly, fastidiously—and too harshly. Ullathorne could do nothing in such a brief visit—except provoke Conolly's complaint to Bishop Morris that Ullathorne was too young and not Irish. However, the Tasmanian situation was degenerating rapidly. Conolly's parishioners—there were about 5,000 Catholics in a total Tasmanian population of 45,000—held a protest meeting, and approached the government to send out a better priest. Conolly replied with a libel writ against one of the parishioners. A visit from Ullathorne failed to produce any settlement.

When Bishop Polding, on his way to take up his episcopate in Sydney, visited Tasmania in August 1835, he left one of his party, Father Cotham, behind as a means of remedying Conolly's neglect. Many Catholics had fallen away. Of those who were still prepared to acknowledge their religion, a number had not practised it for thirty or forty years: they had to be instructed like children. Cotham found the strain nearly unendurable: 'what with one thing and another, our religion degraded in every place, the just complaints of the Catholics on every side, without one friend to assist or console me, I am nearly distracted, nearly mad.' No church could be built because Conolly claimed that the government grant of land was his private property. Polding journeyed from Sydney to settle the affair, but when he heard of this, Conolly transferred the land to three of his relations and removed himself to the interior of the island. Polding then withdrew his faculties as a priest, whereupon Conolly issued a libel writ against him, dropping it only after protracted unpleasantness. Thereafter, matters improved briefly as Polding sent out more priests. Conolly died in 1839. In the previous year, Father Therry had been appointed Vicar-General of Tasmania. Soon, from 1844, Therry too was locked in a long, bitter and obsessive dispute with his Bishop, Willson, again over the ownership and control of church lands, and again the outcome was suspension. Once more, as under Conolly, the affairs of the Tasmanian church languished and grew sour.

Ullathorne arrived, unexpected, in Sydney in February 1833. There he met Therry, 'the most singular character I ever knew'. When Ullathorne produced his credentials as Vicar-General '. . . Father Therry immediately went down on his knees. This act of obedience and submission gave me great relief. I felt that he was a truly religious man, and that half the difficulty was over.' So it was. Therry, in his strange mixed character—'pious, zealous, obstinate', Polding described him—was instinctively submissive to ecclesiastical authority, though part of him also clamoured against it.

Like Therry himself, the religious situation that Ullathorne found in Sydney was singular. There was no church: St Mary's had no roof, a church was half completed at Campbelltown, another had been begun and had fallen into ruins at Parramatta. The law courts served as churches throughout the country. Clergymen? Conolly—derelict in Tasmania; Dowling—embittered in Newcastle; Therry—truculent and factious in Sydney; and McEncroe—prey to melancholy and drink. Religious observance was confined to a small section of the nominally Catholic; as Father McEncroe had reported to the Archbishop of Dublin at the end of 1832, there were 16,000 or 18,000 Catholics, 'not one half of whom hardly ever see a priest'. Sexual morality was, to say the least, lax. Marriages between Catholics and Protestants were frequent, and often led to loss of Catholic faith. Sacramental life was at a low ebb. Ullathorne was told that he had more communicants on his first Easter Sunday than there had been in the whole of the previous year. And the community was poisoned by the reason for its existence. Ullathorne was appalled by the vice, corruption and harshness. Nonetheless, he faced the situation squarely, compassionately, and with a deepening detestation of the convict system: 'At every step in this dreadful system springs there up a new source of corruption.' The convict world was aggressively hostile to religion. 'In most cases, the practice of religion is a thing unrecognised, the power of ridicule forbids it to appear openly . . . how many newcomers have I known to have stolen into the woods to hide their prayers, trembling to be discovered on their knees, as though they were doing some guilty thing.' The prevailing spirit was one of 'irreverence and dissoluteness'. It was a world which crushed human feelings, warmth and affection. 'The feelings of the convict are petrified by the hardness of everything about him. He never feels the touch of kindness. Wonder not that his vital warmth dies, and he becomes a haggard, insensible thing.' It was in this that Therry's virtues were luminous: his compassion went out without hesitation or reserve to those most degraded and abandoned. So did Ullathorne's, but Therry, instinctively it seems, sought for the lost sheep. He had that indefinable touch which could open spiritual communication with such men, more directly, more immediately, than could the tutored intellect of Ullathorne.

What did Ullathorne see? An atmosphere thick with crime, a land spread with obstacles, a terrible shortage of priests—and a people shamefully fallen. Here was no mission in the ordinary sense. The urgent demands of the European population prevented any especial attention being given to the Aborigines. But Therry had done something, and Polding was to do more. In 1833 these demands were still mainly those of a prison chaplaincy. Redemption meant the saving of souls at the most primitive level; religion existed at the level of emergency. There was little time or place for normal pastoral affairs, none for contemplation. Priestly functions were concerned mainly with deaths and executions, nearly always with transitory contacts; it was a ministry without visible continuity, as a continual procession of souls, some going to their final destiny, others to remote places, swirled past. Small wonder that Conolly had broken; the wonder was that Therry had endured. Ullathorne had, as protection, the resilience of youth and the detachment of intellect. More important, the penal world he found was soon to shrink and disappear.

And what of the established practising congregation? Could it have numbered a thousand? In large part it was little removed from ignorance, held curious beliefs bordering on superstition, and was, of course, riven by Father Therry's disputes. Books virtually did not exist among them, and were, in any case, little appreciated by a people substantially illiterate. In 1830 Catholic schooling catered for eighty-eight children; according to Ullathorne, even Father Therry 'could not put two ideas together on any subject'. So identified was Therry with religion that he was popularly thought to be some sort of saint, certainly a man favoured by God. It was believed that the full efficacy of the sacrament of baptism depended on Therry's personal ministrations. Infants were brought long distances to him: his baptism was a guarantee of good luck, and regarded in later life as a mark of good character. His popular following was large and intense, his influence like a spell. When it was known that he was in Sydney, a crowd of suppliants would assemble at his door every morning, with personal problems, with papers to be signed, with a host of requests, both temporal and spiritual.

Polding saw deep into the strange contrasts that made up Therry's character when he accounted as a great achievement Therry's keeping alive 'the embers of religion when a few more capable persons without his peculiarities would not have done half as well.' This achievement was not without grave cost. He had split the Catholic community. Yet, as Polding saw, but for Therry's peculiar ardour and faithfulness, would there have existed a Catholic community to be split? However highly Therry's successors might value the essential creation of his stewardship—the Mystical Body of Christ now lived in that penal world—they had to deal with what he had made, and that was seriously flawed, at least on the human level. Therry had, Ullathorne judged fairly, 'kept everything from consolidating'. Some of the laity had become deeply involved partisans in Therry's marches and counter-marches. Most were thoroughly tired of constant dissension and dispute, and the scandal so caused.

It is difficult to measure Therry's responsibility. Certainly he was a principal in all disputes, but if he maintained them, did he cause them? Therry had arrived in 1820 to find a lay group which had determined its own affairs in the preceding years. His decision not to build the tiny church they were prepared to pay for, and to proceed with a large and expensive cathedral far beyond the immediate needs of the Catholic community, sharply divided the laity. It was a situation in which both parties had valid arguments—the anti-Therry section that a cathedral was an absurd extravagance, the Therry party that they must look to the future and to the establishment of a fitting public stature for the church. But, whoever was to blame, once involved in faction, Therry became incurably addicted to it. Ullathorne's own arrival had been preceded by Therry's campaign to obtain promissory notes from the people, pledges of their future donations to the church, in an attempt to get future ecclesiastical revenues firmly into his own hands. On Ullathorne's arrival, Therry, relishing faction, promptly confronted him with the situation. Ullathorne responded decisively.

The next morning, as I came from Mass, Father Therry met me and said: 'Sir, there are two parties among us, and I wish to put you in possession of my ideas on the subject.' I replied: 'No, Father Therry, if you will pardon me, there are not two parties.' He warmed up . . . and replied, with his face in a glow: 'How can you know about it? You have only just arrived, and are as yet so inexperienced.' 'Father Therry,' I said with all gravity, 'listen to me. There were two parties yesterday. There are none to-day. They arose from the unfortunate want of some person carrying ecclesiastical authority. That is at an end. For the present, in New South Wales, I am the Church, and they who gather not with me, scatter. So now there are no longer two parties!

Nor were there, at least for the moment and on that issue. Tackling firmly the hostility which had been aroused by his superseding Therry, Ullathorne called a meeting of Catholics at which he secured harmony and placed the St Mary's project in the hands of trustees. Soon the church had a roof, and was sufficiently complete to be dedicated in June 1836 by Bishop Polding.

Ullathorne was totally wrong in thinking that lay faction was at an end. It had scarcely begun. He had achieved a temporary success in pacification, a success which arose from the situation at least as much as from Ullathorne's ability to handle it firmly. From Therry, Ullathorne had taken over a church which had been Therry's achievement, the outcome of his long fight. Ullathorne's contrasting diplomatic authority and charm came at the right moment to secure peace, at least for a while.

Therry found it hard to knuckle down to Ullathorne's authority, and continued to mix challenge and deference in the same breath.

> Now and again [wrote Ullathorne] his highly sensitive nature got so moved, and his head so heated with the notion that I was doing him some grievous wrong . . . 'Pardon me,' he would say, with reddened brow, and mincing manner, bowing all the time, 'I do not wish to offend you. But you are my greatest enemy. You are very learned, but you do not understand this colony. You are very unjust to me. Oh, pray don't think I wish to say anything displeasing to you or inconsistent with your office.' And after this . . . would come out some vague expression of a grievance, or perhaps very strong words, always balanced with apologies.

Was Therry right? Did Ullathorne understand the colony? Not fully, no—though who could claim such absolute knowledge? Ullathorne did not, at least in 1833, understand the necessities which had forced Therry to fight. He did not understand that such fights inevitably increased factionalism, and he did not understand that factionalism was far from dead. If Ullathorne had his insights, so did Therry have his.

Therry, in the first of his several translations, was soon moved to Campbelltown, in full charge of that area. There he exercised his remarkable pastoral gifts, the itinerant priest going wherever, and doing whatever, he thought necessary for religion. The shadow of his frustrating Tasmanian career lies dark across the remainder of his life, but he died, venerated, in May 1864 as pastor of Balmain.

So, rapidly, peace—temporary peace—within the Catholic community spread with Ullathorne. A major factor in this was the tolerant attitude of Governor Bourke. Ullathorne's description of his meeting with Bourke shows that a new spirit had entered Catholic-state relations.

> The fine old soldier was one of the most polished men I ever met. In his younger days, he had been a good deal under the influence of the celebrated Edmund Burke, and was a man of extensive information, as well as experience. Though not a Catholic, he had a great respect for the Catholic religion, and had many Catholic relatives and friends. He received me with kindness, and soon we understood each other.

Bourke was opposed to an Anglican religious monopoly, and in 1836 his Church Act provided for an equitable division of public funds for the support of the principal religious bodies in the colony.

Soon, Ullathorne was writing to Dr Polding at Downside monastery, insisting on the necessity for a bishop in Australia. Episcopal rule from distant Mauritius was totally unsatisfactory, as had been obvious long before his own arrival. Local authority was necessary. Even more important was the need to attract priests to Australia: only a bishop could do this. Naturally, Ullathorne turned to his Benedictine superiors, for theirs was the religious responsibility, conferred by the Holy See in response to the wishes of the English government. Equally naturally the Irish in Australia turned to their own religious origins and ecclesiastical authorities; the Archbishop of Dublin was under increasing pressure from Irishmen in Australia to come to their religious aid. When he met Ullathorne in Tasmania, Father Conolly's immediate criticism was that the new Vicar-General was 'unacquainted . . . with the habits and manners of the Irish who chiefly constitute the Catholic population in the Colony'. For his part, Ullathorne was not impressed by Conolly's habits and manners. There was ample room for discord in the differences between the English and Irish brands of Catholicism. The Benedictines might regard their spiritual dominion as natural, and a common Catholicism more than sufficient to contain national differences, but the Irish became increasingly determined to apply to Australia a religious home rule—not Australian independence, but Irish ecclesiastical imperialism—and given the nobility and greatness of that principle, they seldom paused to count its cost. Or if they did, they weighed it as nothing against their great missionary achievements.

2

The Benedictine Dream 1835-1865

In June 1834 John Bede Polding, novice-master and subprior of the Benedictine monastery of Downside, was consecrated in London as Australia's first bishop. Before leaving England he issued an appeal for help in his mission. Its theme was to echo and re-echo down the rough and unsecluded cloisters of his future life—the plea to charitable and generous hearts to assist in the salvation of wretched sinners. Scripturally, it followed the Gospel of St Luke: 'What man of you that hath an hundred sheep: and if he shall lose one of them, doth he not leave the ninety-nine in the desert, and go after that which was lost until he find it?' For 'there shall be joy in heaven upon one sinner that doth penance, more than upon ninety-nine just who need not penance.' Polding's life was dedicated to the search for that which was lost.

The great redemptive image of the Good Shepherd found in Polding a clear, untroubled reflection. It was from those ninety-nine left in the desert, those just men who needed not penance, that his main cares and troubles were to come. Those just men, with a zeal for souls which they shared with Polding, were to seek the frustration and destruction of his ambition to impose the temporal forms of the Benedictine religious life on the spiritual mission of the Catholic church in Australia.

On his arrival in Sydney in September 1835, Polding plunged into that sea of wickedness he had expected to find, his first concern the confessional, the sacred tribunal to which he found it 'Oh! . . . so difficult to bring these people'. Before all things else, the immorality of the convict population claimed the greatest share of his pastoral energies. He was then forty, a man in the prime of life, and in excellent health. His pastoral vigour was inexhaustible. 'From week to week we have been employed in hearing the general confession of individuals, who, on account of their circum-

stances, or through negligence, have remained in sin for
forty or fifty years and even a longer time', so Polding
reported to Rome.

> We commence at an early hour in the morning, and place
> ourselves in the Church, or house used for that purpose, and
> remain there until someone comes to confession. At 10 a.m.
> the sacraments of baptism and matrimony are administered;
> afterwards the hospitals are visited, the prisons, the jails,
> and finally, the sick living in the city and suburbs. Thus is
> occupied the day until the evening, when the funerals are
> attended. Then only can we repose for a while, and apply
> ourselves to our spiritual exercises, although they are fre-
> quently interrupted, and even our sleep during the night.
> In the evening we instruct our converts. It need not be added
> that the Sunday is a day of incessant occupation. Each one
> celebrates Mass twice, and it is necessary to give two or three
> instructions, besides continual attendance in the confessional.

So Polding toiled, through this and nearly forty subsequent
summers, his confessional an oven of heat and sour with
the stench of sweat, yet a cool oasis of peace in a desert of
vice.

And there were ceaseless other activities—he administered
the sacrament of confirmation for the first time in the
colony; he became a familiar figure moving among the
chain gangs. With Ullathorne he devised a scheme to attend
to the spiritual needs of new convicts as they came. When a
convict ship arrived, the government permitted all the
Catholics to be entrusted to Polding for four or five days.
They were marched to St Mary's at 6 in the morning, remaining until 11, and returned again in the afternoon from
3 to 6. There they were given spiritual exercises, exhortations
and instructions, beginning—for most of them knew virtually
nothing—with the simplest of truths, the existence of God
and the immortality of the soul. It was typical of Polding
that, as these convicts assembled, he should weep over them;
for he saw himself surrounded by men whom providence had
led through an immense tribulation so that they might be
rid of sin; he saw God working through evil itself, a great
and most moving consolation to him. He was in his confessional more frequently, and longer, than any of his
priests. His confessional was besieged by convict penitents,

who at times moaned aloud with the burden of their crimes. Often as congregations waited impatiently for Mass or for his preaching, Polding had to be persuaded to leave, still weeping, the confessions of convicts: 'Others I could leave to another time; but these poor creatures who have no one to care for them, I cannot.' His preaching brought a similar opening of hearts and minds. His style was homely, yet the doctrines stood forth in firm simplicity; it contained exhortations which made both preacher and congregation weep, yet the great dogmatic truths were there too, leaping out of his meditations to transfix and transform listening minds.

This was merely Polding's ministry in Sydney itself. The impact of his prodigious spiritual campaign was swift and clear, well beyond the limits of the growth of veneration for Polding himself. There was a surge of renewed spiritual life, obvious in a sharp increase in the number of communions. In previous years, many convicts committed new offences soon after their arrival. By 1837, 1,400 newly arrived convicts had passed through Polding's system of spiritual exercises: only two had found their way back to Sydney gaol. By 1841, 7,000 Catholic convicts had gone through this system. Public authorities acknowledged a drop in crime and a general increase in tranquillity.

On this basis of social reformation, Polding approached the government in May 1836 for an increase in the number of priests, admitting that, for all his labours and despite ample evidence of success, the problem was so vast that all the present clergymen could do was to keep religion from entire decay. Like Ullathorne, Polding saw that their priests' time and energy—to the very limits of exhaustion—were taken up in running hastily from place to place, to meet emergencies and supply only the most pressing needs, and that inadequately, to administer the rites of religion to the child and to the dying man.

Polding wept not only in compassion, and in the face of wickedness, but at the sheer immensity of his task. His efforts in Sydney were often wasted because of the lack of religious ministry in the interior of the colony, a wilderness of spiritual neglect, and promiscuity. Yet, to Polding's wonder and consolation, even in remote places might be found those who did persevere, who, in the absence of any priest, still prepared themselves as for Mass and the sacraments, week by week: in 1836 it seemed to him that only priests were necessary to make the country Catholic. Seeing the want, Polding made its remedying a very personal obligation. He began a life of constant travelling, all over the colony, away for weeks or months at a time, visiting every Catholic who conducted himself well, passing those who gave public scandal, stopping for protracted missionary efforts where he found religion most neglected. His greatest difficulty was to get couples married, and their children baptised: having adopted the laws of nature they often could see no reason not to continue in them. In September 1838 he was away for a month in which he rode 900 miles. 'I live when I travel,' Polding remarked in 1837, 'entirely on bread and tea, now and then an egg, nothing more . . .' In later life, bad food (damper and acid bread) tended to impair his health on such trips. Polding, an excellent horseman, loved the country and was excited by its strangeness. Often, at the end of an arduous day's riding, he was less fatigued than the young clergy who accompanied him. His description of his journey to Western Australia in 1852 may be taken as typical of the more strenuous of his many journeys:

> . . . hundreds of miles through a wild uninhabited country, travelling days and nights without meeting with hut or man; at night resting on the wet ground, it being winter time, and storms most fearful; branches broken off and whirling about through the violence of the wind, and tumbling on every side; vast trees torn up by the roots, and large lumps of ice cutting one's face until the blood streamed . . . Twice was I swept off my poor jaded horse by branches hanging down in the dark, and falling on my back, and yet not hurt.

What did Polding achieve? Ullathorne, critical of Polding in many ways, touched the essence when he said that Polding 'raised the Catholics into a religious people'. And by his example he inspired a vigorous missionary spirit in his clergy. It was nothing for his inland clergy to ride up to five thousand miles in a year of ministry. Success in what Polding valued most—the search for souls—cost him what he valued next dear, his own dream of the earthly organisation of that ministry.

Polding had come to Australia with the firm intention of setting up a Benedictine monastery as the centre and form of Catholic life. He believed that the salvation of that sinful land lay in revealing to it the beauty of holiness; the ordered loveliness of religion would shine forth to the colonists in the exemplary lives of a monastic community which would manifest the ideal Christian life. This vision was, with Polding, more than a hope. He was quite certain that without the establishment of a Benedictine monastery, 'we can do no good'.

In part, this conviction reflected Polding's personal faith, as a Benedictine, in the redemptive power of his own rule, and his belief in its peculiar applicability to the colony's situation. He was obsessed by the destructive potential of a clerical pursuit of wealth: 'the vow of poverty alone can prevent the accumulation of wealth, the bane of the Church and the destruction of the individual.' He was appalled by the 'grasping at money' characteristic of some of the Anglican clergy, and fearful lest this canker should corrupt secular priests, that is, those priests who were not members of a religious order and thus free to accumulate possessions. Lack of money hamstrung many of Polding's own efforts, particularly in education, but his attitude was quite simple: 'As for means of support, we have quite enough; more than Peter the Fisherman, and Paul the tent-maker.' Personally, his circumstances were ascetic; his room was a ˙tiny cell, with a small iron bed, a chair, a table, a wardrobe and a bookcase. And he was very critical of what he took to be the greed, the pursuit of money, which he saw in some Irish priests: he failed to realise that many of these priests, coming from families desperately poor, were supportiing their families with remittances to Ireland. To such Irish priests and their families, the priesthood was a way towards temporal as well as eternal salvation.

There was his belief in Christian poverty. There was also Polding's conviction that vice and irreligion were to be conquered by the vital example of virtue and dedicated religion publicly established and lived out. It was in this way that he linked the naturally divergent aims of monastery and mission. Essentially, the monastic life meant the individual sanctification, through worship and contemplation, of the monks themselves, within the monastery walls. In contrast, the mission was as wide as the colonial world, as dispersed as Christ's flock, and to all conditions of men. Polding dreamt of a mission in which a monastery would give focus and ideal meaning.

There was at stake the honour of the Benedictine order, too. The failures of Bishops Slater and Morris in the Mauritius mission had harmed, to the extent of disgrace, the Benedictine reputation in Rome and elsewhere. Benedictine hopes of rehabilitating the missionary good name of their order rested squarely on Polding, a responsibility of which he was very conscious (both he and Ullathorne were aware of being pioneers for their order in the post-emancipation age).

Polding had left England with three priests, three sub-deacons, two catechists, and a boy, which he intended as the nucleus of a Benedictine monastery. When he arrived, he found that there was no money for such a foundation and that the country desperately needed not monks but missionaries. Immediately he became a missionary himself; his office as bishop in effect became secondary; his vocation as monk a poor third. And he sent his priests to the interior. Much has been written about the attempt and the failure to found a Benedictine monastery-mission in Australia. Just as Polding was its great champion, so was he the fundamental cause of its collapse. Its failure lay in Polding's response to the situation he found on his arrival. Had his heart been smaller, his vision and love narrower, he might have chosen the path of an episcopal monk, and his monastery might have stood, a lonely lighthouse, in a land made desert by pastoral neglect.

The fact was that Polding chose, for the greater part of his episcopal life, to work as a simple priest, constantly travelling, preaching, teaching the catechism, hearing the confessions of multitudes, and attending the sick and dying. Indeed to say he chose this is false to the workings of his generosity. It would be truer to say that, finding himself in the midst of a vast pastoral work, he lamented the decay of his great hopes for a monastic ideal. Polding's dream of a Benedictine Australia failed because he did not attempt to achieve it above all else. Working as a simple priest, he failed to act as bishop. When he did act episcopally, it was in the interest of the mission first, and that of his beloved monastery after. His monastery still remained beloved, the object of his loving ambition. He was blind to the consequences of his own generosity, of his consuming love for sinners. He could not see that he, a fisher of men in that dark sin-stained colonial sea, had forsaken all things, even the cherished expression of his spiritual desires, to follow Christ.

If, in retrospect, it seems that the die was cast against Benedictinism by Polding himself, and by all the events that followed, this did not seem so to Polding. He set out firmly towards his monastic goal. Nor did his failure to achieve it seem inevitable to those to whom his monastic dream was repugnant; their claim that its failure was inevitable was part of their campaign to ensure its failure. A dominant theme of the thirty years following Polding's arrival was a conflict over the form, organisation and destiny of Catholicism in Australia.

Polding saw the imperative need for more priests. In June 1836 he sent Ullathorne home to implore assistance. Polding and Ullathorne sought two related things. Firstly, papal approval for the establishment of a Benedictine monastery in New South Wales. This they obtained. Secondly, they wanted Benedictine recruits or, at least, English priests. In this they failed. The Superior of Downside could spare no monks for the mission. Some English priests offered their services, but their bishops, desperately under-staffed, refused to release them. As a last resort, Ullathorne went to Ireland. The Irish bishops received him warmly. At this time they were considering the foundation of a seminary for educating priests for the British colonies and foreign missions. This was to result, in November 1842, in the establishment of All Hallows College in Dublin. In the meantime, the bishops encouraged volunteers, and Ullathorne secured about ten priests from Ireland.

Ullathorne saw clearly what this situation implied. By the middle of 1838 he was convinced that 'To do anything Benedictine in the Colony is now out of the question . . .' The failure of the Benedictine order and the English church to respond had 'destroyed my prospect of Benedictinising the Colony—a plan I thought both feasible and desirable, as did Rome . . .' This, coupled with the Irish response, had 'Hibernicised our Mission'; 'the Colony will become, of course, an Irish mission, and perhaps ought to be so.' The Irish seminary plan, urged by Rome, for the supply of the colonies, and moves in some Roman quarters to bring the colonies under the Irish hierarchy, completed the picture for Ullathorne. Not only was Benedictinism at an end as a goal, but he foresaw future conflict: 'I have much confidence in the piety and present good dispositions of all our new missioners, but doubt much whether the Mission would work well, all the superiors being English, and all the subjects, nearly Irish.' This being so, Ullathorne decided to leave the colonial mission himself, within three years, not in any fit of pique, or because he had lost his missionary zeal, but because he had seen, in a flash, the nature of the situation. His was a Benedictine vocation; he wished to pursue it in tranquillity. He thought that his presence in Australia might be an obstacle to the mission's advancement; he could serve the mission better in England, as advocate or agent.

Ullathorne had the gift of realistic perception. Polding had his holy dreams. He failed to see what Ullathorne saw so clearly—that his Benedictinism must fail. His blindness ensnared all in bitterness. Polding, so transparent in the affairs of souls, was often opaque to the world's realities. He was too absorbed in his dream of Benedictine spirituality and culture radiating from his beloved monastery to see obstacles, however real, however insuperable.

It was left to Ullathorne to unite, in a poised humility, a full acceptance of the universal needs of souls with a full recognition of their particularly human and local bent. Speaking to the laity of Sydney in January 1839, Ullathorne made his submission:

I have had no other will than yours, for in yours I have been accustomed to see the will of God. You spoke and I went forth; you breathed into me your spirit, and that spirit prevailed . . . you were ever in my heart; I lived but for you . . . wherever my steps fell, in public or in private life, I spoke of you and of your wants . . . In whatever I have said or written of you, at home or in foreign lands, I had but one object— to deter poor, weak, ignorant men from crime, and to arouse the zeal of good men to hasten with their help to the fallen . . .

I know of no politics, for I am set apart to religion, I know of no parties or party views—except to lament the disunions and uncharities which grow out of them—for I am a minister of peace.

Fine words—with the ring of St Paul boasting of his tribulations.

In the midst of the destruction of his Benedictine plans and desires, Ullathorne bowed before God:

I have seen strange invisible things as though they were visible. I have seen circumstances and events follow and combine with each other in numerous and strange ways, independently of human will in our regard, that I can no more doubt the finger of a special Providence over our affairs, than if I saw it incarnate before me. I have done nothing, I was but the empty capacious vessel of reception for the gifts of God as they unexpectedly came from many quarters. Ireland, as of old, supplied her saints, and England gave her money . . .

It was Ireland which, in the ways of providence, had supplied the saints: for Ullathorne, the Benedictine dream was over. For Polding, the dream remained untouched, its realisation about to begin.

It was Polding, not Ullathorne, who disputed the ground with the Irish. Ullathorne left to follow his own life. Yet, although it was he who first conceded the Australian mission field to Ireland, and that fifty years before it was formally won, the Irish judgement of Ullathorne has been harsh—a snob. The Irish saw in Ullathorne merely his air of confident superiority. That, he had: all men have their dooms. As in their dealings with Polding, the champions of Ireland failed to consider that the cause of Benedictine monasticism might mean as much to the Benedictines as the cause of Irish religion meant to the Irish. And none took the measure of Ullathorne's renunciation. Who cared for that? It meant nothing to them save their own victory. But the fact remained that Ullathorne could accept the failure of that which he cherished, Benedictinism, as nothing but cause for a passing human regret in the face of his joy in the spread of Catholicism, priesthood, faith and good lives. Essentially, if reluctantly, despite his dreams, Polding possessed the same lucidity. Their opponents within Catholicism were not all distinguished by the same clarity of vision and judgement.

In conceding the future to the Irish, Ullathorne had spoken of providence. The essence of Irish religious ambition was not dislike for English episcopal authority: that was accepted without difficulty in some circumstances—in England itself, for instance. At the core of Irishism lay the conviction that God was on the side of the Irish: they were instruments of his providence. This conviction had in it the makings of a sacrificial heroism—and the seeds of pride, arrogance, and want of scruple. So great was the religious destiny God had marked out for the Irish in Australia, that nothing must stand in its way. In this, and in its failure to separate nationality and religion, lay the doom of Irishism. The Irish were to erect a church of abounding vitality, far more vigorous than any the Benedictines might have made on some English pattern. But the Irish built for their own, no less exclusive a structure than the English one they determined to frustrate. At the time, the Irish structure did not seem narrow or exclusive, for Irish and Catholic then meant virtually the same. As the Irish had denied the catholicity of the Benedictine dream, so the Australian future was to deny the catholicity of Irishism.

In the conflict between Benedictinism and Irishism, the Irish triumph has been both praised and lamented. Lament should be reserved for the fact that the conflict occurred, praise for the fact that the church survived and thrived. If there be anything of tragedy in this conflict, it is in the pity that men of good will, seeking after good, should be at odds; and in the terror that, in obstinacy and blindness, they should hurt each other, and harm the cause they all, fundamentally, held dear.

Ullathorne returned from Europe in December 1838. He was immediately swept into a vortex of controversy which was to leave him with the public brand of 'Very Reverend Agitator-General of N.S.W.' When Polding had left England in 1835, his mission had provoked some indignation: it was taken to amount to government approval of the aspirations of popery. He was soon confronted by a similar situation in New South Wales. Anglicans, particularly the militantly conservative Bishop Broughton who was appointed Anglican Bishop of Australia in 1836 and held a seat on the Executive Council, clung tenaciously to their ideal of an Anglican establishment. They persistently sought to undo the church legislation of 1836-7 which placed Anglicanism on equality with other denominations. Catholics defended this legislation, for it was their charter of religious liberty, but it was not an entirely unmixed blessing. It led to an influx of Protestant dissenting clergy—Presbyterians, Methodists, Congregationalists—and with them came a virulent strain of anti-Catholic animus less obvious before.

To Anglicanism, Governor Bourke's church legislation seemed entirely bad. Broughton was opposed to Protestant dissent. He was even more opposed to Catholicism, and, from the middle of 1836, led a public campaign against it. To him Catholicism was idolatrous, inquisitorial, hostile to Bible reading and socially dangerous in that it was willing, for its own designs, to ally itself with the evil forces of liberalism. Worse, it sought the domination and enslavement of all men: any growth or development of Catholicism Broughton equated with aggression. Polding, using a pseudonym, replied to Broughton in a series of newspaper articles. However, Polding did not regard Anglicanism, for all its abrasive pressure, as a serious religious rival. 'To suppose that the cold forms of Protestantism can ever have effect on our abandoned population is absurd. Zeal amounting to enthusiasm is required. So long as Methodism does not come in, we have no rival to fear . . .' Nor did he value highly the dedication of other clergy: 'I doubt much whether Methodist Ministers would persevere long. Money is to be made more rapidly by tending the quadrupedal than the biped flock. Hence, most of those who come out here to preach the Gospel, sink into woolgrowers and herd feeders.'

Polding regarded most of the anti-Catholic prejudice and bigotry that existed in the colony as political—Tory—in origin, not religious. Such animus sought, basically, the political oppression of Catholics; Polding wondered what would have happened to the rights of Catholics if Plunkett, the Attorney-General, had not been a Catholic. And, in large part, Polding was right: the anti-Catholicism of, for example, the *Sydney Herald* was directed towards preserving the existing ascendancy by the exclusion of a Catholic mob from the franchise. In contrast, Broughton's prejudice was religious; his attacks, as such, might be endured. Those of Mr Justice Willis could not.

In July 1838 Willis publicly denounced 'the undue assumption of spiritual power, the adoption of unauthorised traditions and idolatrous worship' of the Church of Rome. Polding presided over the Catholic public meeting of protest which demanded Willis's removal from the bench—no Catholic could feel secure in impartial justice while he remained there. Polding disliked controversy; he sought peace, and counselled peace—'the greatest of all temporal blessings' —but he was determined to get rid of Willis: 'the decision on this case will either attach or detach the affections of the people to the Government. If they uphold Willis, good-bye to peace and union for many a long day. Remove him, and we shall never again be disturbed.' His instructions to Father Heptonstall, who acted on his behalf in London, were vigorously explicit: 'Spare no expense, no trouble; oust Willis, and you will save us folios of controversy.' Willis was transferred to Melbourne, and later removed from the bench. His fate was a measure of the public distance Catholicism had travelled since Therry's dismissal as chaplain thirteen years before. The folios of controversy, however, were merely beginning to be written.

While in England in 1836-8, Ullathorne had published two pamphlets, *The Catholic Mission in Australasia* and *The Horrors of Transportation briefly unfolded to the People,* and had given evidence before the Select Committee on Transportation. All his efforts strongly condemned the evils, vices and degradations of the convict system, and this had aroused fierce indignation among those colonists who wanted transportation continued, those who regarded it as an economic necessity, those who possessed virtually free convict labour. As Ullathorne remarked: 'I had deeply wounded both freemen and emancipists, in two ways, had touched them, in two most sensitive points, in their pride and in their pockets.' Ullathorne, and the church generally, came under scarifying fire. A letter of the *Sydney Herald* gives the flavour:

The cloven foot, which Jesuitical cunning for some time endeavoured to conceal, is again put forth—the tyrannical and
exterminating spirit of Popery again rears its head—now,
viper-like, insidiously stinging those whose too great liberality
and charity have restored to the serpent its venomous fangs—
now again boldly trampling under foot all that resists its
blighting progress.

Within clerical ranks, the attacks of Dr Broughton were
supplemented—and outdone—by those of Dr John Dunmore
Lang, that tempestuous, acidulated Presbyterian minister
who regarded the Pope as the Man of Sin, and local
Catholics as his diabolical minions plotting to dominate New
South Wales. Besides abuse, Lang's efforts were directed
towards securing Scots and Ulster immigrants to balance the
Catholic Irish. Meanwhile Broughton, with constant reference to the Statute Law of England and the Oath of
Supremacy, challenged every Catholic claim to public equality, and notably Polding's appearance at the Governor's
levees in his garb as a Catholic bishop.

Polding summed up the core of this attack when he
observed that he had been 'classed with the infidel and the
socialist; was described as the enemy of truth, and as linked
with Satan . . .' In July 1839 he issued a Pastoral in reply,
denying any Catholic provocation, or intention to seek
worldly power: 'Our aim has been, and will be, to mind our
own business, to fulfil the end of our ministry, that we may
render a good account to Him who has called us into it . . .'
However, Polding declared, Catholics would fight for religious
liberty, and 'repel every attempt that may be made to
establish a privileged denomination of Christians amongst
us.'

Ullathorne joined in this counter-attack, defending himself and the non-aggressive nature of Australian Catholicism.
He asked the pertinent question:

> What is our crime? we have mingled in no party strife or
> political contention, we have not sought to make ourselves
> a property, we have taken none of our time, or of our small
> means from our people to ourselves—acts which are readily
> excused in the clergy of other creeds . . . what is our crime,
> but that we have laboured and striven to present our people
> to the Government better subjects, to employers more faithful

and trustworthy dealers, to masters more orderly and better servants, to society better men? If we have failed in this attempt, whom have we injured? If we have at all succeeded, where is our guilt?

The Anglican claim to superiority, and its bitter anti-Catholicism, made certain that Catholics would take their stand on liberty and equality—an enduring theme in Australian Catholic history. Polding and Ullathorne stressed this, and a public meeting of Catholics in July 1839 resolved that 'Perfect equality amongst all religious denominations is our sole object, and that we are determined to uphold'. The same meeting sought the removal of Broughton from the Councils of the colony, as being required by legislation imposing religious equality.

Insistence on liberty and equality was logical for a minority religion. It was also a *liberal* argument, in its emphasis on liberty and equality as the principles of state policy towards religion—ideas then being propounded as ideals in European Catholicism, particularly by Lamennais in France—and condemned by the papacy. Obviously, the demand for liberty and equality was the only possible Catholic policy in Australia, but this demand had a marked tendency to translate what was possible into what was desirable: the campaign for 'perfect equality' soon became one in which equality represented perfection. The importance of this translation in determining Catholic attitudes in Australia can scarcely be over-estimated. For many Catholics the ideal public religious situation (outside the personal life of the soul) became one in which their religion would be separate but indistinguishable from any other. To take a stand on equality in a world where Protestantism was to decline was to risk sharing that decline. And there can be no doubt that the pursuit of equality was an aggressive one. As Ullathorne put it: 'we had to meet the long cherished traditions of Protestant supremacy, and to *assert* that equality before the law, which the law itself has given us.' Thus equality became further elevated towards an ideal, the more vigorously it was asserted—and denied.

Whatever its faults, the aggressive Irishry which character-ised the Australian church in the later part of the nineteenth century and earlier years of the twentieth, had one enormous, saving grace: it provided a firm, distinctive and meaningful Catholic identity at a time when other religions were crumbling into the amorphous and the nondescript.

The 1838 Catholic defence did not halt the Anglican attack. It entered a new phase of hostility with the publication in 1840 of Judge Burton's *The State of Religion and Education in N.S.W.*, in which Catholicism was denigrated and Anglican establishment advocated. Ullathorne hit back with his sensational *Reply to Judge Burton.* The Catholics now had a voice in the *Australian Chronicle,* founded in August 1839 by a group of leading Catholic laymen, as a defence measure. In September 1840 a branch of the Catholic Association of Great Britain was established to deal with the Protestant Tract Society; Ullathorne was a prominent figure. The Association accused the Tract Society of promoting enmity and division between two classes of Her Majesty's subjects, and, by representations to the Colonial Office, forced government officials to withdraw from the Society.

Polding had seen that anti-Catholic animus was largely political, that is, directed towards excluding Catholics from positions of political or social influence. He did not realise that this would certainly provoke a political response. Efforts to remove Judge Willis, Bishop Broughton, and government officials from the Tract Society were all, essentially, political activities. However, the Catholic body was predominantly Irish, and if it was forced, as a body, to take political action, it would be Irish political action. The effect of Anglican efforts to secure dominance was to rouse a vigorous Catholic—and that meant Irish—determination that they would not. The first Australian sectarian equation was a simple one: aggressive Anglicanism produced aggressive Irish Catholicism.

The beginnings of an organised Irish response are apparent in the circumstances of the laying of the foundation stone of Sydney's second church, St. Patrick's, Church Hill, in August 1840. Shortly before this, Polding and Ullathorne had had an interview with the Governor, Sir George Gipps, concerning his scheme for reorganising the elementary education system on a non-denominational basis, plus Bible reading. They strenuously opposed Gipps's views, to which he eventually replied: '. . . I must adhere to the strongest party, and I don't think you are the strongest.' Polding and Ullathorne then decided to make a public demonstration of strength: if the Catholics were not the most numerous, they were the most united. They decided upon the laying of the St Patrick's foundation stone as the occasion.

Soon the demonstration showed signs of escaping their control. 'Hitherto,' Ullathorne wrote, 'national distinctions had been instinctively avoided in the Colony; all prided themselves as being Australians.' But as the day of the ceremony approached, 'a warm national feeling' was raised among the Irish Catholic population, and they resolved to make it a national demonstration. Green banners, scarves and other Irish emblems were prepared. This alarmed the government, which feared an Orange counter-demonstration, ending in a riot or, at the very least, organised social factions. Polding, unwilling to go against the enthusiasm of his flock, would not intervene. Eventually, Ullathorne, with one of his remarkable demonstrations of persuasive ability, induced the organising committee to abandon the Irish emblems. The procession was the largest and by far the most impressive seen in Australia up to that time, with bands, 300 girls in white, and thousands of marching Catholics (then comprising 14,000 of Sydney's population of 40,000).

Ullathorne records that many non-Catholics were impressed; he does not refer to the many who must also have been alarmed by the show of strength. Irishry was on the march. So were the Orange Lodges, strongholds of ultra-conservative Protestantism, which had opened in New South Wales in the mid-1840s. The Irish hurling matches which Father McEncroe took care to organise in Hyde Park on 12 July, the day of the Orange procession, were not regarded as any joke at that time. The second sectarian equation was that aggressive Irish Catholicism produced aggressive Orange Protestantism.

Polding left Australia for Europe in November 1840, enjoining peace and harmony but with the din of sectarian strife ringing in his ears. His objective was to remedy the grave need for priests. He was accompanied by one of his priests, H. G. Gregory, and by Ullathorne, who was not to return.

Polding had once said to Ullathorne: '. . . we made a complete man between us, and that I was needful to supply in those points in which he was deficient.' To another priest he had confessed: 'I cannot live unless those about me, into whose souls I may pour my thoughts freely and uncontrolled by any apprehension, be of the number [of intimate friends].' Polding could not live in himself. In his missionary work this was a prodigious virtue, indeed it was the whole meaning of his character; his love went out without stint. The result was that by October 1839 Ullathorne could say: 'The moral face of the country is showing a new set of features'. By that time about 3,500 of Sydney's 14,000 nominal Catholics were attending Sunday Mass regularly, and there were about 650 monthly communions, which was a tremendous advance on the previous practice of religion. In 1835 there had been three priests, three churches in course of construction, ten schools and 200 communions. By 1841 there was a bishop and twenty-four priests, nine churches completed, six being built, thirty-one schools, and—here his spiritual impact lies revealed—23,130 communions. There was, of course, still a long way to go. In 1842 the average Sunday Mass attendance in all the Australian colonies was about 9,000, roughly one-fifth of those nominally Catholic. This low attendance rate is only partly explained by dispersion of population and shortage of priests. Nevertheless, Polding's work had transformed the situation.

As another man might crave power, or drink, Polding craved the hearts and souls of men—for God—and here lay his great missionary zeal; but this also was important for himself: he could not live without friends, confidants, a person or a group on whom he depended. And in Polding the Bishop, this was a grave weakness. His friendship was an enormous burden to Ullathorne. Obviously, administration fell to him. The Bishop was overworked, mainly in the confessional and catechetical instruction. He was seldom at home during the day, away on visitations, often in the country, hardly ever at his desk. He had no administrative routine. Correspondence with the government was neglected and unanswered: his entire business was in arrears and confusion. Ullathorne did what he could, in anguish:

> No one but who has experienced it, knows the pain of the evil effect on self, of being obliged to govern and almost command your own superior and he a Bishop. God help me! . . . Understand me: the Bishop is doing vast good as a missioner, and is idolised by the people as he is beloved as well as pitied by his clergy; only God never made him to govern or transact business.

Ullathorne's problem was not simply one of remedying neglect; he also had to deal with Polding's terrible inability to make decisions. When faced by problems, he sometimes floated off into a playful optimism, a cheery assumption that all would somehow come right. More often, particularly with difficulties involving public opinion, or likely to make him unpopular, he would lapse into depression and paralysis of will. Although he knew his own weaknesses—procrastination and indecision—he could not defeat them. It was Ullathorne's task to rouse Polding from his utter misery, and persuade him to look such problems in the face. Thus, when confronted by the problem of what to do about the planned Irish demonstration at the foundation laying of St Patrick's in August 1840, Polding eventually allowed Ullathorne to act. When Ullathorne succeeded, Polding, in tears, flung himself on Ullathorne's shoulders crying that he was always saving him. Invariably he put things off: often, real prudence lay in prompt decisions, which he was always most reluctant to take, even under Ullathorne's constant urging. His failure to write important letters frequently led to needless misunderstandings, and, sometimes, serious trouble. Or, at a whim, or on an impulse, he would make some unfortunate decision, leaving Ullathorne with the consequences.

The Bishop had made it clear that Ullathorne, as Vicar-General, was expected to bear the brunt of attacks on the church, to do the odious things, and to protect the episcopal office from unpopularity. Ullathorne was ready to do this, but not, eventually, without resentment. He found that while Polding's public reputation was that of an angelic Catholicism, charitable and tolerant, his own image was that of 'medieval bigotry and intolerance'. Worse, Polding would not stand by his friends when they needed him. When a torrent of abuse descended on Ullathorne after his criticism of transportation, Polding, who completely agreed with that criticism, was confused and dismayed, and would say nothing in Ullathorne's defence. Nor would he defend him from the envy and denigration of other priests, until Ullathorne demanded that he do so.

By 1840, Ullathorne's health had deteriorated under these pressures. He was nervous and depressed, and beginning to be convinced that he would be better off without the colony, and the colony better off without him, for every sectarian disturbance seemed to centre on him personally. In any case, when Polding pressed him to accept first a coadjutorship, then the Bishopric of Tasmania and later that of Adelaide, Ullathorne was adamant in his refusal: 'I had seen sufficient of bishops, I said, to compassionate them, but not to envy them . . .' So, despite Polding's implorings, Ullathorne remained in England. He became a bishop in 1846, and died as Bishop of Birmingham, and one of England's leading ecclesiastics, in 1889. Ullathorne had been able to protect Polding from the consequences of his shortcomings. For the next two decades, until 1860, this task fell on the shoulders of H. G. Gregory. The problems of those decades far outweighed those of 1835-40, and Gregory was far less well equipped than Ullathorne to deal with them.

Ullathorne, however, made one last impression on Polding. He persuaded him to seek, in Rome, the formation of a hierarchy. Van Diemen's Land was obviously in need of its own bishop. In May 1839 Polding had sent the Irish Franciscan, Patrick Geoghegan, to establish Catholicism in Melbourne, where settlement had begun in 1835. Ullathorne himself had gone to South Australia in May 1840 to organise the church there. The church was growing—and dispersing—too rapidly for Polding's authority alone to be adequate.

Accepting Ullathorne's plan, Polding placed it before the Roman authorities in November 1841. He stressed the excessive size of his jurisdiction: to visit it entailed great expense and waste of time. Besides, visits were ineffective; residence was required; division of territorial authority was imperative; more bishops were necessary for discipline. Polding submitted that such bishops must be both ordinaries and vicars apostolic. The appointment of ordinaries, with local territorial jurisdiction, would solve legal problems, avoid unease or discontent among the laity, and stop Protestants representing them as foreign intruders: the existence of Anglicanism, which had an episcopal church government, was a potent factor in prompting Polding to establish other dioceses in order to forestall the Anglicans. At the same time, vicars apostolic, with their wider, roving authority, were necessary for the firm establishment of discipline in a missionary situation.

In March 1842, Rome approved the setting up of episcopal sees in Hobart and Adelaide, with a Metropolitan Archbishop —Polding—in Sydney. In 1845 a West Australian bishopric was established, and that of Melbourne in 1847. The honour conferred by his archbishopric pleased Polding, but he still felt strongly the pull of the convict mission. 'Were I to follow my own inclinations, I would prefer moving to Van Diemen's Land, since the prisoners are sent there, and not to N. S. Wales. They gave me my vocation, and to their instruction I feel strongly attached.' With the stopping of transportation to New South Wales in 1840, Polding's real interest—his vocation—became less and less relevant to the actual situation.

The British government acquiesced in the foundation of an Australian Catholic hierarchy, the first to be erected in a British possession since the Reformation. In the colony Bishop Broughton protested that Polding's assumption of the title of Archbishop of Sydney was 'an act of invasion and intrusion on the part of the Church of Rome'; he refused to serve with Polding on a charitable committee. Australian Catholicism's first Provincial Council, in September 1844, was important as an effort to promote Catholic unity and solidarity in the face of a continuing Anglican offensive. However, the Anglican onslaught was weakening as that church's internal problems worsened with growing Evangelicalism, the High versus the Low church issue. It was secularism which was to be the threat of the future.

Polding also obtained, on his visit to Rome, a rescript recognising St Mary's as a monastic cathedral, with a Benedictine monastery annexed. Here was papal recognition of Polding's dream: there would be regular recitation of the

Divine Office, in choir at the canonical hours; Sydney would know Matins, Lauds and Vespers. At last, Polding believed, there would shine forth 'the beauty of the holiness which is the ornament of the Catholic Church'. 'I would wish to keep choir . . . this would give tone and form to the good work.' And the good work would be done by men of the Benedictine Order 'brought up in simplicity and obedience, in habits of retiredness and of self restraint, which We know from experience to be the best preparation for the future Apostolic Missionary.' The vows of poverty and obedience would unite all the clergy of the diocese, be they English, Irish, or Italian, into one monastic, missionary co-operation, conforming their individual wishes to the common good, as marked out by the authority of the Bishop.

Holy dreams. The reality was very different. From the beginning Polding had insisted on the great need for care in selecting clergymen for the colonies. 'They live so continually in the eye of the Public, their conduct must be spotless, or Religion vitally suffers.' Their missionary work 'with men coarse and addicted to vulgar habits', 'indifferent to everything except money and drink', meant that 'prudence and steadiness are as necessary as zeal; and perseverance!!' But Polding did not take his own advice. His selections were frequently unsatisfactory. So anxious was he to get monks to implement his dream that he would take anyone, suitable or not; those who presented themselves were often the most unstable, fired by romantic illusions about colonial life. Since Polding's arrival in 1835 there had been plotting, jealousy and insubordination within the small group of Benedictines. In 1838 he had opened his ecclesiastical seminary. Its progress was very slow: in 1843 he ordained seven priests, but he also dismissed three from his monastery.

And what about 'the object I have most at heart—after the propagation of religion, the diffusion of sound taste and a love of the arts'? The main obstacles were general illiteracy and sheer incomprehension. Even among those Catholics who did value the arts—a small section, but far from being any Benedictine preserve (indeed some Benedictines were not in it)—few shared Polding's tastes. When, in 1839, he set up a choral society, he found that he could not change the tradition of Irish singing: 'I must now have chants from

Ireland which I detest . . . modifications of that Gregorian chant which I loved so much in dear Downside.'

To change a tradition of singing was a much simpler matter than to change a whole religious outlook. Yet that is what Polding, in effect, set out to do when he returned to Australia in March 1843, his Benedictine enthusiasm glowing under the papal benediction. He did not hope that other priests would join his monastery, he *assumed* that they would. Writing to the Archbishop of Dublin in October 1843, he made the assumption that Irish priests being trained in All Hallows College for the mission would join the Benedictine Order upon arriving in Australia. The first such priests, arriving in 1847, made it clear that they would not, and that to think they might was something of a joke. But even in 1842, other Benedictines could discern that Polding was dreaming, and that if he continued to do so there would be trouble. The Benedictine Bishop Brown told the Prior of Downside in June 1842:

> The clergy and people in Australia are almost all Irish, having a strong national feeling. Dr Ullathorne, and I think Dr Polding, told me that the Australian Irish clergy, and their countrymen, including the Bishops in Ireland, were sore at being under an English Bishop and a Regular . . . what will it be when new Bishops, foreigners as they may be termed, shall be appointed, and the resident clergy and even their nation of which the Irish are most jealous shall be overlooked. Let Dr Polding recommend Irishmen for Bishops, and more good will be done.

There was, obviously, much truth in this; and Polding did not foresee that the erection of a hierarchy was to make it even more certain that his dream of a Benedictine Australia would never come true. Nevertheless, it is quite clear that the Irish-English friction was only one, and not the major one, of the causes of the internal turmoil that seized the church over the next twenty years. Of the five bishops Polding appointed in the 1840s, three were Irish—Francis Murphy of Adelaide, John Brady of Perth, and James Goold of Melbourne. Bishop Willson of Hobart, and his own coadjutor, Davis, were English. Sydney and Hobart had serious troubles, but so did the Irish-led dioceses of Adelaide, Perth and Melbourne. The Sydney disaffection had many English leaders, and the Irish martinet, Bishop Quinn of Brisbane, who led the new wave of Irish bishops in 1861, suffered similar challenges from Irish sources.

Basically, the ferment which troubled Australian Catholicism from the 1840s to the 1860s was a questioning of authority—any authority. Its sources were mainly three: the radical equalitarian movement within colonial society generally at that time, the insubordinate reaction of fifty years of Catholicism lived without the authority of clergy, and currents of thought associated with the Liberal Catholic movement in Europe and England.

Because Catholics came mainly from the lower social and economic orders, they were closely identified with those democratic, anti-authoritarian pressures which, about mid-century, were determining Australia's future character. The carry-over of secular attitudes into religious affairs, to question clerical authority, was a natural transference.

Again, there had been a notable absence of customary church discipline. In 1841 Polding's case for a hierarchy stressed the need for bishops to ensure discipline and order. Not until 1835 did any episcopal authority exist; that is, nearly fifty years after the first settlement. Even then, Polding's role had been missionary, transitory, sacramental: no hierarchical church existed in practice. Priests were few, far between, and essentially itinerant; independent in remoteness, they pleased themselves as to how they conducted their ministry. Lay Catholics, usually without a priest, conducted their own services. The erection of a hierarchy, with its stability and order, its growing resources of priests, and its efforts to ensure closer supervision and centralisation of policy, was a sharp constriction of the old free and easy order. Any real episcopal authority was bound to conflict with a tradition of independence which had been established by both laity and priests, and difficulties and friction were likely.

Added to this was the effect, from the 1830s, of liberalism, that is, ideas centred around the key concepts of liberty and equality, on those few Catholics who were cultivated and intellectual, those natural leaders.

Polding's first troubles surfaced when he was away in

1840-3. He had left Francis Murphy, Ullathorne's Irish priest of 'six-priest-power', as Vicar-General. He returned to find that Murphy had allowed Irish nationalism and factionalism to call the diocesan tune. The major casualty was W. A. Duncan, ejected from the editorship of the *Australian Chronicle*.

The idea of a Catholic newspaper had been initially McEncroe's: he had been trying to establish one in Sydney since 1837. With his American experience, McEncroe had argued that in order to rid themselves of social and political disadvantages, Catholics urgently needed the leadership and the voice of a newspaper. And these were the aims to which the *Chronicle* aspired, financed by a number of wealthy Irish Catholic emancipists. W. A. Duncan had been Polding's choice as editor.

Duncan came to the colony with Ullathorne, as a schoolteacher, in 1838. He had been a convert—at the age of sixteen—from Scots Presbyterianism, had a wide and diverse cultural background, and was still, for all his remarkable development of cultural and personal qualities, very young—twenty-seven when he arrived. He had intelligence, vision, integrity and will-power, all to a high degree—too high a degree perhaps, for his unusual self-reliance and independence tended towards a head-strong obstinacy, even irresponsibility; and his intellectual brilliance tempted him into self-righteousness and acid intolerance of lesser abilities. Duncan's energy and power—and his editorial policy of social and religious liberty and equality—had by 1840 made the *Chronicle* second only to the *Herald* in circulation. Polding was writing articles and some of the leaders. The original arrangement with the Irish emancipist owners was that Duncan would have complete control of policy. This was satisfactory while Duncan combated sectarianism and asserted emancipists' claims to equality in the colony. However, in Polding's absence, Duncan's policy, and his aggresive tone, brought him into conflict with the owners, who had the support of Murphy, the Vicar-General.

Duncan antagonised this group on two major counts. Obsessed with the ideal of social equality, he was the enemy of all privilege, and championed, in particular, a radical extension of the franchise—wealthy emancipist backers did not want this. They, and also the Vicar-General, found Duncan's forcefulness distasteful, for they feared it would offend Protestants and thus hinder their own social acceptance. Murphy was of this cautious temper, believing that the church should be unaggressive and should not engage in attacks on privilege. He regarded Duncan as a fomenter of dissension, and thus a hindrance to the progress of Catholicism: Duncan's criticism of Murphy as wanting in zeal was the reverse of that coin. However, such Irishmen as Murphy and the wealthy emancipists, while seeking the ways of quietude locally, were often rabidly nationalist in relation to Irish affairs. And here Duncan offended again. He refused to give the *Chronicle*'s support to the movement, led in Ireland by Daniel O'Connell, for repeal of the Act of Union between Great Britain and Ireland. Worse, he said he was against repeal. Indeed he was against any form of Irishism in Australia, believing that Irish national feeling transported to Australia was a disease, particularly when it afflicted Catholicism: 'Our religion is neither English nor Irish, but Catholic.'

So the owners, with Murphy's blessing, ejected Duncan from the editorship of the *Chronicle*. The *Weekly Register*, which Duncan founded to give himself a voice, was excellent in quality but not a financial success. Polding returned to find Duncan furious and embittered, and the Irish element triumphant. He asked Duncan to withhold criticisms of Murphy, while he, Polding, redeemed the situation. Typically, Polding failed to do anything. Duncan went his own way, into the civil service, and in the 1850s let loose shattering criticism of Polding's administration.

And how did Polding deal with Murphy, with whose performance he had been ill pleased? Murphy was appointed the first Bishop of Adelaide in 1844, which was punishment enough—and Murphy felt it to be so. South Australia was a poor mission, with neither church, nor chapel, nor schoolhouse, and only 1,200 Catholics in a population of 20,000. Those Catholics were scattered and poor: Murphy often slept in the open, his saddle his pillow. The Victorian goldrushes in 1851 left Adelaide almost deserted and almost destroyed the mission. The Bishop himself taught in the primary school for three days in the week, and survival—

poverty-stricken survival—was made possible only by one of his two priests appealing for aid in Victoria. It was typical of one side of Murphy's character that he should be, in 1847, the first bishop to reject a government grant rather than submit to what he regarded as government interference; typical of the other side that he should be popular among Protestants and acquire a public reputation for mildness and enlightenment. He died, of consumption, in 1858. Patrick Geoghegan, from Melbourne, succeeded him, but cancer was already robbing Geoghegan of his energies. By 1864, when Geoghegan died, there were twenty churches, nineteen schools and eighteen priests: the church existed in South Australia, but at that stage it had little character or dynamism, though this was to develop rapidly.

Bishop Murphy had disciplinary problems with the erratic, liberal intellectuality of one of his priests, Francis Coyle, but his bishopric was relatively untroubled in comparison with that of the Englishman Willson in Hobart, and that of the Irishman Brady in Western Australia—and in neither case can Irishism be blamed fully for what occurred.

Bishop Willson, an English secular priest, and contemporary of Polding's, had a reputation for good sense, calmness and benevolence:

> The imposing feature of his countenance was his brow. Square and well advanced above the eyes, the upper part presented an extraordinary development, which rose like a small second brow above the first ... Spurzheim was lecturing on phrenology in the Town Hall of Nottingham when Father Willson came in, removing his hat as he entered. The celebrated phrenologist interrupted his lecture and asked: 'Who is that gentleman? He has the largest development of benevolence I ever saw in a human head.'

Even this degree of benevolence was inadequate to the demands made on it by Father Therry, Vicar-General of Tasmania since 1838. Before accepting the Hobart bishopric, Willson insisted that Polding accept two conditions—that the church be out of debt, and that Therry, whose factious reputation Willson knew, be recalled from Hobart before he, Willson, arrived. Polding, who had Therry's assurance that there was no debt, agreed, but, in character, neglected to do anything. When Willson arrived in Hobart in 1844, he found Therry in full control, with a recently incurred debt of £3,000, strong lay support, and unwilling to hand over church property to Willson unless the Bishop accepted full responsibility for all debts. Furious, Willson immediately asked Polding to come to Hobart to settle the matter. Polding's intercession was in vain, and the dispute dragged on until 1857, embittering many years of the lives of all involved. Despite this, Willson achieved much good. With the end of transportation to New South Wales, his charge was similar to what Polding's had once been, a penal colony with all its problems: 'this huge jail,' Willson called it. Willson was no scholar, but he had an intense practical interest in criminology which he applied to reform.

However, Tasmania's major contribution to church life from 1844 to 1857 was the Therry *v.* Willson dispute: its influence was as wide as Therry's reputation, and as deep as the blind and passionate loyalties he commanded. The first damage this caused was to the relations between Willson and Polding. When, in 1844, Polding seemed to have persuaded Therry to give in, he found, to his astonishment, that Willson would not accept these terms, and even went so far as to protest against Polding's interference in the temporal affairs of the Hobart diocese. 'Vesuvius in a blaze,' remarked Polding privately. 'An apparently mild man in a passion is, to me, of all things the most awful.' Later, Willson wrote a deeply wounding letter to Polding, telling him that he had no confidence in him, that he formally and deliberately renounced his friendship, and that Polding had forfeited his title to be considered a just and honourable man. This breach was never healed. At first Polding was prepared to accept, ruefully, his blame in the affair; later he grew impatient. With increasing age and illness Willson became more and more critical of the Benedictines in Sydney.

Willson's whole life and ministry were soured and blighted by his dispute with Therry, whom he regarded as insane or, at least, totally without discipline. In 1849 Polding's co-adjutor, Davis, set out the essence of the Therry problem:

> . . . to be at variance with him is to be exposed to odium from all quarters, so much is he esteemed and loved by all

amongst whom he has been labouring during the last 30 years.
He is the queerest mixture of good and evil . . . that ever
crossed your path; benevolent and charitable in the extreme,
indefatigably zealous, and of extraordinary devotion . . . yet
. . . he will not scruple as to the means of annoying anyone
that unfortunately comes in contact with him.

This was to see Therry as a perplexing psychological
problem: to be forced to cope with that problem as a
practical one was to risk distraction and destruction. Willson
did not have the resources to escape these dangers.

Nor, for that matter, did Polding. He was intensely
worried by the repercussions of the Therry-Willson conflict
in Sydney:

. . . the people here are beginning to talk and canvas this
unfortunate business; parties are again forming which we
had well-nigh extinguished. The utmost prudence is required
to steer aright. If I am kind to Therry, Dr Willson will
misinterpret it as upholding him in opposition; if I am not,
all my people will lose confidence in me.

Perhaps this exaggerated Therry's influence, but not grossly:
in Sydney his influence was discerned in every dispute or
faction, and usually with some accuracy—he was, for instance, probably involved in the campaign against W. A.
Duncan. Both his real influence and Polding's fear of it were
potent factors in diocesan affairs.

So again, from Tasmania, Therry's influence returned to
cast its magic, divisive spell, raising up partisans wherever
his opposition to Willson was known. Whatever the rights
on Therry's side, and there is no doubt that he had a case,
basically the dispute arose from his unwillingness to accept
authority, and his popular lay backing. It happened that this
was cast in an Irish *v.* English form; but this was not the
essence of the dispute, though many thought it was.

The Therry-Willson dispute did much to accentuate divisions already developing in Sydney. It invited mainland
Catholics to take sides on principles which were already
agitating them—liberty and equality as against authority
and hierarchy—and in Tasmania the cause of liberty seemed
identified with the immensely popular and reputedly saintly
Therry. Here, then, were foreshadowed situations which

were to face other bishops, particularly Polding. Polding did not foresee this: all he saw was the existing damage to the work and reputation of the church. Out of patience with both disputants, he considered both in the wrong: 'There has been a sad want of heroic generosity, and too much, by far, of human calculation.' Indeed, knowing Therry, he was harsher on Willson: 'However unpleasant, Dr Willson ought at once to have taken the responsibilities, as I did.' This was inaccurate and unjust: Willson had received Polding's assurance that his conditions would be honoured. That the dispute did so much harm reflected the faults of the protagonists; but that it occurred at all was Polding's own responsibility. The Tasmanian dispute smouldered on.

Meanwhile, in the late 1840s, spectacular problems erupted in Western Australia. In 1843 Polding had sent John Brady, an Irish priest supposed to have a particular interest in the conversion of the Aborigines, to Perth as Vicar-General. Brady was then forty-three. He had come out in 1838 and had been prematurely aged by unremitting work and a remarkable asceticism. He was appointed Bishop of Perth in May 1845. Cardinal Moran recounts that Brady's first episcopal residence was a room formed by encasing with boards the four wooden posts that supported the church bell. As the room was only about four feet square, Brady could not lie down—he slept in his chair; an umbrella was his only protection from sun and rain—there was no roof. When he moved to better accommodation, his new home invited the description of hovel. His diet was in keeping with his surroundings—coarse, poor and insufficient. Brady's personal circumstances reflected not only his utter disregard for his own comfort, but also the parlous state of his diocese, and Brady expected that those priests and religious who came to share his missionary labours should also share his abject poverty.

After visiting Europe, Brady returned to Perth in January 1845 with about thirty priests, nuns and ecclesiastical students. This large contingent was grossly out of proportion to the number of Catholics, a scattered 300 in a total population of 4,600, and to their ability to support such a large mission. It was, in fact, tailored for the two million Aborigines whom Brady believed to be awaiting the call of

Christ. He determined on three missions to the Aborigines; only one succeeded, that of the Spanish Benedictines led by Dom Serra and Dom Salvado, who, after surviving the initial diet of lizards and insects, eventually built up the New Norcia mission until it was self-supporting.

By 1849 the West Australian colony as a whole faced bankruptcy and extinction. So did Brady's mission. He had accumulated a debt of nearly £10,000; diocesan affairs were in disorder and decline; Brady's house was besieged by his creditors; he was fighting a bitterly anti-Catholic government. Dangerously near breaking point, in health and mind, he asked Rome for a coadjutor, and was given Serra, in July 1849.

Serra, a strong-willed Spaniard, was already a bishop. In August 1849, he had been appointed to a projected see north of Perth, which never eventuated. Instead of solving Perth's problems, Serra's appointment led to worse troubles. Under the influence of Father Urquhart, his Vicar-General, Bishop Brady decided to dispute with Serra for possession of the diocese. He engaged Serra in various law suits in the civil courts, and eventually suspended him. Serra decided to withdraw to Guildford, taking the New Norcia Benedictines with him when Brady took possession of that mission. In Holy Week 1850 the New Norcia Benedictines walked for three almost waterless days to Guildford: 'On Good Friday we were very tired, but considering how much Jesus Christ suffered for us walking to Calvary, we derived great comfort from the thought'—so wrote Martin Griver, a future Bishop of Perth. (On that journey, Griver carried his own cross, wooden and thick, a foot long, with five iron spikes that entered his flesh, fixed by a cord to his back between the shoulders; but that was not known until his death in 1886.)

The Brady-Serra dispute was referred to Rome, and Brady went there in 1851 to present his case. He was confronted by an angry Pius IX, who suspended him, took Perth under his own authority and appointed Serra as administrator. It seemed that the affair was at an end. But Brady returned again to Perth in December 1851, in breach of papal authority, bent on dispossessing Serra by further legal action. This time, the result amounted to schism: the Catholic community divided into Serraites and Bradyites holding separate religious services, both appealing for public recognition.

To settle this, Polding, as Metropolitan, travelled from Sydney to Perth, overland to Adelaide, in long horseback rides, conducting missions on the way. He spent eight months of 1852 in Perth. In July, Brady, in front of the congregation gathered for Sunday Mass, knelt before Polding to submit to the papal suspension, and to Polding's authority, and to express deep regret for his actions. Still insubordinate, part of the Bradyite congregation protested against this humiliation. Polding promptly and sternly excommunicated them. Brady retired to Ireland, where he died, still Bishop of Perth, in 1871. Serra took over full control of the diocese, but some of the grievances of the schism period still rankled. His halting English and his Spanish authoritarianism (his colleague Salvado commented wryly: 'Bishop Serra wants to make a saint out of me, and that rather quickly') did not endear him to a mainly Irish laity. Conflict between the Irish and the Spanish was one of the elements in the Perth affair, but again, not a basic one. Outside the important personal issues—Serra, touchy and alone; Brady, rash, zealous but unbalanced, obsessed with his debts—the issue was one of authority, even, in Bishop Brady's case, a temporary obduracy in the face of the papacy itself.

Hobart and Perth were symptomatic but peripheral: the future of Australian Catholicism was being determined in the metropolitan diocese of Sydney. In March 1837 Polding ordained Henry Gregory, who had come out in 1835 from Downside. Gregory took Ullathorne's place, becoming Polding's companion and confidant—their relationship was that of father and son—and in 1844 he was appointed Vicar-General. It was a disastrous choice.

Gregory was a dedicated man. In him religion took a blunt, direct form. Physically he was strong and muscular, mentally he was aggressively decisive. When he became Vicar-General, he was only thirty, completely lacking in monastic, or indeed any other, experience, but devoted to Polding. Gregory compensated for his inexperience, and his basic lack of self-confidence, with an arbitrary and autocratic manner, devoid of tact or wisdom, or respect for others' feelings; he thus rendered even his trivial decisions distasteful. He ran the Benedictine monastery as a martinet. Lacking ability to handle men, he invariably relied on stern demands for subjection to authority. Outside the monastery, in the public—and particularly the Irish—view, Gregory seemed the epitome of the arrogant Englishman.

Polding consigned much of the implementation of his Benedictine dream to Gregory. The dream was already doomed, but Gregory's faults were of major importance in deciding the particular time and manner of its destruction.

Even while the first peal of monastic bells rang out in January 1844, the dream was languishing. Polding knew why: 'with all our multifarious duties, we have but little time to give to the novices; and that little, by reason of necessary absence we are often compelled to deprive them of.' The mission ruled their lives. Gregory, as Vicar-General, was too busy to find time to train Benedictines, and, in any case, he usually accompanied Polding on his numerous journeys. Polding knew that his ideal of a Benedictine Australia depended on the training of native-born Australian priests, hence the establishment of his seminary in Sydney. The problem was that not nearly enough seminarians presented themselves to stock the rapidly growing mission: by 1846 there were only fifteen candidates for the priesthood in his seminary. To strengthen this tiny community, to secure a coadjutor, and also to try to settle the Willson *v.* Therry case, Polding left for Rome in February 1846, leaving Gregory as Vicar-General. He brought back two Benedictines from the English congregation, but within a year he was to lament that their discontent had 'disturbed almost to destruction the peace and well-being of my infant community'. Polding's diagnosis of the origin of his problem was superficial. The new arrivals were not the most substantial source of the dissatisfaction and indiscipline which had existed from the monastery's beginnings. Having once entered in, the demon of unrest proved impossible to exorcise.

Much happier was Polding's choice of a coadjutor, Henry Charles Davis. A Benedictine, to whom Polding had been both spiritual director and friend, Davis arrived in Sydney at the end of 1848 as Bishop of Maitland, which he was never to visit. Bishop Davis was thirty-three, a delightful, charming man, but in weak health. At root, Polding had sought a coadjutor not so much to assist in his work, as to act as an episcopal substitute for him while he was away missioning: when Davis arrived Polding was talking of spending the next four or five years riding over his vast diocese, paying visits to Sydney only now and again.

Davis turned willingly to the administrative role Polding had marked out for him. Some things he found flourishing, such as the school attached to the monastery which by 1848 had eighty-five boys, well taught by Messrs Sconce and Makinson, former Anglican clergymen who, in February 1848, had embraced Catholicism in a sensational conversion case. In most other matters Davis found problems, particularly financial. Deprived of Ullathorne's supervision, the archdiocesan accounts had lapsed into confusion. By 1844 Polding was lamenting that he was at least £24,000 in debt: 'What will become of me? I am ready to hang myself when I think of it.' Debt distracted and paralysed him: 'I hate this debt; it disturbs my rest. I cannot exert myself with the millstone about my neck.' Davis achieved some semblance of order, but he too found in Polding the defects which Ullathorne and Bishop Willson had found—muddle, indecision, inertia and caprice.

By linking the aggressive, blundering energies of Gregory to Benedictine aspirations, Polding gave his dream a hard abrasive edge. In 1850 Gregory made his attitude and assumptions clear in a report to Propaganda in Rome. He had deleted from the first draft a reference to 'the somewhat lesser mental and social habits of the laity and clergy of Irish extraction', which obscured for Protestants ('a class possessing a tolerable share of intellectual cultivation') the genuine worth of Catholic faith and morality. His report did include a glowing reference to Benedictine influences:

> . . . great as are their benefits, they are of a kind not at once nor strikingly apparent to the vulgar, at least in their most valuable forms, and consequently the arduousness of the task is two-fold; we must not only labour to produce the results of a sound and liberal education, but we have also to create amongst our people the taste and power to appreciate them . . . Among the indirect means by which the Divine Blessing may render it possible to elevate and refine both the intellectual and religious perceptions of the people, may be reckoned

as not the least influential, the presence of the Benedictine Community in Sydney . . . nearly the whole population of the Colony, have before them constantly the spectacle of the religious life, the unceasing daily round at Divine Office, and the instructive and striking ceremonials which take place in the progress of a monastic institute. The people, both the Catholic and the Protestant, are compelled and attracted to recognise and contemplate the existence and the nature of a higher life than any which presents itself to them in the ordinary course of the world.

This last was a very telling point—a public witness to holiness in a land, as Polding remarked, 'neither inspired nor directed by religion'. But, in general, the ideas and attitudes revealed in Gregory's report were either incomprehensible or repugnant to the Irish, as redolent of snobbery.

Usually, the Benedictine dream is conceded to be noble, if unrealistic. Yet, Gregory's report reveals that aspect of the dream which was the pursuit of conformity, the seeking for acceptance by the Protestant intellectual and cultural establishment. Their vow of poverty testified to the Benedictines' personal rejection of material wealth; they distrusted wealth's corruptive power; yet they found, in their work, the preserves of wealth, the establishment, to be their most natural habitat. Polding's monastic school sprang from 'a solicitude for raising the sons of the settlers who were acquiring property, that they might take their suitable position.' In settling the Benedictine nuns at Subiaco on the Parramatta River in 1842, the Archbishop insisted, 'it must be as a means of providing the better, that is, the richer classes of society with the means of education.' Of course, this emphasis was not confined to Australia. It derived from the English Benedictines' concern with, and derivation from, the English upper classes. In England, this orientation was a barrier between the Benedictines and the ordinary clergy and laity: it spawned numerous misunderstandings, including the charge that the Benedictines were worldly in spirit.

Similar processes operated in Australia, where most of the Irish found the Benedictine ethos odious and intolerable. The Irish also, in the main, rejected intellectualism. They did not reject the pursuit of conformity, particularly in that area which the Benedictines had repudiated, the pursuit of conformity in wealth and possessions. None saw this more clearly, or with greater sadness in his old age, than the man who most assisted the Irish in their struggle for social progress, Father John McEncroe.

For some years after his arrival in 1833, McEncroe had kept, as much as he could, to himself, and to the duties of a convict ministry. He was conducting a private war with alcoholism. Ullathorne, who trusted and admired McEncroe, described this:

> He was subject from time to time to have his mind overcast with a terrible melancholy, accompanied by great internal heat and a peculiar twitching of the mouth; and then came on an intense longing for drink on this otherwise very sober man. If then I took his shoes and his hat and locked his door to save him from sallying forth, he so far lost his senses as to get out of the window as he was and cross the park to some Catholic house, where he would implore the people for the love of God to put the light wine used in the country down his throat. And I used to have to go and seek him out and drive him home in my gig like a log. When he came to himself nothing could exceed his distress and self-humiliation.

And few could have exceeded his strength of will: by about 1840 he had conquered his failing, never to fall prey to it again. The gigantic struggle was written on his face—square and firm, with sunken eyes and deep-etched lines—and stamped indelibly on his character: his own weakness had taught him humility and compassion, and that, with God's help, weakness might be conquered. He was convinced that intemperance was the greatest single cause of sin and human degradation, and he became a vigorous campaigner for Total Abstinence.

Father McEncroe became in a way—a much saner, more balanced way—successor to Father Therry. Irish Catholics came to look on him as a leader of their causes. Lead them he did, towards temperance and social equality, against Protestantism—and against Polding's dream.

McEncroe had once thought, with Polding, that the Benedictine monastery could supply the diocese with priests. By 1851 he had changed his mind; it was obvious that the monastery could not do so. Perhaps in twenty or thirty years it could, but not before. What McEncroe believed might happen in the meantime perturbed him so greatly that he wrote directly to the Pope. He urged that new dioceses of Goulburn, Bathurst and Brisbane should be formed, under Irish bishops who would soon get priests from Ireland, the only country that could spare them. If this was not done, he told the Pope, 'the faith will be nearly extinguished in the numerous Irish Catholics, and their children will grow up without any religion, become indifferent, or turn Protestants.' There was also the problem of authority: if more bishops were not appointed he feared the growth of indiscipline such as had plagued the American church.

However, the main problem was want of priests. McEncroe submitted that Irish priests would not come in existing circumstances, because they had heard that Polding intended to supply his mission with Benedictines, and that Irish clergy would be employed merely as assistants. McEncroe reported that Irish priests would go to Adelaide and Melbourne because of their Irish bishops, but not to Sydney. He was wrong, at least in part: Irish priests would not go to Adelaide either, because the diocese was too poor to pay them enough. Matters of preferment, ecclesiastical promotion and parish revenue were very important indeed, but McEncroe could not see past a simple Irish-English problem.

He explained to the Pope:

> Unfortunately the Irish and English characters are very different in their nature, and when any difference takes place between an English Bishop and an Irish priest, then national antipathies and mutual distrusts spring up, and prevent a proper understanding, and thus perpetuate bad feelings. In my opinion very few Englishmen know how to guide or govern Irishmen, whether lay or ecclesiastical.

This was very true, as far as it went, but it did not go nearly far enough. It did not explain the problems of Irish bishops, problems at times identical with Polding's, nor did it explain Polding's problems with his English Benedictines and English lay people. Nevertheless, his central point was both practical and valid: additional priests were desperately needed. To McEncroe, Polding's great vision seemed irrelevant. What was urgent was not some great blending of culture and religion, but an immediate solution to the actual practical problems which faced the church; or, simply, many more priests.

By the 1850s the discovery of gold and an enormous increase in immigration had revolutionised the old missionary situation. Free emigration to New South Wales had begun in considerable numbers in the late 1830s, so that by 1846 the population had nearly doubled to about 200,000. From 1847 onwards, the Great Famine in Ireland had brought heavy immigration to New South Wales and particularly to Victoria. The gold rushes after 1851, with their substantially Victorian location, drew a flood of further immigration, trebling Victoria's population in four years. In 1846 Victoria had 9,000 Irish-born, about a quarter of the population; twenty-five years later, there were 100,000 Irish-born among Victoria's 170,000 Catholics.

Much of the immigration of the 1840s was female. Bishop Davis reported in August 1850 that in the previous eighteen months nearly 3,000 female orphan immigrants had arrived from Ireland. So vast was this immigration problem that Polding had to revive the religious arrangements he had made for convicts in 1835: the immigrant ships were met on arrival and their occupants given brief religious retreats before they dispersed.

But the major Catholic contribution to the moral and social good of immigrants was made by that astonishing woman, Mrs Caroline Chisholm. In New South Wales from 1838 to 1846, she made over her life, her anxiety to do good for Christ's sake and her immense organising ability, to the cause and comfort of the immigrant poor, favouring neither country nor religion, only need. In her many journeys into the bush, she personally settled 11,000 people on the land. All this was the instinctive response of a warm but highly efficient and informed sympathy. Between 1846 and 1854 Mrs Chisholm pursued her crusade energetically in England, leading in 1848 to the formation of the Family Colonisation Loan Society, to assist the poor to emigrate as families. She saw the family unit as the crying need of the new Australian society: 'All the clergy you can dispatch, all the schoolmasters you can appoint, all the churches you can build and all the books you can export, will never do much without God's police—wives and little children.' Then in 1854, still only forty-six and with six children of her own, she went back to Victoria to do what she could in the turmoil of the gold rush. But from 1857 ill health overtook her, then poverty: she had to pawn the medal that Pius IX had given her as acknowledgement of her work. And in 1877 she died, poor, bed-ridden, and in obscurity. Despite the venomous attacks of Dr Lang, Mrs Chisholm was no Romish agent. Her Catholicism was vivid, and dear to her: she required it to be respected. But her object was the moral good of all. She sought for herself salvation, but of earthly rewards she sought one alone, which she knew herself and wanted for others: happy homes.

As well as enormously accelerating population growth by immigration, the discovery of gold posed other problems for the church. It suddenly altered the geographic pattern of religious needs. In ten years Melbourne's population shot up to 125,000, from 23,000 in 1851, and the gold rushes swung the major impact of immigration from New South Wales to Victoria. Everywhere, old centres of religious ministry dwindled relatively; some, such as Adelaide, teetered on the verge of extinction. Many new settlements, Ballarat, for instance, appeared from nowhere, with pressing religious demands. The gold rushes led to the need for establishment of country dioceses, not only because of the growth of new towns but because of the development of farming activities.

Polding did not welcome this rapidly changing situation. The discovery of gold saddened him. He could see in it no promise of good for religion. 'I apprehend this gold mania will be productive of many moral and physical evils amongst us,' he wrote in September 1851. 'I expect we shall have an invasion of worthless characters poured in upon us. And I fear very much that the abundance of gold will make more world-loving the souls of people than they are even now. No part of the world is in such spiritual poverty as we are.' Nevertheless, the numerical problem of many more souls had to be faced, and Polding showed little disposition to regard this demand as an emergency. By 1852 the Catholic population of Australia had jumped to 87,000 in a total of 338,000. Despite growth—Melbourne in 1852 had a bishop and fourteen priests—the supply of clergy was gravely inadequate. McEncroe's suggestion seemed the only remedy. However, Polding was coming increasingly to distrust him because of his continuing campaign for Irish bishops and priests.

The truth was that Polding found himself more and more enmeshed in difficulties arising out of his efforts to realise his Benedictine dream. There were signs of progress: Subiaco was full, with twenty-four pupils; in December 1852 Lyndhurst Academy, intended to meet the wants of upper-class students, had been opened with thirty-five scholars. But the centre of Benedictinism, the monastery, was in turmoil; serious trouble had arisen, reaching the ears of Rome. And then there was the continuing, debilitating dispute between Bishop Willson and Father Therry. So worrying were his problems that, suddenly, in 1854, Polding decided to go to Rome, and took Gregory with him. He attended the solemn promulgation of the doctrine of the Immaculate Conception, and is credited with intervening in a preceding discussion to bring about acceptance by the assembled bishops of papal authority: this was a great comfort to him, for in all other things he suffered reversals.

Polding left Davis in charge in Sydney. Already, though he had been in Australia only six years, Davis's warmth and charm had won him wide affection. He was more approachable than the stately, venerable Polding, and invited a degree of familiarity which the Archbishop did not. The contrast between the two men is apparent in an incident which occurred during one Holy Week when Davis was so ill that Polding insisted that he remain in his room. On Good Friday he ordered Davis to drink beef-tea. 'Your Grace is turning me into a complete heathen,' smiled Davis. Polding replied seriously: 'Obedience is better than sacrifice.'

Davis excelled as a musician. An excellent organist, he composed and arranged and sang—and improved the voices of his choir with a generous egg-flip of his own invention. Even in that austere Benedictine community, which rose at 4.30 a.m. to prayers and mass, then breakfasted on tea, bread and butter, where life was hard and food sparse, Davis was reputed abstemious. He was a great believer in hydropathy. After celebrating mass at 5.30 a.m., he always

took a long draft of pure cold water which he relished as
if it were champagne. He was often ill. When well enough,
he bustled about on his religious duties, and worked actively
as a foundation member of the Senate of the University of
Sydney, his major contribution to public life. He died, in
Polding's absence, in May 1854. In death, as in life, his
remarkable spiritual quality was revealed. In a lucid interval
before his death, he asked his attendant to read a passage
he recalled in a magazine. It described some of the impious
practices of Italian revolutionaries. The Bishop listened—
and then remarked that he had been hoping that his memory
had been deceiving him. Deeply grieved, looking death in
the face, Davis said that he could not have believed that
men would let themselves sink into such an abyss of wickedness.

Even Davis, blending firmness with sympathy, had been
unable to prevent an explosion of discontent in the monastery. Restlessness had been growing since 1851. Indeed it
had been an anti-Gregory campaign within the monastery,
and also Polding's feeling that his own public popularity
was waning, that prompted the Archbishop to go to Rome.
Soon after his departure, the monastic situation came to a
head in a petition to Propaganda from some members of the
St Mary's community, then numbering thirty-two. This
petition set out their doubts concerning the validity of their
personal religious vows and profession, requested secularisa-
tion if their vows were valid, and asked for Gregory's
removal from all authority.

The petitioners argued that the Australian mission would
never succeed unless it came more into the hands of a secular
clergy. This, they reasoned, was because there was no hope
otherwise of building a native clergy, for the people were
prejudiced against regulars; absurd this might be, but the
prejudice was invincible—Benedictines in Sydney were suspected or despised or hated. They further contended that
monastic discipline was a great hindrance to the mission.
The monks did not reside among the people; they were not
free enough to minister vigorously and successfully. Twenty
years before, Ullathorne had made this very point: 'Efficiency
. . . depends upon residence amongst his [the priest's] people,
and familiar acquaintance with its habitudes and dispositions.'

Indeed Polding's whole life testified to the truth of this. He had not lived the enclosed monastic life, but had moved freely and frequently among the people; the nature of the colonial mission had pressed this on him. It is not surprising that other Benedictines should see its weight as well, feel the dynamic excitement of the growing colonial society, and yearn to be involved directly.

Unedifying, contumacious, but not surprising—the same might be said for the Benedictine attack on Gregory. The petitioners complained that they had no confidence in him, that he was arbitrary, persecuting, unpopular, and also that he had no love for Rome. Again, there was truth in this, especially from a subordinate's viewpoint. That such complaints sprang, in the main, from turbulence, from envy and malice, and were unscrupulously furthered, is another matter. The net result, however, was to do Gregory's reputation serious damage in Rome, worsened by an incident during a papal audience which suggested to the Pope that Gregory was at fault and that Polding supported him. The outcome was that Propaganda let Polding know, in mid-1854, that it could no longer approve of his plan to make Sydney an entirely Benedictine diocese. The Benedictines might remain, but as one religious element among others: the abbey diocese dream was at an official end. Polding, accordingly, resigned as Archbishop. Propaganda refused to accept his resignation. The Pope himself comforted him. But Polding remained seared by this abrupt termination of his visionary ambitions. Nearly ten years later, he remarked of this visit to Rome: 'What I suffered . . . has impressed a sort of horror: I shrink from the thought of visiting Rome.'

The whole affair was further branded on Polding's mind by what he found on his return to Australia in January 1856. By October 1857 he was writing: 'I often look back with a sort of regret to the first years. If the labour was great, so were the consolations, and our difficulties were not of that harassing character of the present.' The monastery showed signs of disintegration. Legitimate recreations, such as boating and bathing, led on to a number of scandals, mainly tipsyness. Monks began to leave. The monastery—a community of thirty-two in 1846—had dropped to twelve in 1874. Whatever contribution the monastery had made to

Christian life was dwindling rapidly. And Polding found McEncroe still agitating for new dioceses and Irish bishops, an agitation which was growing. This was a challenge to his concept of the Australian church, already damaged beyond repair by the Roman decision. A related but much more serious challenge came from the leaders of the laity and a section of the clergy. They questioned, and agitated against, Polding's understanding of proper government and authority within the church.

At first it seemed that unity was growing, not departing. The campaign to construct a college for Catholics within the University of Sydney aroused remarkable and widespread enthusiasm. Land was secured and a sum equal to voluntary subscriptions offered by the government. Polding opened the appeal for funds for St John's in a Pastoral Letter of June 1857: the financial response was instant and overwhelming.

In his Pastoral, Polding made three major points. He stressed the opportunity now given to Catholics to acquire intellectual culture, to demonstrate their love of knowledge and their desire to pursue the cultivation of taste and refinement: to Polding religion and culture went hand in hand, and to that extent the St John's project promised the integral realisation of the principles of his Benedictine dreams. However, he also pointed out that the Anglicans had already begun a University college—St Paul's—and that higher education would bring 'the social advancement of yourselves and children, and again, the increase of your political influence.' It was these last two points which gave the St John's campaign popular meaning—not being outdone by the Anglicans, and the prospect of worldly betterment. Two-thirds of Irish immigrants, like those from England and Scotland, were illiterate. Obviously, they were in no position to understand, let alone cherish, the worth of culture and scholarship. They valued education as a key to getting on in the world, as a means of acquiring necessary practical skills of everyday utility. So Polding's Lyndhurst Academy—which produced some of the best Greek scholars at the University of Sydney—was never popular. Before closing finally in 1877, it was forced to amend its studies programme away from the classical and towards the practical, in order to meet public demand. Even more basically, there was widespread popular suspicion of education of the Lyndhurst kind: its value was not understood; its cultural orientation was distrusted as erecting a barrier against the ordinary community; it was suspected of breeding snobbery, pretentions, and the noxious airs of superiority—in all, of setting itself up as an area of exclusion, above the rest of men. The foundation of St John's College became a popular cause, and also the issue on which lay opposition to the Benedictine regime came to a head.

Following the *Chronicle*'s eventual collapse, McEncroe had established, in June 1850, the *Freeman's Journal,* around which there grew up a group of active, vocal laymen, best described as Liberal Catholics. McEncroe himself, influenced by his earlier life under American democracy, was well disposed towards the Liberal Catholic movement then the current vogue overseas. This movement sought, in emphasising freedom of conscience and thought, to reconcile Catholicism to the modern liberal world. In particular it stressed the rights of the laity within the church.

The *Freeman's Journal* purveyed news, particularly Irish news; it was a journal devoted to the cause of Ireland in Australia. Its political attitudes reflected McEncroe's personal democratic predilections, and, more generally, the dominant dispositions of the Australian Irish, reinforced as they were by the surge of nationalism that followed the 1848 rebellion in Ireland. This meant that the *Freeman's* was against transportation, squatters, oligarchs and any tendency towards fostering privilege or aristocracy: it was for a land of equal opportunity.

McEncroe's role in furthering such aims was very important. He actively identified himself with the socio-political cause of Irish Catholics, becoming a public champion of the interests of the under-privileged. This brought him into conflict with such wealthy Catholics as Plunkett, the Attorney-General, who had no faith in democracy or any government based on it. And it brought McEncroe some odd allies—Henry Parkes and the Reverend J. D. Lang, for instance. (Lang, a political radical of remarkable popular energy, carried over his convictions into religion—or was it vice versa?—denouncing the arbitrary despotism of popery

with fiery perseverance. Anti-popery was a constant feature
of Lang's political programmes after the envenomed Port
Phillip election of 1843 when he secured the defeat of the
Catholic candidate, and firmly established Orange Lodgery
in Melbourne. Lang achieved a tribute not accorded to any
other man: Polding's call in 1867 for a day of prayerful
reparation for Lang's blasphemies. As Protestantism atrophied, it bequeathed its anti-Catholic venom to the secularism
which replaced it; if any single man might be said to be a
living example of this process in action, it was Lang.)

Despite his political interests, McEncroe was no Catholic
variant on the Lang parson-politician theme. McEncroe
believed that the less that clergymen engaged in temporal
affairs the better for them—and for the spiritual welfare of
their people. He saw his own activity as a mere stopgap
until the laity could provide their own leaders, such as a
representative of their faith on the new Legislative Council
of 1851: no one but a Catholic, McEncroe believed, could
fully understand their needs or faithfully present their views
on such questions as education. Encouraged by McEncroe,
Catholics did enter politics in increasing numbers. In 1864
McEncroe surveyed, with stinging contempt, the outcome of
this process: 'I would be glad to find a proper number of fit
and intelligent Roman Catholics returned to the next Parliament, but I would be better pleased to have honest,
enlightened and intelligent gentlemen of other persuasions
elected in the preference of time-serving or self-seeking
Catholic candidates.' His American experience had alerted
him to a major danger of democracy—that the Irish would
become the creatures of insipid or worthless politicians. Free
and religious men, in a free and strong church, in a free and
noble state: in 1864 McEncroe was contemplating in disillusion the ashes of his dreams. Polding was not the only
religious dreamer whom Australia was to disillusion.

Before the 1850s, Catholics had been busy, and unitedly
busy, fighting for religious rights: these were their politics,
by and large. But by mid-century, with the introduction of
responsible self-government in Australia, political battles
were cutting across religious divisions and taking the form
of warfare between privilege and the advocates of liberalism
and radicalism. As did prominent Anglicans, some leading

Catholics carried these secular principles into church affairs, questioning the authoritarian structure in which bishops governed and laity obeyed: fundamentally, the growing assertion of lay claims, and intensifying criticisms of Polding's regime, sprang from a lay acceptance of liberal ideals. By the mid-1850s the *Freeman's Journal* was reflecting this trend, becoming much more concerned with the church's internal affairs and increasingly critical of its authoritarian structure.

The *Freeman's Journal* became the spearhead of an attack, mainly lay but with some clerical elements, on the *status quo*. In 1856 Polding succeeded in removing from the editorship Sheridan Moore, an ex-Benedictine monk who was under church censure for having violated his vows. J. K. Heydon, whom McEncroe appointed to succeed him, was hardly less critical, if not as bitter. Neither Heydon, nor W. A. Duncan, who figured prominently as an invited contributor, held any brief for ultra-Irishism. One was English, the other a Scot, both held strong liberal views, and were convinced of the importance of a free lay opinion, and of the necessity of lay action within the church leading to a situation of healthy co-operative government. Both attacked Benedictine rule openly and trenchantly. Theirs was a formidable indictment. A clergy must be fit to lead its flock; an Australian clergy must be devoted to the mission, not a monastery; it must be constantly active; it must seek co-operation, on terms of equality, with the laity in determining policy matters. Judged on these counts, they found the Benedictines unfit to lead.

Others jumped on the *Freeman's* bandwagon, taking up the cry of greater freedom for the laity for other reasons and purposes, but particularly on the assumption that the Irish must be free from English rule. Because the Benedictine monastery was the centre of church authority in Sydney, it was natural that the lay protest against authority as such should prove a convenient vehicle for Irish antagonism. This was obvious at a public meeting held immediately after Polding's departure from the colony in 1854, at which complaints were made that Polding obstructed everything non-Benedictine, everything Irish. While some of the laity were concerned that he should have power to obstruct, others were much more concerned that his alleged obstruction should be of the Irish. By the middle of 1855, the *Freeman's Journal* was complaining that Englishmen looked down on the ignorant Irish. The Benedictines were being ridiculed for their 'Cawtholic' pretentions. From 1856 the malcontent Irish element became more and more aggressive. They were erecting the control of the Australian church into a goal to be fought for and won, for Ireland.

The Irish champions of freedom and liberty were not liberals at all. They exploited the current of liberalism, unleashed by others, who were not Irish, such as Duncan and Heydon, in order to substitute for English authority another form of authoritarianism—their own. Certainly they appealed to public opinion, not in principle, for itself, but because that public opinion was Irish. And of course they destroyed liberalism, which, in its enmity with authority, did not distinguish between English and Irish brands. They also destroyed, swamped rather, the small educated elite, gifted and pious if perhaps obsessive and irresponsible, that had led the liberal attack. But, for a while, all English and Irish were one in their crusade to burst the bonds of Benedictinism. Under the catch-cry of freedom, Polding's affairs met a barrage of bold explosive criticism, as illiberal, reactionary, anti-Irish and snobbish. The major target was the vulnerable Gregory, the Vicar-General; an attack on Polding seemed to these critics too dangerously near the very bone of the church itself. For all their acerbity, these critics loved the church. Indeed it was their love which called forth their protest.

In this setting, the establishment of St John's became the *Freeman's* chosen battlefield, where the laity fought Polding for supremacy. In December 1857 St John's was incorporated into the University of Sydney on terms identical to St Paul's, the Anglican college—that is, with strong lay representation, and ecclesiastical influence kept, constitutionally, at a minimum. The first election of Fellows saw animated public meetings, and two contending tickets—a list of names proposed by the Archbishop, another by the *Freeman's* lay group. The election of June 1858 amounted to a defeat for Polding, with a strong group of his most prominent critics being elected to the governing body of the college which was to have been so integral to his dream.

Just before this, Archbishop Polding, and Bishops Willson
and Goold, met in Melbourne and issued a Pastoral Admoni-
tion to the clergy, warning them against that 'insolent and
most foul liberty, which does not hesitate to commit to
public print what each one may think concerning faith,
discipline, authority and ecclesiastical individuals . . .' Its
terms of denunciation of malcontents were strong indeed.
'Following in the footsteps of Luther and other authors of
heresy, they profess the greatest veneration towards the
Church, and still raise their voices and write in various ways
concerning abuses and shortcomings; they hold Bishops in
honour, and condemn Episcopal rule.' The Pastoral spoke
of 'corruption and blindness', of 'poisoned pasturage', making direct reference to the *Freeman's Journal*. Utterly
unrepentant, the journal responded by intensifying its
criticism.

Thereupon, Polding tried another tack. He called a conference of clergy at Campbelltown, and invited the laity to
submit a list of grievances and suggestions. The *Freeman's*
lay group held a public meeting which petitioned Polding to
form a lay organisation to assist him in bringing to New
South Wales clergy of all orders, and to expand the mission,
and also to advise him on other archdiocesan policy matters.
Not only was this, for its time, an extremely radical proposal
(and totally un-Irish as far as church government went), but
it was released to the press before it was given to Polding.
He responded coldly to what he regarded as unfilial and
contemptuous behaviour.

His feelings towards McEncroe were much warmer—fury.
So indignant was Polding with McEncroe's continued financial connection with the *Freeman's Journal*, that he
considered depriving him of his archdeaconship and even
withdrawing his faculties as a priest. For McEncroe, while
condemning some of the *Freeman's* articles, would not condemn the paper as a whole. He quite strenuously attempted to
exercise a moderating influence on the *Freeman's* group, but
fundamentally he sympathised with them. He confessed to
Bishop Goold that, as all other means of promoting the good
of the church seemed to have failed, the pressure of popular
opinion, however unruly and unpleasant, might work the
oracle.

However, in September 1858, at the conference of clergy at Campbelltown, McEncroe's opinions received strong clerical support: the clergy declared for new dioceses with Irish bishops, and for lay participation in church government. This assisted McEncroe's cause when he went overseas at the end of 1858. His declared purpose was to secure a rector for St John's College. He also set up a campaign headquarters at All Hallows College, in his drive to recruit Irish priests for Australia; and he went to Rome to hammer his Irish arguments there.

McEncroe, for all his unceasing Irish activity, was not a member of the extremist Irish clerical camp which had been formed in Australia. One of the reasons why the onslaught of the laity was so uninhibited was its support by a small group of Irish priests. By the late 1850s more than three-quarters of the Australian clergy were Irish, and almost all of these were graduates of All Hallows. Maynooth attracted the more prosperous, educated aspirants; All Hallows drew on the less privileged sectors of Irish society. Its outlook was missionary and practical, not scholarly. This reflected the demands of the mission. As an All Hallows priest wrote back to his college in 1860: 'I have given up study, in fact my whole time is taken up in collecting for the Church.' All Hallows graduates were often men to whom the priesthood meant a substantial jump up from social origins in poverty.

Polding had failed utterly to persuade these men, as he had hoped, to join the Benedictine order. The differences were very great, and of much importance in producing friction. Benedictines and Irish viewed each other with distaste across the social gulf. To the Benedictines the Irish were crude and uncultured; they were not gentlemen, and their vulgarity, violence and factious nationalism made the Catholic religion a travesty, obnoxious to the general community. Some Irish priests themselves made similar criticisms of the products of All Hallows:

> they are very ignorant in polite education and in good manners and this is a great injury to our Holy Religion and a deep reflection on our poor country . . . Some of our young Priests are not able to write even a passable note . . . the note would

be a disgrace to a poor Country Farmer . . . Some of these young Priests are not fit to sit at a well regulated dinner table.

To the Irish, the Benedictines were pretentious snobs who did not understand the real work of the mission, and Polding's policy seemed one of dilatory neglect. A comment from the Englishman, Bishop Willson, throws some light on this situation. Hearing that Rome proposed to send him a learned scholar as coadjutor, he observed that 'long journeys on horseback in hot weather might be found more perplexing than deep problems in mathematics.' But it must be further noted that Polding did not have a high opinion of Irish priests even as missionaries, or as catechists. To his mind the Irish clergy and people in Australia were satisfied with a deplorable infrequency of Mass and sacraments. Yet, contrary to the allegations of his critics, he pressed All Hallows constantly to send him more priests: he could find no others. And he eventually changed his opinion. After visiting All Hallows in 1861 he paid it the greatest tribute he could: he praised it for achievements unparalleled in mission history.

However, it was in Melbourne, the diocese of the Irish Bishop Goold, that clerical criticism of the episcopacy first became strident. Obviously it was authority as such, not merely English Benedictine authority, which was in question, under challenge.

When the Irish Franciscan, Patrick Geoghegan, went to Melbourne in 1839, he found a pioneering situation similar to Sydney's early days but without the convict element. The Catholic laity was poor, mainly Irish, and had kept religion alive by holding prayers in common. Geoghegan, 'a round, chubby, natty little man, a perfect picture of health and cheerfulness', had no pretentions: in the early days he slept on planks placed across beer barrels in the bar of a hotel next to the primitive hut used as a church. By 1842 he had erected a temporary church; in October 1845 the church of St Francis, in Lonsdale Street, was opened. By this time Melbourne's population was about 11 to 12,000, of which Catholics comprised about a quarter, perhaps a third. And by this time Orange bigotry was well established: the incident in which Father Geoghegan was shot at in the street is well enough known—in fact Geoghegan informed the Archbishop of Dublin in August 1846 that 'three distinct attempts were lately made on my life'.

James Alipius Goold was Melbourne's first Bishop, appointed in July 1847 to a long episcopate which ended only with his death in 1886. Goold was Irish and an Augustinian monk. When he arrived in Melbourne in 1848, he was young, only thirty-six, and had come to New South Wales with Ullathorne ten years earlier. Pastorally, Goold was in the Polding tradition, itinerant, hard-riding, following the life of missioning, but more in the routine sense of organised programmes of prayers, sermons, confessions. In contrast with Polding he lacked imagination and colour; his cast of mind was matter-of-fact, orderly and thorough. Nor did he have Polding's warmth; towards his people he was reserved and retiring. His strongest assets were, personally, his simplicity and piety, and episcopally, his energetic activity, capable administration, his stability and sense. He was more than adequate for the problems of prejudice and bigotry that pressed in on him: Anglican challenges to his title as Bishop of Melbourne, disputes over ecclesiastical precedence, public agitation against Irish immigration, in fact a similar range of antagonisms to those experienced by Polding.

The gold rushes revolutionised Goold's episcopate. To meet the vast demands of the unparalleled situation was impossible with the nine priests available in 1851, but Geoghegan (Goold was in Rome) did what he could. Father Patrick Dunne joined the rush to Ballarat in 1851; in Ireland Goold mustered priests; in 1848 Victoria had two churches, thirteen years later it had sixty-four.

The situation in Sydney of lay criticism of the church was not unique: in Melbourne a similar group of laymen clamoured, to Goold's annoyance, for a greater share in church government, but there it was a relatively minor problem. Lay attitudes were substantially determined by John O'Shanassy, who arrived in the colony in 1839, entered politics in 1846 and remained politically prominent until his death in 1883. O'Shanassy's Catholicism was both unashamedly direct and conservatively orthodox: Goold had full confidence in him. His leadership was sufficiently pervasive in the Catholic community to absorb even the secularism and anti-clericalism associated with the 1848 rebellion in Ireland, and imported into Australia through the transportation of the rebellion's leaders, detained in Tasmania, and by Gavan Duffy, a voluntary exile in Victoria. Even the brilliant Duffy, who was no lover of clericalism, and advocated national education, trimmed his jib to suit the Victorian Catholic climate. Nevertheless, the Eureka Stockade in 1854 made it very clear that if Victoria's Irish Catholics were not religious radicals, they were certainly political and social radicals.

O'Shanassy's influence—and a simple preoccupation with gold—protected Goold from the scarifying gales of lay criticism that swept across Sydney. Instead, it was clerical winds that blew against Goold. He had a firm and high conception of his own episcopal office and authority; towards his clergy he was invariably the strict disciplinarian. This grated on some of his priests, particularly those of greater intellectual brilliance than the rather ordinary Goold, and notably on Patrick Bermingham and Michael McAlroy who had been recruited by Goold on his trip to Ireland. Goold had posted Bermingham and McAlroy with Patrick Dunne to the Geelong mission in 1854, where they very soon established a turbulent reputation as 'the clique'. By 1858 they were leading a defiant full-scale attack on the administration of the Melbourne diocese by Goold and Geoghegan. They charged that maladministration had plunged religion in the diocese into a deplorable state. Goold, they claimed, was, as an Augustinian, prejudiced against all secular priests, particularly those from All Hallows. His injustices had scared away potential priests and driven others out. They asserted that the laity, having no confidence in the Bishop, would not contribute to church funds. Indeed, by 1858 Bermingham was claiming that Melbourne was nearly lost to Catholicism. Such charges were either false or absurdly exaggerated, which was apparent in Victoria but not to church authorities in Sydney, Rome and Ireland who were bombarded by the correspondence of this gifted trio. These men were activated by an unshakeable conviction that they, not Goold, knew best what Australian Catholicism needed— an Irish episcopacy and clergy—and they were determined to have their way.

I Father Therry in the 1830s

II Archdeacon McEncroe

III The young
Bishop Polding

IV Archbishop
Vaughan

Goold's efforts to crush or silence the clique were fruitless. In 1858 he took his problems to Rome, where the Pope observed of such men that they were the greatest enemies of religion, 'persecuting religious in the name of religion'. Meanwhile the clique had found a home in the Sydney diocese.

Goold, who was intensely loyal to Polding, already had misgivings about where Polding really stood, and about his prudence. He had stayed on in Rome in order to defend the Australian hierarchy against the clique's slanders and to preserve their interests and powers in the face of McEncroe's representations for Irish control. To Goold, McEncroe seemed 'bent on mischief'. In Rome, he met McEncroe who was busy furthering his Irish case—with the aid of a warm introduction from Polding. Goold's patience with Polding was to be more sorely tried. Polding, in need of priests and misreading their Victorian activities, accepted Bermingham and McAlroy into his own diocese: Goold had hoped for their removal from Australia.

Bermingham and McAlroy were given charge of the Yass area, where in ten years they built up a large semi-private religious empire. Their energetic zeal and devotion to religion stood forth in a remarkable, prosperous multiplication of churches and schools. But they promptly demonstrated, in New South Wales as in Victoria, to Polding's remorse and Goold's chagrin, their factious unwillingness to accept authority, their brazen ambition to become bishops, and their astonishing lack of veracity and scruple. They continued to pour out to Ireland and to Rome in correspondence and personally—as in Bermingham's 1862 visit—alarming criticisms and misrepresentation. Cardinal Cullen, Archbishop of Dublin since 1852, had been Rector of the Irish College in Rome from 1833 to 1849. He, and Patrick Moran, his nephew and secretary, had the unlimited confidence of the Curia, with whom they were most influential. Moran in particular was regaled by Bermingham with all the Australian scandal, with every item detrimental to the image of the Benedictine diocese. Thus was built up, in the areas of highest authority in Dublin and Rome, a picture of serious discontent and gross maladministration. Neither Polding nor Gregory did much to counteract this. They were contemptuous of such denigration, yet, if only in part, it was being believed.

The enduring effect upon bishops in Australia of clerical insubordination, such as that of the Bermingham-McAlroy clique, and of other misconduct among priests, can scarcely be overestimated. From Adelaide, in 1847, Bishop Murphy had laid down to All Hallows what qualities he wanted in his priests: 'I do not [want] great talents in those whom I wish to cultivate the vineyard in Australia but I principally wish for docility, piety, humility & perfect disinterestedness.' With the clerical agitation of the late 1850s, a heavy emphasis fell on docility. In 1860 Bishop Geoghegan expressed his fear of receiving the wrong sort of priests, those who would spread schism in new lands and simple hearts. In 1877 Bishop O'Connor of Ballarat wrote:

> It will be a great matter to impress upon my young friends [student priests] the great duty of obedience and cheerful, unquestioning submission to the ordinances of Authority. At home young priests are very much encouraged by the example of the veteran priests of the diocese who have grown old in the good service . . . Here unfortunately all are young nearly and there [are] therefore fewer breakwaters against the impulse of ardent temperaments.

Above all, the danger of clerical indiscipline worried Goold, who had suffered most from it. It became almost an obsession with him. In contrast with Bishop O'Connor, Goold wanted young men, whom he could mould, not old ones who would lead the young astray.. Astray signified, however, much more than insubordination: 'the chief difficulty,' wrote O'Connor, 'arises from a fatal affection to drink strong drink.' This was what Goold was referring to when he complained: 'We have suffered much from the indifferent & selfish, not to speak of others whose example has been productive of great scandal.' Others were afflicted by the craving that had beset McEncroe, but some had less success in mastering it. But these were few, and, to some extent, particularly Goold's problem. As a Tasmanian priest noted acidly in 1862: 'Victoria is certainly a great mission. Its greatness & richness assist its ruin—or at least the ruin of some of its pastors. Better for them if they had some of the

Poverty of Tasmania to contend with.' What Goold wanted, he made clear, was 'good seekers of souls & not of money'. There were ample of these, the overwhelming majority who went about, in obscurity, their daily religious ministry.

In February 1859 the mounting tension in Sydney exploded. Gregory had appointed a distinguished Protestant surgeon, Dr Bassett, to a seat on the Board of Management of the Catholic Orphan School at Parramatta. The *Freeman's Journal* took this action, which was intended as acknowledgement of Dr Bassett's kindness, as an insult to the Catholics of New South Wales. The journal contended that Dr Bassett's appointment implied either that no Catholic was as fit as Bassett for the post, or that the hierarchy did not trust the laity. It headed its outburst 'Treason against Holy Church and the lambs of her flock', and announced a public meeting. At that meeting the wantonly brilliant lawyer, D. H. Deniehy, moved that the Catholics of New South Wales could no longer have confidence in their ecclesiastical administration. He proposed a lay committee to deal directly with the government in the administration of Catholic institutions until the affairs of the church were in the hands of dignitaries worthy of their trust. Despite strong opposition, these resolutions were carried.

This Polding could not ignore. Criticism was one thing, flagrant refusal to accept his authority was another. He called on the revolutionaries to withdraw and renounce under pain of excommunication. They submitted resentfully and, they claimed, only temporarily, and only to edify Protestants and allow them time to appeal to Rome, notably against Gregory whom they likened to a madman. On his side, Polding withdrew Bassett's nomination. Rome tactfully avoided the laity's appeal by pointing out that it had not been made according to correct canonical procedure: the laity took this, intended as a rebuff, as implicit recognition of the strength of their case, and the *Freeman's Journal* pressed on with its fierce onslaught against what it considered was Polding's infringement not merely of religious rights but civil rights as well. The journal assembled all the ammunition it could muster with which to bombard the existing ecclesiastical edifice. The present difficulties and disputes were magnified, dead problems disinterred. The journal pounced on anything that might be used to suggest that religion was decaying and that Benedictine rule was to blame.

Unfortunately for Polding, there was ample such ammunition to hand. A variety of related problems had arisen from his efforts, in dealing with secular priests and other religious orders that he had brought to Australia, to bring all Catholic elements into some ideal relationship of subordination to a central and pervasive Benedictine influence. Even the Benedictine nuns had great difficulty in coping with the intrusions of Polding's benevolent paternalism. Polding had tried to absorb others—subordinately—into his Benedictine dream. Conflict arose from the seculars' refusal to accept this, and from the fact that other religious orders had differing ideals, and differing rules of Christian life to which they were dedicated. These orders had a clear sense of their own rightful independence, under their own Superiors, but Polding and Gregory showed scant respect for such independence once an order had settled in the colony. The result was conflict and casualties, the first affected being—though other factors were involved—the Italian Passionists.

In 1843 Polding brought back with him five Italian Passionist priests to conduct the Aboriginal mission. He had high hopes of protecting the natives from 'the destructive breath of a civilisation which is neither inspired nor directed by religion.' However, he gravely underestimated the difficulties. To him the natives seemed intelligent, cheerful, and ready to accept Christianity. The Passionists' experience was directly to the contrary, but Polding would not recognise this. He became very critical of them as inept, and very resentful of their claims to an independent jurisdiction, for which the Passionists had full Roman authority. Frustrated both by the nomadic habits of the Aborigines, and by Polding's refusal to provide adequate funds to meet their difficulties (which arose mainly from having to support the Aborigines), the Passionists abandoned their mission in 1847. Or rather, in the *Freeman's Journal*'s terms, they were driven out by Polding.

The journal put forward the case of the Christian Brothers in a similar light. The chief obstacle to the success of the Australian mission, Polding contended, was the want of schools and of competent teachers, and after Roman representations on his behalf, he secured, in 1843, the services of three Irish Christian Brothers. The Brothers came on conditions to which Polding had agreed—their own house, the right to follow their rule, control of their own schools, and with the Archdiocese to support them. By 1846 they were in direct conflict with Polding over his partial failure to observe these conditions as they understood them, and his efforts to subject them to his own authority and jurisdiction. They left Australia, in bitterness and misunderstanding, in 1847.

However, it was the question of Polding's—or rather Gregory's—treatment of the Sisters of Charity which supplied the *Freeman's Journal* with one of its major specific grievances. While in Dublin in 1837-8, Ullathorne arranged with Mrs Aikenhead, foundress of the Sisters of Charity, for five sisters to return with him. They went to Parramatta, and took over the care of the female prison, which held up to 1,500 prisoners, and the Orphan School. Their impact on this situation was astonishing: 'Where, heretofore, all was noise and ribaldry and obscene conversation, you may now see the quiet of a well-ordered family. Not an oath nor curse nor brawling word is heard; and a general desire to frequent the Sacraments prevails.' More gentleness prevailed: laundry and needlework took the place of breaking stones and sawing wood. So deep was the impression made by the nuns on some prisoners that the nuns sometimes found it difficult to prevent prisoners making their confession to them. Polding interfered with the autonomy of the Sisters of Charity, but Mother Aikenhead had foreseen the possible need for a separate Australian Congregation. This is what eventuated, but not before some difficulties, conflicts and disputes arose. As was typical of him, Gregory's treatment of the Congregation was authoritarian.

This was the background to a complex series of incidents regarding the religious administration of St Vincent's Hospital, culminating in May 1859 in the departure of a Sister de Lacy for Ireland. Sister de Lacy was one of the first Sisters of Charity to come to the colony. She had been connected with St Vincent's Hospital from its beginnings in

1855, when McEncroe was in charge of the Archdiocese following Bishop Davis's death. The Irish regarded St Vincent's Hospital as a project peculiarly their own, and the *Freeman's Journal* made an enormous issue out of Sister de Lacy's departure, claiming that she had been forced out, a victim of 'the terrible absolutism which governs our ecclesiastical affairs'. In reporting to Propaganda, Polding described Sister de Lacy's version of the affair as 'fairy stories', but it was the *Freeman's* account, picturing Sister de Lacy as a Christian heroine, and stressing the total incapacity of the reigning ecclesiastical dynasty, which carried the day.

By May 1859 both McEncroe and the *Freeman's* group had petitioned the Holy See to send an Apostolic visitor to the colony. While this was being considered in Rome, Polding continued to recoil in horror and anger from those few 'wicked men' who had that 'infidel paper' at their command. He found particularly distressing that aspect of the lay attack which wanted the abolition of state financial assistance to religion, and the substitution of a voluntary system. This was a central feature of the lay onslaught, appearing as early as 1846 among the Tasmanian laity, and led to victory in the New South Wales parliament by W. B. Dalley in 1862. Polding saw in the Catholic campaign to abolish state aid to religion the presbyterian spirit he regarded as characteristic of lay agitation: 'a desire to subvert the discipline of the Church and bring her ministers into an unseemly, intolerable bondage . . . They would subvert the divinely appointed hierarchy, and introduce a presbyterianism controlled by the wretched tyranny of money· or loud-tongued oligarchs.' In this threat, Polding (and also many Anglicans) saw the destruction of all religious discipline, and an arbitrary anarchy of lay control which would destroy all religion. The principle of state financial grants to religion, as a Catholic petition put it, 'recognises as its utmost function the maintenance in some tolerable degree of the principles of natural Religion . . .' Polding saw abolition as a victory for secularists over the previous acceptance by the state that it had a religious character and religious responsibilities. No doubt Polding's view of the abolition of state aid was narrow and simple (Dalley was no secularist), but seen in these

terms—and also in terms of the fear that its logical extension would be the end of state aid to religious education—
no further explanation is needed why Polding resisted abolition, and the corpus of thinking of which it was a part, with
all his power.

The outcome of the anti-Benedictine campaign was not an
Apostolic visitation, but Abbot Gregory's recall to England,
at the end of 1860, by the President-General of the Benedictines at the express order of the Holy See. Gregory was
made the scapegoat for the Benedictine failure, his dismissal
was the price of peace. Charges had been laid against him,
fabrications of immorality apparently. He was not told precisely what the charges were, nor was he invited to Rome
to defend himself. In fact, these specific complaints were
unimportant. He was recalled for the sake of peace, sacrificed
to end the disturbance of the troublesome group in Sydney.
The Roman attitude had been seasoned by the Bermingham
clique, by the failures of Benedictine bishops in Mauritius,
by complaints against the order in England. Even had this
not been the prevailing Roman picture, the number, fre-
quency and vigour of complaints from Australia could not
be ignored. Gregory, the major focus of these complaints,
must go. This marked the Roman decision that Polding's
Benedictine dream, even as limited to Sydney, must end; but
it did not, of course, signify the end of rule by Benedictines.

Gregory's fall marked the climax of lay agitation. Polding's lay critics claimed that Rome had acted in their favour:
they were jubilant and self-righteous. Polding and Goold
smarted under what they saw as a frontal blow to their
authority. Polding claimed that the relative peace that
followed Gregory's departure was really due to Heydon's
retirement, in June 1860, from the editorship of the *Freeman's Journal*. He felt keenly the wounding injustice of the
whole affair, felt too the lack of Gregory's understanding
companionship. Later, he tried to persuade Gregory to
return, but he would not. Gregory had left with considerable
dignity, acknowledging at least some of his mistakes and
shortcomings, his unfortunate manner, his contempt for
criticism. He died in 1877.

Was Gregory's downfall a triumph for Irishism? No. The
core of the *Freeman's* group was as much English as Irish.

The first attacks on Gregory came from within his own monastery, where faction had been bred, and some of his own religious brethren were heavily implicated in the anti-Gregory campaign throughout its duration. The destruction of Gregory was a victory for democracy against authority, but also a striking demonstration of the swift and decisive—not to say arbitrary—authority of Propaganda, in the person of Cardinal Barnabo. As the democracy was overwhelmingly Irish, it opened the way for that later phase in which democracy and authority would be in harmony, complimentary, two aspects of the one Irish whole.

Despite the sharp reverse which the recall of Gregory represented, Polding's energies and ardour were apparently undiminished. Sadder he was, yes, and perhaps left with a tinge of bitterness, yet at heart there was no deep gloom in him, but rather a more profound movement of love and forgiveness as he went forth again to do vigorous battle with his enemies—sin, and detractors. In December 1861 a letter from Polding to Gregory contained comments on the Gregory affair and on attacks on his administration, and also the plaint: 'I am tired out of life'—and a description of a six weeks, 1,100 mile missionary tour he had just finished in northern New South Wales. (Truly, it could be said of Polding at his death: 'What forest has he not travelled? What stream has he not crossed?')

In 1862 he was devising plans to deal with the Bermingham clique. Geoghegan, Bishop of Adelaide since 1858, had achieved immense progress there. Polding wanted to move him to Goulburn as a means of crushing the factionalism and insubordination of Bermingham and McAlroy, whose 'vile, anonymous calumniations' were angering the Archbishop beyond endurance. Their other activities included the direct sabotage of Polding's higher educational structure: they persuaded their parishioners to send their sons to Ireland for education rather than to Lyndhurst and St John's. He was also busy making arrangements for the second Synod of Australian bishops, the first having been held in 1844. The Synod was held in October 1862; its major concern was education. It also discussed the establishment of an Australian seminary for training priests, and the problems of divorce and mixed marriages; it congratulated the poor on their generosity, and rebuked men of great wealth, whose generosity the church had not experienced.

Throughout the 1860s Polding was fighting a losing battle over the appointment of new bishops. This had been McEncroe's special cause, and still was. In 1863 he was still reporting to the Archbishop of Dublin that very many Catholics never saw a priest, nor had the opportunity to receive the sacraments; that the young were growing up with little knowledge of religion; that 'hundreds of our practical Catholics are being lost to God and the Church all for the want of more Bishops and priests.' Polding did not differ from McEncroe over the setting up of new dioceses, but over who should be their bishops. He recommended a list of Benedictines, including Gregory. The Irish response to this was obvious in a letter Polding received from Dr Quinn, the new Bishop of Brisbane. '. . . I find he strongly advises to leave the election of Bishops to the Holy See, and to have them all from home, and to follow out the wishes of the Conference held at Campbelltown. He states he knows little about those recommended by us.' To which Polding added, plaintively, 'What do we know of those recommended from home?'

Polding's preferences were, however, becoming irrelevant. The Irish case—McEncroe's case—had won the day in Rome, even, to some extent, in its most extreme form as purveyed by the Bermingham clique of 'wretched liars'. Polding deeply resented the interference of the Irish clergy and hierarchy in his affairs. A choice case of this is that of the irrepressible McAlroy who wrote to Polding in 1863, from Ireland, saying that he had just heard that new bishops were to be appointed to Australia, and that he had been favourably recommended by some of the Irish bishops. Polding was further astounded and humiliated to receive, in December 1863, a letter from Cardinal Barnabo, in charge of Propaganda, charging him with having appointed two Englishmen as administrators of Armidale and Goulburn, Fathers Hanly and Austin Sheehy: both were in fact Irish. His guilt assumed, he was further charged with fomenting lay discontent by his policy of appointing Englishmen to all offices. Polding's most extreme Irish critics described those Irishmen the Archbishop appointed, or sought to appoint to

office, as being under his influence, his tools, Anglicised.
Their conclusion was that all new appointments must come
direct, and thus uncontaminated, from Ireland. Such episcopal
appointments came, in a bunch, in a few years from 1865—
Bishop Murray to Maitland, Bishop Quinn to Bathurst,
Murphy to Hobart, O'Mahoney to Armidale, Lanigan to
Goulburn. They all had studied at the Irish College in
Rome and all were relatives or friends of Cardinal Cullen.
The Irish episcopal invasion had begun.

In fact, it had begun a little earlier with the appointment
of James Quinn, another of this group and head of the
Harcourt Street school in Dublin, to the new see of Brisbane.
Quinn pioneered, in an extreme form, the Irish episcopal
autocracy. While Polding's autocracy crumbled, the new
Hibernian form was emerging in prototype in Queensland.

Queensland's growth had been slow. When Bishop Quinn
arrived in 1861, the colony's population was under 30,000,
with about 7,000 Catholics. As to Brisbane—'Where is the
city of Brisbane?' asked Quinn, as he looked across it for
the first time. Quinn's religious impact was immense. On his
arrival there were two priests, 7,000 Catholics, four schools
and four churches. Ten years later there were thirty priests,
30,000 Catholics, twenty-eight schools and thirty churches.
Even the increase in the number of Catholic colonists was,
in part, Quinn's achievement. He found on his arrival a
venomous anti-Catholic press and a legislature bitterly hostile
to Catholicism, oligarchical in structure and outlook. Believing that the government's immigration policy deliberately
discriminated against Catholics, Quinn launched his own
immigration scheme, and founded the Queensland Immigration Society in 1862. In three years the Society brought out
6,000 Irish. But public fear that Queensland was becoming
'Quinnsland' led to the Society being dissolved in 1865.
Quinn's episcopate, until his death in 1881, was distinguished by the way in which his astonishing success in building
the church provoked accusations that Catholicism was aim-
ing at political domination.

Quinn's achievements were remarkable not only in their
extent, but also in the autocratic means he used to attain
them. He believed rigidly in authority, particularly his own.
The presbyterian spirit was just as repugnant to him as it

was to Polding and Goold. While dedicated to 'Irishing' the Australian episcopacy, he proceeded with caution, as he was determined that this would take place from above, not in response to pressures from below—as was threatened by the popular democratic agitation associated with the Sydney laity, or Father Bermingham. Authority must be preserved.

It was probably his contempt for the failure of Polding and Goold to preserve their authority unchallenged that led to Quinn's ignoring them, or scarcely bothering to disguise his conviction of his own superiority. However, the 1860s were a time when Irish authority was still authority like any other: in 1862 Father McGinty, one of the two priests who had pioneered Queensland Catholicism since 1843, challenged Quinn's administration to his face in a protracted bout of unruliness during which McGinty formed a lay party to support him. Quinn counter-attacked with threats of excommunication and, eventually, McGinty's suspension. McGinty stood firm and the dispute did not end until after he had petitioned the Queensland parliament against Quinn. Throughout the affair, Quinn stood immoveable on his dignity, brandishing the weapons of authority.

The McGinty affair taught Quinn nothing. So harsh was his rule that in 1867 six of his priests left the diocese for ever, without his permission. His interference in the organisational affairs of religious orders was so arbitrary and high-handed that the Sisters of Mercy attempted to return to Ireland; Quinn prevented them, by command, manoeuvre and even by intimidation, from doing so. The Sisters of St Joseph withdrew from Queensland because they could not tolerate the utterly authoritarian claims that Quinn made in order to subject them to his authority. When the Bishop went to Ireland on a recruiting campaign in 1870, so odious were the rumours about the manner in which he ruled his diocese that he could not persuade even one Irish priest to return with him: so much for McEncroe's claim that Irish bishops would automatically attract Irish priests to Australia, merely because those bishops were Irish. Quinn had to settle for foreign priests, from France, Italy and Germany.

Quinn had enormous energy, gigantic drive, and zeal. In the pursuit of his vast plans of religious expansion, he was passionately determined that all his resources would be subordinate to his conception of the interests of the Australian church. One such resource was money. He was constantly pressing for it, so strenuously as to dismay some of his clergy. But it was money to be used in the service of the church. The same for human resources: the State paid nuns as teachers, but Quinn kept this money in an education fund. The nuns had to keep themselves with music lessons and raising poultry; their housing was bad, their food poor, their clothing insufficient. The casualty rate was high. In 1879, when a nun aged thirty-four died, Quinn wrote: 'Her age is about thirty-four, and she is the oldest but one of twelve, whom we have interred within the last ten years . . . but we do not regard ourselves as loosing them. We believe, on the contrary, that they are forming a band of advocates for us in Heaven, whose pleading will be irresistible.' Quinn is not an attractive figure. His holiness seems heartless, his vast plans for expansion have the ring of ruthless ambition rather than love or foresight. Too hard, too unyielding, was the verdict of Bishop Reynolds of Adelaide when Quinn died in 1881. He left vast property, a situation Reynolds thought regrettable, in the interests of religion. Yet, as Quinn's panegyric said: '. . . all that is great and good and glorious, all that is valuable will be found costly and of the highest price . . . he who sowed the seed sowed it in privation and tribulation. He sowed the seed which even in his own lifetime brought forth its fruit fifty and one hundred fold.'

The future lay with the dynamic realities of Irish imperial autocracy, though none perhaps as despotic as Quinn's. What of the waning fortunes of Polding's dream and ambitions?

At that very time when the financial fortunes of his church were at their lowest—in August 1862, state aid was withdrawn from all New South Wales religious denominations—Polding opened an appeal for the completion of St Mary's Cathedral: 'A building is to be completed which shall express to all beholders the store that the men of Australia set upon a due outward expression of their religion.' But on 29 June 1865 St Mary's Cathedral was destroyed by fire. The earthly centre of Polding's Benedictine dream took on, in the moments of its destruction, a terrible grandeur: 'The cold frosty air, blowing on the rafters caused them to glitter with resplendent brilliancy. The flames, like innumerable serpents of fire, hissed and crackled along every part of the building; and as they swept from one interior fitting to another, assumed most singular shapes.' Nothing was insured; the material loss was about £50,000.

When the news reached him by electric wire at Bathurst, Polding was prostrated with grief. In Sydney, it was McEncroe, the architect of the new Irishism, who presided over an immediate public meeting to open a rebuilding fund. At the formal meeting a week later, Polding, in calling for a new and even more glorious St Mary's, bridged the gap between what had been destroyed and what was to be built anew: 'Resurrection, my friends, is not a "creation" . . .'

3

The Education Question 1865-1884

By the mid-1860s the attention of the Catholic church in all the Australian colonies was beginning to swing away from internal problems towards a question of major public importance—education. This question was being framed in such a way as to constitute, in the church's eyes, a fundamental menace to her mission. Essentially, the education question of the 1860s and 1870s came to this: will government money be withdrawn from any support of religious denominational education, and be devoted exclusively to a public educational system which would be free, compulsory and secular? That is what it came to, but at first the question was much less pointed—how to devise some national system which would meet the increasingly urgent demand, as Australia's population grew, for universal elementary education. This became the centre for what was probably the most passionate, fundamental and continuing ideological conflict in Australia's history, the Australian focus for a confrontation that was world-wide; between Catholicism and all those varieties of nineteenth century thought which came under the general heading of 'liberalism'.

The education question was resolved so as to exclude religious schools from any share of public money. Since that time, Catholics have agitated for a reversal of this decision, an agitation which has, to some extent, obscured the origins of the controversy. For, in the 1860s and 1870s, the church faced two related questions. One concerned the future of Catholic education: if government money was withdrawn, how could Catholic schools continue? The other was, what should be the Catholic attitude to the creation of a secular education system, a system without an acceptable religious content, enforced upon all Australian children and their parents? Historically, this last question came first.

Since the 1880s, Catholic relations with the state on

education matters have been restricted, it might seem, to a continuing pressure for financial aid. These appearances are deceptive. The very existence of the Catholic education system is a continuing repudiation of, and challenge to, the prevailing values of the secular state system.

The origins of this repudiation lie in the 1860s and 1870s when, faced by the growth of the secular education movement, the Australian bishops defined their stand. This was a stand taken from their viewpoint of national interest, not on narrowly Catholic grounds:

> . . . a system of national training from which Christianity is banished, is a system of practical paganism, which leads to the corruption of morals and loss of faith, to national effeminacy and to national dishonour . . . What can be more false, what more fatal to men, to families, and to States, than to call this education.

The enduring confrontation of Catholic church and liberal state on education stands out obdurately in the 1879 Pastoral Letter of the Archbishop and Bishops of New South Wales:

> . . . we, the Archbishop and Bishops of this colony, with all the weight of our authority, condemn the principle of secularist education, and those schools which are founded on that principle. We condemn them, first, because they contravene the first principles of the Christian religion; and secondly, because they are seedplots of future immorality, infidelity, and lawlessness, being calculated to debase the standard of human excellence, and to corrupt the political, social and individual life of future citizens . . . parents . . . could not do a greater service to religion or to the State than to upset, by constitutional means, a system which, whilst it is a crying injustice to themselves, promises to be a source of incalculable evil to the colony.

Here indeed was a scathing indictment of secular values, and a declaration of uncompromising hostility. How had this confrontation come about?

In the early years of the penal colony, education seemed scarcely relevant to the affairs of what was merely a prison. A few schools did exist, monopolised by the Church of England and thus repugnant to Catholics. Father Therry did what he could to provide education for Catholic children; when Ullathorne arrived in 1833 there were about ten Catholic schools. Polding tried to improve the position, particularly by bringing out lay teachers from England. When W. A. Duncan came out as a school teacher in 1838, he found few schools, primitive buildings with little furniture or none, perhaps one child in six with any kind of book, and teachers who seldom knew more than how to read and write at a rudimentary level. Comparatively, such Catholic schools were not remarkable: they were similar to most other colonial schools, and representative of the poorer class schooling of an age prior to universal education. But Polding, in whom the pursuit of religion and culture were integrated things, found this intolerable: 'Our schools are in a very low state', he complained in 1840.

A fundamental cause of this was parental negligence. Polding lamented publicly in 1839, that 'through the apathy of parents, the *street* is the school frequented by very many children—an apathy not confined to the lower orders . . .' Having had no education themselves, or very little, many Catholic parents could not see any value in education for their children, particularly as it meant the payment of fees, usually twopence a week.

No less basic was want of money. Governor Bourke's revocation, in 1833, of the Church and Schools' Corporation ended government financial support of the Anglican educational monopoly and introduced the denominational system, a partnership between the government and all churches that wished to provide schools. However, Bourke's plans were much more ambitious. He wanted to construct a single educational system, acceptable to all denominations, in which all children would mingle in the one school, receive Bible instruction together, but separate for denominational instruction from their own pastors. This scheme, based on the then Irish national education system, aroused a Protestant outcry, led by Bishop Broughton, claiming that it infringed church authority over education, and did not allow for adequate and appropriate religious instruction. Bourke therefore dropped it. Later, a somewhat similar proposal from Governor Gipps, including Biblical instruction but excluding denominational teaching, was also defeated, again mainly by Broughton.

The total Anglican opposition to Bourke's proposal, though undoubtedly genuine, seems not unrelated to a natural pique at the earlier destruction of the privileged Anglican position. Similarly, Polding's generally favourable, though not enthusiastic, reception of Bourke's scheme seems to have been partly derived from his reaction, at a time when he was under Anglican attack, against anything Anglican. In 1842 he described Anglican criticism of Bourke's proposal as showing 'prejudice and fanaticism'. Yet, two years later he was contending, as Broughton had done: 'We shall not have the Irish system; I am glad of it, for it would ruin religion in this country.' Nor was Polding uninfluenced, in regard to Bourke's scheme, by the parlous state of Catholic schools: any scheme would be better than the existing situation.

That situation, which was to continue for about forty years, was one of small government grants to aid existing church schools. The grants were grossly inadequate, as even at their most generous they lagged far behind needs, let alone demand. Polding could make no real educational progress: 'On account of the low salaries we are alone able to pay we cannot secure a sufficient number of efficient teachers for our schools.'

Bourke's scheme, and that of Gipps, pointed the way to the future—some national system of education. By the 1840s, education was being recognised as an inescapable social problem with which governments would have to deal systematically, but obviously it was a problem complicated by difficulties of meeting the requirements of the various churches already operating schools. The 1844 Select Committee on Education recommended against the denominational system; the Legislative Council voted thirteen to twelve in favour of the Irish national system; but both Anglicans and Catholics stood firmly by denominationalism, and nothing was done. However, the Committee's investigations had shown that of the 25,675 children in New South Wales of school age (four to fourteen) more than half were receiving no schooling whatever; the Committee believed that the denominational system—or lack of system—itself was largely at fault in leaving this majority uneducated.

Obviously, organisation and central regulation were needed to cope with this problem, which was Australia-wide. In the late 1840s governments sought to solve it by establishing administrative boards—a board to control the public schools which were increasingly needed, especially in rural areas, and a board for denominational schools. Religion was left entirely to individual schools.

From the first, Bishop Goold distrusted the Victorian denominational board, being suspicious of its composition, and objecting to its prescribed textbooks. His attitude was exceptional. The other bishops welcomed their denominational boards, seeing in them the promise of the spread of improved educational facilities. And indeed, in the early years of the denominational boards, their financial policies were generous and encouraging. While their grants did not make education free, they made it possible wherever local interest was sufficient to provide some enthusiasm and partial financial backing. Under these boards, Catholic schools in Australia increased from fifty in 1848 to nearly two hundred in 1858. Nevertheless, the problem was still much greater than the attempted solution. Bishop Davis wrote in 1850: 'Our means for the education of the poorer classes of Catholics are very limited, and parents, either through poverty or apathy, neglect their children exceedingly; and thus we have hundreds of children growing up in a state almost of barbarity.'

Moreover, hardly had the denominational boards begun their work than governments began to seek new solutions to the educational problem. Administrative policy began to swing against fostering the denominational system. The trend was first reflected in legislation in South Australia in 1851, spreading to Tasmania and West Australia, and then in the 1860s to Queensland, Victoria, and, last, New South Wales. Government aid to church schools shrank rapidly, while governments sought increasingly to intervene in their control.

This pressure was only partly the product of hostility. It also derived from economic and administrative necessity. Bishop Davis's complaint in 1850 had a much wider appli-

cation than New South Wales: 'Our present Legislative
Council is chiefly composed of a fearful set of infidels. They
will, I fear, soon succeed in introducing a system of national
education calculated to destroy all principles of religion . . .'
But while he saw their endeavours as infidel and anti-
religious, these men regarded themselves as reformers
seeking the creation of what was undoubtedly necessary, an
efficient national system of elementary education.

The great flaw of the denominational system was that,
because of competition between the various denominations,
it led to a proliferation of uneconomic schools, as too many
different schools vied with each other in one place, and
produced large areas of complete educational neglect where
there were no schools at all in places where they were
desperately needed. In addition, the quality of teaching was
often very low. The 1855 Report of the Schools of New
South Wales stated that the condition of schools was in
every respect unsatisfactory, with denominational schools
worst of all. In Catholic schools, it was noted, teachers were
'quite unfit and wholly incompetent', the children being 'in
a deplorable state of ignorance'. As employment, teaching
was regarded widely as a last resort; in the mid-1850s,
more than half the teachers in Catholic schools, as in those
of other denominations, were completely untrained. Bishop
Goold blamed this, as Polding had done, on the niggardly
government grants, but another very powerful factor was
the general failure of local school boards, as the parents
themselves lacked any real interest in the schools.

Whatever the causes, it was obvious in all colonies that
the education system required reform if a minimum of
efficiency was to be achieved. However, moves towards
greater efficiency—welcomed by the bishops—were accompanied by pressures on church schools of a kind which
aroused their profound misgivings.

In the 1860s denominational boards were refusing to
sanction any other textbooks but their own, which were
usually Protestant in content and tone. There were difficulties over syllabuses; Goold, in particular, was extremely
cautious. He required, for instance, that science teachers,
even if they were priests, submit an outline of subject
matter for his approval. Such requirements contributed to

the growing tension between bishops and boards.

The clerical reaction to this degenerating situation took two major forms—the search for a solution in the use of political pressure, and the search for some acceptable compromise. In New South Wales Archdeacon McEncroe had become virtual director of Catholic schools. As early as 1855 he told the clergy there that:

> It is the bounden duty of the clergy to urge on their respective congregations the obligation that the Catholic electors are under to their God and to their offspring to vote for no candidate who will not pledge himself to use his best exertions in Parliament towards securing a proportionate share of the sums voted for educational purposes, for the Catholic schools established, or to be established, in accordance with the practice and principles of the Church . . .

So was announced a theme of enduring significance in Australian political affairs. However, at that time, and thereafter, many Catholics paid little heed to such considerations. The prominent Catholic, Michael Fitzpatrick, a politician from 1869 to 1881, and Leader of the Opposition in 1880, was an open enemy of church schools, but he continued to receive Catholic electoral support. There were other similar cases.

By the early 1860s the denominational system was under such hostile pressure that the Australian bishops were faced with the question of how far they were prepared to go in compromising with the states' conditions in order to continue to be eligible for government money. In South Australia, where withdrawal of government aid was furthest advanced, Bishop Geoghegan was firm for independence. The great majority of the clergy, in states where this erosion was less advanced, did not think in such terms. To them, a separate Catholic educational system was inconceivable. To them the question was: what concessions to the state could be made, in keeping with Catholic principles, in order to preserve state aid? This raised the question: what were Catholic educational principles?

The 1860s saw these principles defined, under Archbishop Polding's influence. The first step was taken at the Provincial Council of 1862, attended by the Bishops of Hobart, Melbourne, Brisbane and Sydney. The Council noted that attempts were being made to deprive Catholics of liberty of conscience, to curtail Catholic freedom to 'train our children in secular learning, quickened by Catholic faith, and guarded by Catholic discipline.' It denounced 'National Education' as 'persecuting sectarianism', since it would compel Catholics to accept a system vitally defective.

> Catholics do not believe that the education of a child is like a thing of mechanism that can be put together bit by bit—now a morsel of instruction on religion, and then of instruction in secular learning—separate parcels . . . We hold, that subjects taught, the teacher and his faith, the rule and practices of the school day, all combine to produce the result which we Catholics consider to be education.

Worse than defective, the system was 'corrupting and dissipating'. The Council warned parents against seductive promises that national education would be scholastically superior, and advised them to proclaim, publicly and politically, their determination to retain religious education.

The tide continued to flow relentlessly against denominational education. When Polding returned, in August 1867, from what was to be his last visit to Rome, he had been absent for nearly two years. Thwarted in Rome in his efforts to secure a coadjutor and to rehabilitate Dr Gregory, the Archbishop recoiled in dismay at the sea of troubles that threatened to engulf him. Darkest among them was Henry Parkes's Public Schools Act, which Polding saw as 'An infidel system of education': 'The heaviest blow that could have been struck at the welfare and true liberty of our people . . . by destroying gradually denominational education.' Yet, surely Polding should have anticipated it. Similar Acts had been passed in South Australia in 1851, Queensland in 1860, and Victoria in 1862. All of them brought national and denominational education under central boards or councils which were, essentially, hostile to the denominational system. Soon Polding was to observe that the governments 'were every day giving proof of a deadly hostility to the Catholic schools.' To combat this, he set up a Catholic Association in November 1867, to defend, improve and raise funds for Catholic schools.

Throughout Australia, Catholic schools—as their historian

Brother Ronald Fogarty recounts—were gradually being forced out of the government system by administrative policies which drastically tightened the conditions for granting aid, allocated the worst teachers to Catholic schools, inspected them harshly, and then deprived them of certificates of proficiency.

Two months after his return, Polding wrote to Gregory: 'You cannot imagine how changed the country is—all spirit seems gone, all depressed under tyranny and despotism.' In part the change was in Polding himself. Advancing age— he was in his seventies—the frustration of all his plans, nagging loneliness, had intensified his tendency to depression and his sense of inadequacy. In the late 1860s and early 1870s he constantly complained to Gregory of his unfitness to deal with the problems that confronted him, of his inability to shoulder responsibilities, repeating again and again his wish to retire, if only the Pope would accept his resignation, or appoint a coadjutor. If only he could retire to the humble missionary work he loved: to return to Sydney after a missionary visit to outlying areas had become almost unendurable to him. Sydney meant coldness, reserve, misery, intrigue, debt; a host of seemingly insurmountable problems rendered hideous to him by his old and known enemies, procrastination and indecision. In anguish he wrote to Gregory in April 1868: 'I fear I shall lose my own soul, and the souls of others. Ah! I know what ought to be done, but I have not the animus to do it. Pray for me.' Soon, he was to confess to near despair, to periods of inability to preach, or even to appear in public. He feared both death and life. He told Gregory in 1870: 'I begin to long for a release from this life, though I contemplate the after judgement in fear—great fear . . .' Yet: 'I fear I shall live to see all I have endeavoured to establish prostrate.'

The change of the mid-1860s was partly in Polding as he turned, almost obsessed by his episcopal imperfections, to face a death that was to be still long denied. But partly the change was in the church itself, and in the world in which the church lived. Polding told Gregory in April 1870: 'A change has come over the Colony since the advent of the [Irish] Bishops, such as I could not have contemplated;

not that I connect the two except that having an access of strength, our trials have been intensified in the all-wise ways of God.' In fact, Polding did connect the two; and, in fact, they were connected.

On his return from Rome in 1867, Polding had found religious animosity of a kind and intensity which had not existed before. He observed in October 1867:

> Just as I expected and as I forewarned them at Rome, this 'importation of Irish Bishops', as Parkes and the Ministerial party term the coming of Mgri. Quinn and Murray for Bathurst and Maitland, has been the unfortunate cause of, or pretext for, raising a No Popery cry, and has been used to influence the votes for the passing of that most obnoxious Education Bill.

For this situation, Polding blamed Parkes in no uncertain terms: 'What a curse that man is to this noble Colony!' He described Parkes, whom he detested, as 'a determined unscrupulous enemy to Catholics and to Irishmen'. This description probably misses the real Parkes, the politician of genius, but it records accurately his image among most Catholics.

However, Polding also blamed the Irish bishops, and militant Irishism generally, for playing into Parkes's hands. Their aggressive self-assertion, amounting to outright clan leadership, gave Parkes, and all those who saw political advantage in it, or harboured hatreds, the chance to encourage and exploit sectarianism.

Certainly, by now Polding was becoming isolated from his people as they swung behind the new bishops of their own race. While he was on superficially good terms with these bishops, and they accepted his decisions, little confidence existed between him and them, nor would they give him aid, but in fact intrigued against him and his policies. The consecration of William Lanigan as Bishop of Goulburn in June 1867 amounted to an Irish declaration of episcopal independence. The consecration was hurried ahead so that it could be performed by three Irish bishops—the Quinn brothers and Dr Murray—in Goulburn not in Sydney, while Archbishop Polding was still overseas. Then the four Irish bishops held a conference at which they adopted several resolutions reflecting their own policies, which they forwarded as suggestions to Rome.

Such was the Irish bark. The Irish bite was worse. Polding's pet educational establishments, Subiaco and Lyndhurst, decayed rapidly in the late 1860s as a result of strenuous and successful efforts to attract Sydney children to boarding schools established at Bathurst and Maitland. So marked was the success of the new Irish bishops in winning the allegiance of what Polding regarded as his flock, that he began to believe that religion itself was in rapid decline. He became convinced that there was 'some secret party' against him: in fact the whole tide of clerical and lay opinion was flowing strongly against his idea of religion, now that the Irish bishops had given the movement decisive leadership. Decisive it was. They established schools to draw away Polding's pupils; they actively fostered, as Polding complained, 'a spirit of nationality and party'. When, during the 1869 Provincial Council, he inveighed strongly against anyone being other than Australian in outlook, and condemned the nationalisms of the old world, every bishop, except Dr Sheil of Adelaide, dissented, wishing, as the dour Lanigan put it, 'not to forget our Irish national history as being connected so closely with the Faith.'

These bishops' wish not to forget one thing led them to forget another. Certainly the faith and Irish history had been closely connected—in Ireland. To impose the connection on Australia was to forget the basic fact that Australia was not Ireland. It was to forget, too, the darker side of Ireland's religious coin. The Irish bishops were fired with a holy ambition: 'to build up in Australia an Irish Church, that in the coming time will rival in sanctity and learning the unforgotten glories of the ancient church of Ireland.' Had they forgotten that the history of Ireland and the Irish church was also a history of deep divisions, passionate bitterness, and corrosive bigotry? In creating Irish splendours in the antipodes, could they avoid importing also the old hatreds, the old malignant wounds? The task would be difficult, because the unique greatness of the Irish church from which they came was that of a church built deep and firm in the face of persecution.

Militant Irishism was one factor bringing about the

atmospheric change of the 1860s. Events were another. The spectre of Irish rebellion was abroad again. In 1858 the Fenian Brotherhood, an oath-bound secret society dedicated to the violent overthrow of British rule, had been formed in Ireland. Its planned insurrection collapsed in March 1867, but throughout that year violent and deadly Fenian activities in Britain itself aroused a wave of anti-Irish fear and indignation that spread to Australia. The Sydney *Freeman's Journal* responded with what Polding described as 'Fenianism and anti-English tirades'. Then, in March 1868, Prince Alfred, Duke of Edinburgh, who was visiting Sydney, was shot at and slightly wounded by a young Catholic Irishman named O'Farrell.

Immediately a surge of fury and apprehension swept across Australia. The attempted assassination was seized upon as evidence of a Fenian revolutionary plot. The extraordinary fear and panic which gripped the colonies may be gauged from the fact that a rumoured Fenian invasion by sea sent Melbourne into a state of virtual siege in March— a gunboat in the harbour, the military guarding strategic points, and volunteers on full alert. O'Farrell had acted, on his own admission, to strike terror into England, but he had acted alone. However, Sydney was packed with police, ready to prevent expected Fenian riots. None came, but. Parkes, and the Premier, James Martin (an ex-Catholic), exploited the tension to split the community and focus its fears on the Irish and the Catholic church. At this time, and later, Parkes demonstrated his remarkable political ability to use 'No Popery' to his own political advantage, as a way of whipping up support and avoiding other inconvenient political questions that pressed in on him.

The O'Farrell affair aroused bitter, corrosive and enduring sectarian animosity throughout Australia. A Protestant Association spread rapidly in New South Wales and beyond; its object, like that of the Orange Lodges, was to exclude Catholics from all positions of power or influence. As in the colony's early years, Irish Catholics were accused of sedition and disloyalty: these charges were to be heard constantly thereafter, reaching a shrieking climax during the First World War and in the years immediately following it.

Parkes was also president of the New South Wales

Council of Education, which administered and controlled education in that colony. With men of this stamp in charge, what could be expected for Catholic education now, when outside the church, in Polding's words: 'There is now abroad a feeling of bitterness more intense than words can express', when within the church Catholics grouped themselves under Irish banners to combat aggressively the hostility with which they were surrounded?

In their Provincial Council of 1869, the Australian bishops defined authoritatively the ground on which they would take their educational stand. Its background was much more profound than the social legacy of the O'Farrell case: it reflected a clarification of the Council's 1862 statement, under the influence of some important overseas developments.

The new Irish bishops of the mid-1860s had come from an Ireland in which, in 1863, the Irish hierarchy had condemned and repudiated the Irish national education system, that is, the system in which religion was tacked on to a programme of secular instruction. There had been similar condemnations of similar arrangements by bishops in Europe and America. Above all, fully state-controlled and purely secular schools had been formally condemned in 1864 by Pius IX in his *Syllabus of Errors;* the 1869 Council made direct citations from the *Syllabus.*

The essential principle laid down by the bishops in 1869 was that education must take place in, and be infused by, a religious atmosphere which would act upon the child's whole character of mind and heart. This did not mean merely, or even mainly, the direct teaching of Catholic doctrine: it meant the interpenetration of a vital Catholic atmosphere in the school, its infusion with a Catholic life and a spirit of prayer. By these standards, all schemes of secular education—including those not directed towards the abolition of religion—were fundamentally defective. Their inherent vice, as Polding remarked, was their sin of omission. Or, to quote Bishop James Quinn's indignation and horror: 'The children come from the [national & government] schools without knowing even how to bless themselves.' Quite simply, any system which excluded Catholic teaching, practices and atmosphere, was not acceptable to Catholics.

Nor would the bishops accept that the secular system had

any moral virtues. Some of its advocates claimed that it would eliminate sectarian divisions and lead to social harmony. The Catholic view was that the vices of hatred and dissension were human weaknesses which could be restrained only by true religion—which the secular education system sought to remove as an influence. As to non-denominational religious instruction, Polding described the attempt to achieve a sort of common Christianity as specious presumption. To the argument that the system placed the responsibility for religious instruction on the parents, where it belonged, the Catholic retort was that many parents, in their poverty, ignorance, indifference, or even vice, could not discharge such a responsibility.

Then there was the question of authority. Education, crucial to man's supernatural destiny, was integral to the church's earthly mission: it could not surrender to the state or anyone else its authority in that sphere, which was to impart religious instruction and ensure that parents discharged properly their serious responsibility to educate their children in the faith. This task ought to be carried out in harmony with the state, but the state had no right whatever to control or impair parental rights of conscience or the authority of the church. In particular, the state had no right to compel parents to violate their consciences by sending their children to schools where an alien religion, or no religion at all, was taught.

The clarifications of 1869 were made in the face of prevalent social attitudes which were overwhelmingly anti-Catholic in two forms, Protestant and secularist. The denominational system had been Protestant as well as Catholic. However, by this time, Protestant opinion had become, in the main, opposed or indifferent to the continuation of the denominational system. If its continuance benefited Catholicism, this seemed to many Protestants to be a good reason to demand that it cease. And generally, religion was declining. Scepticism, agnosticism and indifference were growing, particularly rapidly in the forcing ground of gold-rush Victoria.

Protestant suspicion and fear of Rome were potent factors in the destruction of denominational education. While Dr Moorhouse, Anglican Bishop of Melbourne, could say in

1879: 'If you sow Secularism, you will reap irreverence and immorality', his Sydney counterpart, Bishop Barker, could say in 1876 that Catholic schools would produce a genera- tion of 'aliens, enemies of the English crown, of English laws'. That Catholic schools denationalised Australian youth was a constant theme of criticism. And when Bishop Tufnel in Queensland said he preferred Romanism to infidelity, he was accused of being a creature of Bishop Quinn.

Anti-Catholicism was even more vigorous among non- Anglican Protestants, many of whom opposed all forms of state aid to religion. Many shared John Dunmore Lang's view that Catholic educational claims were part of that church's perennial plotting and scheming for 'power, for pelf, and for the means of proselytising unwary Protestants to Romanism.' In 1872 the Protestant Political Association declared its rationale to be the defeat of 'that political con- spiracy against the rights and liberties of man, commonly called the Church of Rome.' 'United in a sort of suspicious terror', as George Higinbotham described it, Protestantism was determined to frustrate the claims of its Catholic enemy. Such was the attitude of most active Protestants. There was also in Protestantism a strong and growing liberal strand which held that one religion was as good as another, and that a secular education system would remove unreal barriers between creeds and thus unify Australian life.

The other form of anti-Catholicism was unequivocally secularist. This was apparent in the press of the time, in which religion generally (with Catholicism its most obscuran- tist form) was portrayed as the enemy of freedom, progress and enlightenment; the growth of various forms of rational- ism and the collision between science and religion formed the background to this. Secularism was evident, too, among the politicians with whom the future of educational legislation was to lie—for example, Parkes in New South Wales and George Higinbotham in Victoria. Higinbotham thought in terms of some ubiquitous religious sentiment; he distrusted all organised religion, all clerics, all dogmatism, all religious authority. J. W. Stephen, who introduced the 1872 Bill which abolished state aid to religious schools in Victoria, claimed that:

In a couple of generations, through the missionary influence of the State schools a new body of State doctrine and theology would grow up, and that the cultural and intellectual Victorians of the future would discreetly worship in common at the shrine of one neutral tinted deity, sanctioned by the State department.

As it moved towards its various legislative expressions in the several Australian colonies, the movement towards systematising public education and making it universal had taken on a radically anti-Catholic complexion. Partly this was accident, partly design—and partly Catholic fault. Some influential Catholics, clerical and lay, showed (religious issues apart) a marked coldness towards the prospect of compulsory universal education; in part at least, the Catholic reaction was distinctly conservative, and appeared to favour a static social order resistant to the democracy. The educational reformers had some basis for thinking that the church was opposed to reform as such. There were, then, a variety of elements in the hostility which had grown up between reformers and church. The Catholic response anticipated the worst. Victoria led the way. Bishop Goold's consistent and aggressive attacks on secularism, and his brusque refusal to co-operate with state commissions and authorities, were symptomatic of a sense of growing isolation among the Catholic group, prior to the decisive battle.

It came in 1872, and in Victoria; it was no minor skirmish, but a full-scale frontal engagement between liberal, Protestant state, and Catholic church.

A Victorian secular education Bill, championed by Higinbotham, failed in 1867, but the controversy it aroused made the issue thereafter tense and venomously sectarian. Goold had taken an utterly intransigent stand, threatening to excommunicate parents who sent their children to state schools. The brief Premiership of Charles Gavan Duffy in 1871 intensified the sectarian confrontation to an extreme degree. Victorian Protestants had been suspicious and fearful enough of O'Shanassy as Premier; Duffy was intolerable to them. In Ireland, in 1848, Duffy had been a rebel against the English crown. The Protestant assessment of him was as a seditious and treasonable Red Republican, leading what must be a Catholic bid for political domination. This Protestant mood is clear in the claim of one of Duffy's political opponents: 'there is growing up in our midst a movement the main action and control of which is outside the colony'— apparently in Rome or Dublin. Duffy was not one for denials. An interjector at one of his meetings shouted, 'Ah, Irish rebel! Irish Papist!' 'This was too much for some of my countrymen, who made a rush . . . I stopped them good-humouredly saying, "What, boys, are you ashamed of Irish rebel or Irish Papist? For shame!—the gentleman describes me with great accuracy".' That such a man should hold power and patronage was too much for Protestant opinion to stomach, particularly when it was still aghast at the definition of Papal Infallibility in 1870. Duffy's ministry fell.

Thereupon, the question of secular education leapt to the centre of the political stage, with Goold denouncing moves towards a 'Godless compulsory education' as 'hateful oppression and tyranny'. The Melbourne press interpreted Goold's claims as part of the 'huge and hideous fabric of priestcraft'. Thus the Victorian election of 1872 became quite openly a malicious political battle between Catholics and non-Catholics: the Catholics were vanquished, as having attempted to subject the state to the dictation of their church; and the penalty imposed was the Education Act of 1872, which abolished state aid to Victorian denominational schools. J. W. Stephen, to whom Catholic schools appeared as a disfiguring fungus creeping over the colony, expressed the hope that his government's educational policy would 'rend the Catholics asunder', that is, divide Catholics into those who accepted secular education, and those who rejected it. It seemed to Goold that this was a very real possibility. He denounced the promise of free education, free *secular* education, as a 'shameless and demoralising bribe to the poor and weak to put their conscience aside for apparent present advantage.' He feared that many Catholics would accept that bribe.

However much educational reformers had in mind the estimable objective of educating all the people, the circumstances of the Victorian Act of 1872 made the sectarian nature of the new secular education developments absolutely

clear. Secular education in Victoria was the direct outcome
of an anti-Catholic political victory. It was therefore sectarian, and persecuting sectarianism at that, for it obliged
Catholics to violate their consciences, or suffer. Catholics
noted that Protestants were willing to accept such education:
it must, therefore, be also regarded as Protestant—indeed
Bible reading, which such education retained, was the very
basis of Protestantism; church authority was fundamental to
Catholicism. To Catholics, the secular education movement
exhibited a dual character—anti-religious and Protestant—
both aspects of which were repugnant to the Catholic conscience. To demand that Catholics accept this, or make their
own arrangements, and still be taxed to support what they
had rejected, seemed to them to be outright religious persecution and flagrant financial injustice.

But to Protestants and secularists, to accept the Catholic
case seemed an intolerable concession—a concession to that
church whose 'peculiar genius', as Parkes put it, was 'to
thrive on the enslavement of the human intellect'; a concession to what the Anglican Bishop Barker regarded as an
edifice built on fraud and forgery. When Parkes, in 1879,
expressed his wish to 'put a stop forever to the influence of
the clergy in school management', and foreshadowed a Bill
which would spell 'death to their [the clergy's] calling', he
summed up a fundamental element in the secular schools'
movement. It was aimed—and admitted by some of its foremost champions to be so—at the destruction, or at least the
debilitation, of the Catholic church.

The bishops were aware of the nature of the threat. Their
problem was, how could they meet it? No system of
Catholic education had been planned. The bishops had
wanted Catholic schools to continue as part of a government-
financed system. They had not withdrawn from that system,
but, after a procession of concessions and compromises,
they had been forced out. And all their experience suggested
that the prospects for a separate Catholic-supported system
were gloomy indeed.

When Bishop Goold wrote in 1872: 'Our religious progress here is more than ordinary', his terms of reference
must have excluded education: Goold's was a narrow if
holy mind. His field of vision was largely restricted to the

pastoral ministry; after his comment on progress, he added: 'Our success is sure if the guardians of the sanctuary are true and loyal.' The bishop was still fighting his enemies of the 1850s—recalcitrant and rebellious priests. In fact, that battle was over, almost its only existence being its entrenchment in Goold's mind. Now the enemies were external to Catholicism. The education controversy had turned Victorian public life sour. Catholicism was under constant attack. Nostalgia for Duffy's short but glorious reign was useless. Nor did it help to complain, as a Victorian priest did in 1875, that 'the present Government here have no policy at all. They are trading on the prejudices of the people, and are prepared to have recourse to any vile means to keep their place and pay.' By this time it was clear to the Victorian clergy that the education of Catholic children was 'our battlefield'—but it seemed that the battle was being lost. Goold reported in 1877 that in some places the priests were conducting the schools themselves, as efficient teachers could not be found. And all this was despite the fact that, since the gold rushes, Victoria's Catholic population was, proportionally, the largest, wealthiest and most prosperous of all.

The general picture was no less depressing. As state education boards in the 1860s and 1870s became increasingly hostile to Catholic schools, a growing number of those schools were deprived of government money and forced to exist on their own resources. Their performance was generally discouraging. Standards were low; even religion was poorly taught; there was no organisation and no coherent system. The laity had, at best, only vague notions of what Catholic education was supposed to be. Many parents, from ignorance, from apathy, or from worldly motives, sent their children to state schools: in the 1870s nearly 60 per cent of Catholic school children in New South Wales went to state schools. The Catholic Associations set up in different colonies to aid Catholic education all collapsed, that of New South Wales in 1871, which meant that an attempt by Catholics to support their own schools had failed. The basic problem was that Catholic schools depended on government aid. To withdraw it implied their destruction.

These were the facts. The bishops had no other facts. A Catholic education system did not exist. To construct one

V Church progress: the old and the new churches of St Alphonsus at Millicent, S.A., March 1884

VI Members of the hierarchy of Australia at the Plenary Council of 1885. *Left to right:* Most Rev. Stephen Reville, O.S.A., Coadjutor Bishop of Sandhurst; Most Rev. Martin Griver, Bishop of Perth; Most Rev. William Lanigan, Bishop of Goulburn; (*above*) Most Rev. Daniel Murphy, Bishop of Hobart; (*below*) Most Rev. Christopher Reynolds, Bishop of Adelaide; His Eminence Patrick Francis, Cardinal Moran, Archbishop of Sydney; (*below*) Most Rev. Patrick Moran, Bishop of Dunedin, New Zealand; (*above*) Most Rev. James Murray, Bishop of Maitland; (*above*) Most Rev. Francis Redwood, S.M., Bishop of Wellington, New Zealand; (*below*) Most Rev. Rudesindus Salvado, O.S.B., Bishop of Port Victoria; (*above*) Most Rev. James Moore, Bishop of Ballarat; (*below*) Most Rev. John Cani, Bishop of Rockhampton; (*above*) Most Rev. John Byrne, Bishop of Bathurst; Most Rev. Eleazer Torreggiani, O.S.F.C., Bishop of Armidale was a practical problem of enormous dimensions, and a psychological or religious problem no less large—that of arousing apathetic Catholics to a determined enthusiasm to create and support such a system.

Here the Irish bishops came into their own, with the diocese of Adelaide leading the way. By 1860 Bishop Geoghegan had become deeply concerned about the South Australian education situation as it had developed since the 1851 Act. The whole matter was clouded by bitterness, calumny and rancour, but Geoghegan was utterly clear in his uncompromising opposition to the state system. He was clear, too, in what practical consequences that implied: if nothing was done to establish Catholic schools, at whatever sacrifice, then the operation of the state system meant that 'a few years would thoroughly unsettle Catholicity amongst our young people'.

In the early 1860s Bishop Geoghegan began demonstrating that Catholics could establish and maintain their own schools. Bishop Sheil, who succeeded Geoghegan in 1866, rapidly accelerated this development. In 1866 there were nineteen Catholic schools in South Australia, all taught by lay teachers. In 1871 there were sixty-eight schools, thirty-five of them taught by congregations of religious. The number of pupils had nearly trebled.

The South Australian educational revolution, which acted as an example and inspiration to Catholicism throughout Australia, was the work of Father Julian Tenison Woods and Mother Mary McKillop. In 1866 they had founded the teaching order of the Sisters of St Joseph. Mary McKillop had been a pupil of the Mercy Nuns in Melbourne, and was intending to join them when Father Woods suggested that she open a school (in a disused stable) to help in his own concern—but one which was also very widespread—for the education of small pockets of poor children in rural parishes. She agreed: the Josephite order, dedicated to the education of the Catholic poor, provided the staff for the system Woods organised after taking charge of the diocese's educational affairs in 1867. Both Mary McKillop and Woods were young, she in her late twenties, he in his early thirties. They differed considerably in temperament: she was practical, firm, sensible; he was volatile and visionary.

These differing qualities were eventually to lead to conflict between them, but at first the combination proved to be an ideal answer to South Australia's Catholic educational problems.

Despite his comparative youth, Woods had a life of extraordinary variety behind him—England, France, Tasmania, Victoria, work on the London *Times,* journalism in Adelaide, nearly married, exploration in the Australian desert. He had charm, energy, creative imagination, and organisational gifts, all to the degree of genius, a genius which was not without the flaws of imperiousness, unreason and obstinacy. He set out to produce a system superior to that of the state, schools in which Catholic parents could take pride. He financed the enterprise in a way which was to become characteristic, until recently, of Australian Catholic education, by holding concerts, socials, and entertainments of various kinds, which not only raised money, but brought Catholics together socially in the interest of a common enterprise. As editor of the Adelaide Catholic newspaper, he publicised his own efforts. He obtained Catholic textbooks, writing two (on geography and grammar) himself. All this dynamism and organisation was rewarded with tremendous success—remarkable efficiency, very high educational standards, lay enthusiasm, an astonishing awakening of Catholic interest in educational matters, and such popularity for the Sisters of St Joseph that many of the laity wanted no other teachers.

After this initial success came difficulties of a characteristic if spectacular kind. Father Woods, in his vigorous pursuit of his plans, took little heed of the feelings of his brother priests. To many of them he seemed arbitrary, arrogant, and foolishly scornful of the possibility of retaining government aid (Mother Mary would not accept any degree of government interference). The priests' reaction took the form, in 1871, of a deputation to the Bishop attacking the education system, and Woods's maladministration of it. Sheil, who was in that tradition of Irish episcopal autocracy which sought to subject all diocesan affairs to the bishop's personal control, decided to declare himself ruler of the Josephite congregation and to impose new rules on it. The Sisters refused to accept this, and the ensuing difficulties culminated in the bishop's disbanding of the order (for six months) and his improper (in canon law and common justice) excommunication of Mother Mary, an aberration which, however, Sheil, who was dying, soon corrected. But Woods had left Adelaide to take up again a life of wandering, as itinerant missioner and scientific explorer. He died in 1887. When Mother Mary died in 1909, her order had nearly a thousand members.

The South Australian development was being paralleled in other places. The Irish bishops in New South Wales and Queensland had been moving in the same direction, that is, establishing independent Catholic schools and staffing them by religious orders in place of lay teachers. The major difference was that while the Josephites were an Australian foundation, the Irish bishops preferred to import nuns from Ireland, particularly from the Mercy order, on the assumption (not always correct) that such nuns would be amenable to autocratic episcopal control.

Ever since Bishop James Quinn arrived in Brisbane in 1861, he had been extending the work of the Sisters of Mercy, and building up an education fund. He had, correctly, assessed the Queensland education Act of 1860 as the precursor of a totally secular Act, which came in 1875. His brother, Matthew Quinn, Bishop of Bathurst, followed a similar course of authoritarian central organisation leaving the religious teaching orders little autonomy, using Father Woods's methods of vigorous well-organised propaganda campaigns among the laity, who, in Bathurst as in South Australia, responded enthusiastically. In Tasmania, Bishop Murphy began doing the same, and so did the Spanish Bishop Serra in Perth.

But Polding did not. His Benedictine dream had not encouraged, indeed it had suppressed, the development of other religious orders in the archdiocese: only a handful of schools were staffed by religious. Certainly Polding had pioneered the Sisters of the Good Samaritan in 1857, to cope with colonial problems in the Benedictine spirit, but the order had remained small—forty in 1867. In the early 1870s his attitude in the face of the threat of secular education was a blunt refusal to compromise with it. His educational plans consisted of hope in the future.

His hope was justified. Roger Vaughan, who was to become the symbol, and a major architect, of Catholic educational determination, was appointed Polding's coadjutor in 1873. Vaughan at once took over, with efficiency and wisdom, an administration which was in chaos. Polding slipped into the background, into the life of undisturbed pastoral ministry and personal piety which he had craved so long. At first, Vaughan was impatient with him. He thought that Polding had brought many of his troubles on himself: the abbey-diocese plan had been a destructive fantasy. Vaughan and Polding represented the opposite poles of a protracted conflict within English Benedictinism between a missionary and a non-missionary emphasis. Vaughan was convinced that all Polding's troubles flowed from an impossible attempt to combine the two, plus Polding's mismanagement and dependence upon the unwise counsel of foolish friends. To Vaughan, Polding's attempt to found a monastic Benedictinism in Australia seemed disastrous; he proposed to secularise the remaining Benedictines in Australia, to wipe the slate clean.

The slight abrasion between old Archbishop and young coadjutor was not to last long. When, in March 1877, Polding felt the approach of death, he summoned his household to his bedside to humbly ask their forgiveness for any offence he might have given, and he prayed that the Pope would pardon his errors and imperfections in the performance of his episcopal duties. Polding, then eighty-two, priest, monk and bishop, suffered his sense of responsibility to the last: 'In holy fear and holy love fulfil those duties which even angels might dread to discharge.'

When Roger Vaughan arrived in Sydney, he was thirty-nine, a man of commanding presence, compelling power of personality, profound scholarship, and remarkable oratorical gifts—in every way a match for the situation which was to confront him. Writing *en route* to Sydney, he confided to his father:

I think we all love enterprise; and difficulties and sacrifices are quite the wrong sort of thing to try to stop our paths by! Pride! Herbert [his brother, later Cardinal Vaughan] would say. I don't quite know myself what name to call it by; but

anyhow it seems to help me along, and I will not quarrel
with it just at present.

The second son of an English Catholic squire, Roger
Vaughan had five brothers in the priesthood. He was taught
at home (as a boy he had delicate health) and by the
Benedictine order, which he entered. For four years he
studied in Rome; his great love was philosophy, and his
only pleasure, books. Naturally serious and enjoying
seclusion, he was impatient with the frivolous and the
commonplace, yet he had an excellent sense of fun, often
embellishing his letters with humorous drawings. He had
the ability to govern easily and well, and an astonishing gift
of speech. He became professor of metaphysics and moral
philosophy at the Belmont Benedictine Priory; then, from
1862 until his Sydney appointment, he was prior. There he
showed his intuitive flair for administration, his natural
decision and firmness. Even greater were his powers of
speech, which he cultivated earnestly, producing that poised
elegance yet lively reality characteristic of his style. He
also continued his academic work, with a variety of published material, notably his two-volume *Life of St Thomas
of Aquin*, which was published in 1871-2, and received with
a chorus of praise: 'a book truly erudite . . . written with
fascinating freshness and brilliance of style.' Erudition and
style: the book reflected the man.

Here, then, was a cleric of extraordinary abilities, strong-
willed, proud and ambitious in the life of intellectual religion,
an eloquent master of the art of preaching. He was not
wanted in Australia.

Polding had been attempting since 1865 to have Vaughan
appointed as his coadjutor. The reluctance of the English
Benedictines to part with such an able member was one part
of the explanation of Polding's lack of success. The unwillingness of the Irish bishops in Australia—and in Ireland
—to have another Benedictine archbishop was the other.
Polding impressed upon Rome the need for an English coadjutor: Australia, as a British dominion, required a man
superior to all party spirit. His argument had the support
of the British government's diplomatic agent in Rome.

The Irish suffragan bishops totally opposed this, to the

extent of protesting against Vaughan's appointment and of urging Rome to appoint an Irishman. This attitude was quite open in Sydney. Justice Faucett, who presided over the meeting to arrange for Vaughan's reception in December 1873, 'confessed that he might have wished, as others might perhaps have wished, that the selection had come from another quarter.' Some Irish Catholics anticipated, wrongly, that Vaughan would attempt to revive Polding's policy of Benedictinisation.

Vaughan was fully aware of all this. His response was conciliatory—strong praise for the virtues and achievements of the Irish—but in no way self-effacing or apologetic: 'You may call me an Englishman if you will. I am one; but I am a Catholic first. We join in a holy brotherhood, and with the help of God, will fight the evils of the world.'

The major evil of the Australian world was stressed in the clergy's address of welcome to Vaughan:

> We hope to be the better able to protect the education of the rising generation from the blighting influence of anti-Catholic secularism under the leadership of one whose published writings prove him so deeply conversant with the pure sources of sanctity and learning from which the colossal minds of the ages of faith and scholasticism drew their inspirations.

In his reply, Vaughan took up this theme, setting it in a wider context, and relating it to another giant enterprise: he would not be diminished to the size of the immediate emergency.

> There are two instruments, it seems to me, we have in our hands by means of which we may attack what I call earth worship, and overthrow it. In the first place we have that which is a continual protest against earth worship, and that is the commencement of this magnificent Cathedral which is being built now, and which will for generations stand . . . and proclaim . . . that the Catholics . . . manifest their true love to Him from whom all strength proceeds . . . Within these walls we shall worship and praise Him . . . And there is a second instrument, which seems to me to be that of Christian education . . .

The setting of Vaughan's fight for Christian education was a prodigious personal campaign on his part to build the present St Mary's Cathedral. Between August 1880 and October 1881 Vaughan wrote, with his own hand, 1,466 letters asking for donations for the Cathedral: he wrote a thousand letters of reply in thanks for the £16,409 1s 2d he received. True, the Cathedral was still incomplete, but it was opened, with a temporary roof, in September 1882. It had cost to that stage nearly £103,000; Vaughan freed it of debt. Fifteen years before, Polding had been in despair of ever implementing Wardell's expensive architecture. In 1881 W. B. Dalley, addressing Archbishop Vaughan in a public speech, spoke of 'the great distinctive labour of your life . . . You have inspired and sustained the enthusiasm which has led to this triumphant result.' It was not to the Catholic education system that Dalley referred; it was to the Cathedral. And Vaughan, in ten years, more than doubled the number of churches and chapels in New South Wales.

Nor did Vaughan conceive the problem of Christian education itself in any narrow sense. When he arrived in Sydney he took over the rectorship of St John's College in the University, relinquishing it upon becoming Archbishop in 1877, but continuing to reside there. (His uncarpeted sitting room contained only books, a crucifix, and a writing desk on which was a skull; his bedroom was even more austere.) He saw St John's as 'pre-eminently fitted to become the main fortress amongst us of Catholic Christianity'. Here would be produced 'the really Christian gentleman, whilst he is educated so as to acquit himself with honour in the battle of life, he, at the same time, becomes a pattern of what is morally and intellectually beautiful in the teachings of the Gospel—he is a breathing manifestation of Christian truth.' In the tradition of Aquinas, Vaughan firmly linked intellectuality and religion directly, and in apparent paradox: 'a good life is more conclusive than a brilliant argument'.

Vaughan's crusade against secular education derived naturally from his general interpretation of what was happening in the world in which he lived. 'I have perceived an ever-growing body of men, massing themselves together from almost every walk of life, and falling into some kind of shape or consistency through their common attitude of menace to Christianity in all its forms.' Only the Catholic church was capable of resisting this, he believed; all the sects of Protestantism were crumbling away into various kinds of unbelief. 'The gradual melting away of a coherent system of doctrine, and an organised code of practice, is one of the portentous signs of a dark and distressing future.'

Religion was menaced by materialism. And at the centre of materialism, Vaughan contended publicly in 1876, was freemasonry. The hidden spring of freemasonry was a pride in reason. The purpose of freemasonry was to undermine Christian education and the influence of the priesthood: it was a gigantic hideous conspiracy engaged in devastating the vineyard of the Lord (Vaughan's picture of freemasonry had much in common with the ultra-Protestant picture of Catholicism). The public uproar caused by this kind of depiction did not dismay Vaughan: 'It has roused up the Freemasons like a nest of ants. I find that straight speaking, and the whole teaching of the Church does these Australians most good. Religion is looking up and is respected.' Doing Australians good, by straight speaking and uncompromising Catholic doctrine, became the theme of Vaughan's public life. Naturally, this made him a contentious figure.

So, to Vaughan, the attempt to substitute secular for denominational education, while of vital importance in itself, was also symptomatic of a movement aimed at 'the extinction of the Catholic religion, of the Catholic sacraments, and of the calling of the Catholic clergy.'

At first Vaughan was cautious. His adoption of a policy of encouraging religious teaching orders was not automatic. To begin with he wanted to investigate questions of cost and competence, and to assess what had happened in the dioceses of the Irish bishops. He was soon more than satisfied. His decision, in 1874, to vigorously encourage the spread of the Marist Brothers, swung Sydney's educational policy into line with that of other dioceses. Sydney had a lot of leeway to make up. In the previous ten years Sydney had spent £40,000 on schools; Goulburn, Bathurst and Maitland, under the Irish suffragans, had spent £120,000. Having made his decision, Vaughan implemented it energetically. In 1873 Sydney had thirty-four Catholic schools, fifty-four in 1879, and 102 in 1883.

In consultation with his Irish suffragans, and under their pressure, Vaughan also decided to take up the educational challenge in another way. After what had happened in Victoria, the outcome of the conflict between church and state over education was predictable elsewhere. The New South Wales bishops determined to confront the inevitable before it happened. To provoke the crisis was the only way to retain some control over it, and to escape with honour from a shrivelling denominational system which was, the bishops believed, slowly eroding the faith of the people. It was the only way to avoid complete debilitation, to retain initiative among the Catholic people, and to assert leadership on what the bishops regarded as a matter of profound principle.

In 1879 the bishops of New South Wales issued a Joint Pastoral condemning secular schools as 'seedplots of immorality', and challenging in the most decisive terms, as corrupt, infidel and unjust, the existing trends in public educational policy. Its practical recommendations amounted to a grave warning to Catholic parents that they must send their children to Catholic schools, which must be provided, extended and supported at whatever the sacrifice.

The reaction was prompt. Alarm spread through the Catholic community. Within a week, attendance of Catholic children at Sydney's state schools had dropped by about 20 per cent. The Catholic people had been roused. So had everyone else. A sectarian convulsion seized New South Wales as the bishops' denunciation of public schools tapped bitter springs of vengeance. Fierce storms of controversy blew from every corner. Riding on the gales of hate and abuse that swept in on Vaughan, that audacious prelate, that intolerant and seditious priest, came Henry Parkes with the 1880 Public Instruction Act, abolishing aid to denominational education, establishing secularism. The clash between that master of politics, Parkes, and that master of religious principle, Vaughan, produced one of Australia's great public debates. Two conflicting views of man and the world were at battle, sharpened by Parkes with personal thrusts. As Parkes attacked Vaughan with charges of disloyalty and sedition, Vaughan countered with his long and gallant English ancestry, and a challenge to Parkes to prove his accusations in a court of law.

Neither Parkes nor Vaughan believed that the situation

created by the Public Instruction Act would last long, a few years at the most. Parkes, and those of like mind, did not believe that the Catholic stand was one of principle, but the outcome of pride and selfishness: it was merely a brief demonstration, no doubt an attempt at blackmail, which would soon end. Moreover, practically, and financially, how could Catholics provide education for themselves without government aid? To think that they could was absurd. Any attempt to do so must soon fail. And the bishops? And Vaughan? To them it was obvious that 'justice and fair play will conquer', and that it would do so soon. Oppression of such a flagrant kind could not last. Withdrawal of state aid would be a severe temporary strain, but in a few years, justice would be done.

Meanwhile Vaughan began, with optimistic determination, his enormous task. 'I shall show them . . . that we can hold our own without them—I mean without Parkes and his help, and a just deal more than hold our own . . . I will solve the school question, in a way that will astonish them!'

In part, the Joint Pastoral had been directed towards liberating Catholics from the constricting enervation of the old denominational system. Vaughan believed that the old schools had been weakening and impoverishing the faith. Now Catholic schools could be made Catholic without compromise. This was the challenge Vaughan had accepted. On his meeting it successfully, he believed, hinged the future of Catholicism in Australia. He met it with religious orders of teachers, nuns and brothers, and with a succession of warm, moving appeals, pastorals, speeches and addresses, aimed at encouraging Catholics in the holy work of providing schools. Vaughan made the Catholic school the symbol of Australian Catholicism: 'We prize, above all imaginable things, the Faith of our Fathers; that Faith is in peril in a great measure on account of the menacing condition of modern society; and cost what it may, it must be preserved and fostered in the hearts and intellects of the rising generation.'

Into this endeavour, Vaughan, his own imagination caught and possessed by a vision of truth redeemed by heroic sacrifice, infused the magic of a crusade. He saw his own life in crusading terms. 'The spiritual empire, of which we are soldiers, by its very history, stirs up the fires of charity

and zeal in our hearts. Ours is one of the very few causes
in the world worth living for, and dying for, too . . .' It was
his extraordinary gift to be able to communicate to his
people this sense of dedication, to draw out from them a
generosity of spirit truly imperial, in terms of Vaughan's
demand for allegiance to the kingship of Christ. Nor was its
flavour that of some petty squabble: it was nothing less than
a crusade for national redemption. The Archbishop told his
people: 'In these our days we are creating the history of
the future. On those who rule now, or exercise moral influence, depend the future prosperity of the nation. We
mean to do our humble part . . . we shall stand firm on the
adamantine rock of the Catholic faith.'

The rest of his life was spent in quest for religious orders
of teachers, and the building of a system of schools with
these as an essential foundation. At first, these orders were
seen as essential in economic terms, as they would cost a
minimum. Soon they became integral to Vaughan's concept
of schools as holy places. The teaching of men and women
who had dedicated their whole beings to God would transform the Australian Catholic world.

As early as April 1880, Vaughan could say: 'I look upon
the crisis we have gone through as resulting in the salvation
of the Catholic religion in this colony. Nothing less would
have done it. The action of our opponents has been the
greatest blessing that could have fallen to our lot.' Other,
Irish, bishops were well ahead of Vaughan in developing a
system of religious teachers to meet the education crisis.
His greatest contribution was in the realm of resolution and
inspiration. He, above all others, was responsible for transforming the grim lineaments of disaster into the complexion
of joyous providential blessing, the saving of the Catholic
religion. In 1875 the attitude of many bishops was expressed
by Bishop O'Connor, of Ballarat, when he said that he
hoped to support his own schools until better and wiser
counsels prevailed. Vaughan banished such shaky hopes,
substituting in their stead certitude.

Vaughan was soon to die. From 1880 he became increasingly aware that the future was at the mercy of his health.
In April 1883 he left for England, to recruit religious orders
of teachers and to assist Benedictine reforms. He told those

who assembled to farewell him that he was sobered, saddened and depressed; clearly death was already dwelling in him. 'I am struck—I was almost going to say wounded—at the thought of what really might have been done . . . what will my Judge say when I have to give an account of my stewardship before His Court?' Although, with his work hardly begun, he felt the imminence of eternity, the tough realist in him took stock of things as they were: 'Anyhow, let us do our work in our day.' And the warm, genuine love that had grown between him and his people spoke out too: he felt as one leaving a happy home, a home in which the labours had been those of God. In August 1883, in England, life-long heart disease killed Vaughan in his sleep. He was forty-nine. He had been in Australia ten years, Archbishop for six

His remains were laid temporarily in a vault, until the anticipated arrangements could be made for their return to Australia. Two years later, his brother, Herbert, then Bishop of Salford, wrote to Cardinal Moran seeking to clarify those arrangements. The Cardinal replied that the return of Vaughan's remains in Sydney was 'quite out of the question . . . no one in Sydney would wish the matter spoken of, and not one penny would be contributed towards that purpose; and, in the unfinished state of the Cathedral, I don't see how I could give my approval to it.' In reply to Herbert Vaughan's claim that burial costs should be met from the Archbishop's will, of which Moran, as his successor, was sole beneficary, Moran explained that he had already spent the large sum Vaughan had bequeathed: it was up to the Vaughan family to bury him in England, 'but it certainly will not be done at my expense'. In 1946 Archbishop Gilroy had Vaughan's remains brought from England and interred in the Cathedral crypt. For those intervening sixty years, Vaughan's body lay under a tombstone engraved: 'Exultabunt ossa humiliata'—My bones rejoice in humiliation.

This story tells harshly against Moran, perhaps too harshly, for Herbert Vaughan's conduct towards him had long been hostile and provocative. Moran had clashed with him earlier, over Irish affairs, and they cordially detested each other. To Moran, Herbert Vaughan was an objectionable English Tory of the most overbearing kind, attempting to

place him in a position of disadvantage, and to throw unfavourable light on his Sydney administration. He would
not tolerate this, and the toughness of his response was
related to the strength of his antipathy for Herbert Vaughan.
The body of Roger Vaughan, second Archbishop of Sydney,
was the victim of the quarrel.

Vaughan's relatively early death—Polding, Moran and
Kelly lived to nearly twice his age—raises a multitude of
'might have beens'. Some have speculated that had he lived
another twenty years the church may have become more
characteristically Australian, less an Irish religious colony.
Certainly Vaughan set out to build such an Australian
church. He rejected Polding's Benedictine dreams, nor did
he see the church as the Irish did, in terms of party. He
saw Australia as part of the Church Catholic.

> Let us, then, often meditate, during these forty days [he wrote
> in Lent 1881] on the great Spiritual Empire to which we
> belong; encourage in our minds a profound sense of thank-
> fulness that we are members of so glorious a society; and think
> of how we can do our part towards strengthening its hold and
> perpetuating its power in this land of our adoption.

This spirit of universality, notable in all Vaughan's writings,
was particularly expressed in his Pastorals, many of which
pioneered the development, initiated as a policy by Pope
Pius IX and followed by Moran, of the direct dissemination
of papal teaching and encyclicals. Vaughan saw Australia
as part of the Catholic world; Australia's problems were
merely one aspect of the whole. 'If we take the Papal Chair
as a centre, and cast our eyes around the world, we shall
find that the Catholic Church is engaged in almost every
country in a heavy conflict with her enemies.' Again and
again Vaughan insisted to his flock that the secular education
system was merely the form taken in Australia of world-wide
trends which sought 'to make a clear way for the liberty of
the passions and the uncontrolled display of the pride of
man.'

Did he succeed in his efforts to integrate Australian
Catholics into the world at large? Some signs suggest that
he did. His extraordinary abilities, his transparent sincerity,
brillance, power and vigour made an immense impression.

Even his opponents, the *Sydney Morning Herald,* the *Daily Telegraph,* conceded that he was a great man, selfless, a man of Christian rectitude, in all a splendid enemy. And when he left Australia in 1883 it seemed that he had won his people over.

Yet this is to gainsay the facts of Australian Catholic life. It was Irish. Nearly all the episcopacy was Irish, and the clergy, and the laity. How much of Vaughan's support came from the fact that he had followed the educational policies of the Irish bishops? How deeply did his intellectuality, his Catholic universality, penetrate into that resistant soil, that holy Irish ground hardened by the southern sun?

Vaughan had stood at the crossroads of Australian Catholic history and had pointed the way ahead. Thereafter no one could mistake the direction, nor complain for want of inspired leadership. But the way had already been pioneered by Irish bishops, and some of them were already travelling it. Vaughan provided leadership, but no leader can lead unless his followers will, in fact, follow. His stand was not unique. He epitomised, dramatically, the stand taken by others. Hence his success. Vaughan was the medium, a medium of great stature, through which Australian Catholicism expressed its refusal to compromise with a secular world.

4

The Reign of Cardinal Moran 1884-1911

The achievements of Polding and Vaughan may seem, in retrospect, very great. At the time, their deficiencies loomed much larger, especially to the Irish: tragically, dismayingly large. This was not so much a matter of what the Benedictine archbishops had actually done—though there was that, too. Rather was it the Irish vision of what might have been done under Irish episcopal rule. The Irish interpretation of Benedictine control came to this: if the Irish had full charge of the Australian church, more souls would be saved, the church would be stronger, more extensive, more united. Believing this—that souls were being needlessly lost, and religion needlessly handicapped—it was hard indeed for the Irish to endure Benedictine control. Convinced that they were the natural ministers of Catholicism in Australia, it was logical, an imperative religious duty in fact, that they should seek to bring Benedictine rule to an end and substitute their own.

To describe this as Irish ecclesiastical imperialism is not to deny the strong and valid arguments which supported an Irish condemnation of Benedictine control. The Australian laity was Irish or of Irish origin; there had been considerable Irish-English friction; Polding might have done much more to bring priests and religious teachers to Australia, and so on. But the Irish clergy had much more than mere complaints; they had a vision of spiritual empire. They would build, in Australia, a new, free Ireland, a religious realm in which the piety and fervour they know so well in old Ireland would experience an ennobling, transforming liberation, freed from the bitter weight of a persecuted history and the chains of British rule.

This stunning vision of a new religious world, free from the poisons of old, hatred-ridden Europe, had its greatest prophet in Cardinal Moran. It was he who found, on arrival in Sydney harbour, a welcome from his people, so loving and devoted, as to rival, in his eyes, 'the ages of medieval piety'. It was he who explained, when he visited Dublin in 1888: 'In those distant colonies of Australia we are endeavouring, though in a very humble way, to emulate the marvellous fruitfulness of piety that characterises this dear old land.' This, to please Irish ears. He went on to sing Australia's praises: 'Thanks to the prudence and wisdom that have guided our statesmen in modern times in colonial administration, we enjoy legislative independence, we make our own laws, justice is impartially administered, and the blessings of liberty are widespread among our people.' When the blessings of liberty mingled with the blessings of piety, new religious horizons would open out, illimitable in the ways of God. 'Providence has a glorious future for this bright land,' Moran told Australians in 1885. 'Providence has certainly marked out our country for special honour and favour: has marked a course which must lead to power, fame and greatness.' For God had blessed Australia with vast natural wealth and resources, but greater still, with freedom: 'we shape our own destinies and make our own laws.'

If piety, Irish piety, could be brought to shape Australia's destiny, a great religious nation would appear. In Moran's eyes, Australia gave promise of being, in a sense, the Ireland of his spiritual dreams. Ireland born anew, pious and God-centred, but, this time, free. The material to construct a spiritual empire was to hand—pious Irish souls. The climate was favourable—Australian freedom. And the aim was a great nation, religious and free. Besides this staggering ambition, this total vision—the Southern world for Christ—the Benedictine dream pales into insignificance. It was no mere antiquarianism which led Cardinal Moran to assert, continually, and with historical apparatus, that Australia was first discovered in 1606 by the Spanish explorer De Quiros. De Quiros had made his voyages into unknown seas in the belief that he had been chosen by God to discover 'terra australis', the great Southern land, and to bring its inhabitants into the true church, under the patronage of the Holy Spirit. Moran saw himself, and his Irish church, following

in the wake of that holy voyage, with the same vast missionary hopes to capture a new world for Christ.

When John Healy, Archbishop of Tuam, remarked in
1884 that Moran was going 'to govern the archepiscopal see
of Sydney, to which is annexed the Primacy of the Australian
Empire', his terms were well chosen. Denied the cruder,
material imperialism of politics or economic power, Ireland's
holy zeal and idealism, its pursuit of freedom and independent identity, its dynamic expansionist religious energies,
found an outlet in missionary religion, with ecclesiastics the
commanders, the clergy their lieutenants. Moran himself
used the term 'Irish spiritual empire', contrasting it with
existing political and economic empires. The missionary
church became a vehicle for Irish aspirations towards
liberty, and also for their desire to build and create. Their
ambition was to carve out a dominion subject to Christ and
St Patrick, a dominion moulded in an Irish image and
likeness, which was also the image and likeness of God.

Clearly, the dynamic ambitions of Irish ecclesiastics were
not to be measured in narrow factional terms of the further-
ance of Irish-Catholic religion. Rather, their concept of
Australia's future was that of a religious nation, on the
Irish pattern: free, and Irish—where Irish meant true, deep
religiosity. This was a dazzling vision to men who had known
religion only where it was less than free—in Ireland under
English Protestant rule, or embattled or imprisoned in Rome
during the Italian Risorgimento. Moran's coming represents
the high point of that hopeful vision, and also the beginning
of its decline.

McEncroe's prolonged agitation for an Irish episcopacy
rested largely on practical premises. The idea of *imperium*
came with the Irish bishops of the 1860s, in particular with
three of them, James Quinn of Brisbane, his brother
Matthew of Bathurst, and James Murray of Maitland. They
brought with them that unique mixture of politicking and
piety—or, more precisely, politicking in the interests of
piety, which was to become characteristic of the Australian
church.

Their first task was to contest the ground with those
already occupying it. A sorry ground it was, or so they

thought. Matthew Quinn was appalled by what he found on his arrival: 'Oh Dr Murray I was sad, very sad, more sad than I can describe to you . . . May God in his mercy look down on this Australian church. Dr Murray say what we ought to do . . .' Scandals, neglect, lack of real religion seemed to prevail except in those oases they had created themselves, or found preserved by the inherent strength of Irish faith: in these areas, good people lived. For this deplorable situation they believed Polding, that 'poor old man' as they usually described him, carried a terrible responsibility. God would, one day, demand an account of his stewardship, but the Irish bishops were convinced, on their arrival, that he should be steward no longer.

Their revulsion from what they regarded as religious neglect disposed the new Irish arrivals to place the worst interpretation on everything, and, occasionally, to fall into factual error. In 1867, when the Catholic educational revolution in South Australia had begun, Bishop Murray was writing to Dr Moran that the diocese of Adelaide was in a deplorable condition, that nothing had been done there for the previous five or six years, and that education was entirely in the hands of Protestants.

Was Australia a religious desert, as these bishops thought? In their terms it was; they judged true to their own standards. However, their standards were those of the church they knew in Ireland. The startling contrast between the settled piety of an Ireland steeped in Catholicity for centuries, and shrinking in population, and the exploding expansion of the Australian missionary problem was profoundly shocking to these men. The close Irish parish relationship between priest and people did not exist in Australia, except perhaps in some city areas; in Australia a Catholic might not see a priest for months. This seemed scandalous to the Irish bishops, and doubly horrifying because these Catholics were Irish. It was the Irish church that was being neglected.

Nor did these bishops, at first, have any idea of the enormity of the missionary problem. Australia's rapid growth, in population and extent of settlement, far exceeded the ability of the church to provide priests, as these bishops themselves were soon to find. After ten years ruling the Bathurst diocese, Matthew Quinn was still remarking that some parts of his diocese had never been visited by a priest, and that he not infrequently gave first communion and confirmation to persons of thirty years of age. Yet Quinn was much in the Polding tradition of travelling often, and travelling great distances. The Irish bishops, too, lagged behind in the provision of priests, though not as far behind as Polding. And as to that 'poor old man': the Polding they met in the 1860s was indeed an old man, dispirited and alone—and resistant to them and their dynamic plans for reorganisation.

The Irish bishops had expected to find problems in Australia. Their initial experience confirmed the rumours they had been hearing from such sources as Fathers Bermingham and McAlroy. They promptly concluded that Australia's religious future rested on them; that they carried the responsibility of saving the Australian church from grave decline, and of rescuing it, as a matter of urgency, from apathy and indifference. Willingly accepting this duty, the two Quinns and Murray became the new dynamic of the Australian church. Their links were not with Polding, but with Ireland and Rome. They asked Monsignor Kirby, the saintly and influential Rector of the Irish College in Rome, to act as their agent in the Vatican. On arriving in Maitland in 1867, James Murray wrote to Cardinal Cullen thanking him 'for giving me such a good people to look after': these bishops believed that the healthy future of the Australian church rested largely with Cullen, who was constantly consulted in Australian affairs.

Polding did not enter their plans save as their foe and source of most of their difficulties and frustrations. Thus, in 1867, when six of James Quinn's priests quitted his diocese because of his autocratic rule, his brother Matthew remarked that he 'should not wonder' that Polding had instigated this rebellion (which was untrue). The priests' desertion went for consideration to Rome, which asked awkward questions about the Bishop's ability to govern his diocese; the whole affair was a severe and disconcerting blow to Irish pride. The bishops' response illustrates a characteristic of their rule: any challenge to their authority evoked a further assertion of that authority. 'In one word for the protection of episcopal authority, for the interests of religion, and for the purpose of preventing similar abuses in future, the case of the six Priests should be left in the hands of the Bishop', wrote Bishop Murray. So, eventually, it was, but not before the Irish bishops had been sharply discomforted. Nor did Quinn's problems of discipline end. He had to deal with an attempted schism in 1880.

The main area for conflict between the Irish bishops and both Archbishop Polding and Bishop Goold, was over appointments to the episcopacy. In New South Wales this is illustrated by the rival candidatures of Fathers McAlroy and Austin Sheehy for bishoprics. Sheehy was Polding's Vicar-General, and in the late 1860s it had become intensely important to Polding that Sheehy be made a bishop. Sheehy's promotion symbolised Polding's will, authority and judgement. The Irish bishops regarded McAlroy as the 'greatest missionary priest in Australia'. In terms of ministry and buildings, McAlroy had indeed achieved wonders, but Polding, victim of McAlroy's insubordination and misrepresentation, would not hear of him as a bishop. Both Polding and the Irish bishops were determined to have their own way; each was determined to thwart the other. The Irish bishops urged on Rome, through Monsignor Kirby, to Cardinal Cullen, to Cardinal Barnabo in Propaganda, the great virtues and abilities of Father McAlroy, at the same time decrying Sheehy as totally unsuitable for episcopal office.

The outcome was frustration for both camps. Neither McAlroy nor Sheehy became bishops, despite the fact that both parties continued to nominate them at every opportunity. However, victory in general terms lay with the Irish suffragans. They secured a Roman directive that forced Polding to consult his suffragans in the nomination of bishops, and to accept a system whereby there was a ballot selection of three nominees whose names were forwarded to Rome for final selection. Polding did not want to accept this machinery, as the suffragans could always outvote him. The Archbishop recoiled further from the situation that enmeshed him. In 1869 he set out to attend the first Vatican Council. At Aden he turned back, because, it was announced, of failing health. James Quinn, who was travelling on the same ship, remarked privately: 'Health was not the cause of his return.' Polding was certainly ill, but Quinn's cryptic remark raises a question which was in Polding's mind—could he bring himself to face Rome again? Rome had been the scene of his reverses, and was, as he saw it, in the hands of those opposed to him, the Irish.

The Irish bishops had less success in their attempts to dominate the Victorian situation. From their arrival, the condition of the Victorian church distressed them in the same way as they had reacted to the situation that they found in New South Wales. They concluded that it was imperative that new dioceses be formed immediately in Victoria. Just as they had no confidence in Polding, so they distrusted Bishop Goold. When Goold was in Rome in 1867, Bishop Murray assumed he was there to finalise new Victorian dioceses. He warned Rome to be very cautious about appointing as bishops those whom Goold might nominate. Murray regarded those whom Goold favoured as unfit, even going so far as to say that, from what he had heard, 'there are not men in Victoria fit for such a position'. He invoked Cardinal Cullen's influence against whomever Goold might propose. (It was remarkable in this and other cases how the Irish bishops could always find, on the best of authority, evidence of deficient character in those they did not want.)

However, nothing happened in 1867. The Irish bishops in New South Wales continued to press Goold, who became increasingly annoyed by their insistence. In 1869 they urged three new dioceses. Goold would talk in terms of one only—for selfish reasons, the Irish bishops thought. They pressed for Melbourne to be made an archdiocese, but believed that Polding disliked that idea—again for selfish reasons. All this they reported to Rome.

In 1873 the sight of Goold alone fighting the noxious Education Act—ineffectively to their mind—prompted them to step up their pressure for new sees. By this time they were demanding five Victorian dioceses (with McAlroy occupying one). Goold would accept three, but not McAlroy: he had suffered more than Polding from that source. And he was becoming increasingly suspicious of the Irish bishops, more and more resentful of what he regarded as their intereference in his affairs, and increasingly obstructive. Impatient, the bishops blamed not only Goold but also Polding for the delay in creating new Victorian sees.

Meanwhile, they felt, the faith in Victoria was suffering grievously; certainly the subdivision, when it came, gave Victorian religion new life.

In October 1873, with every sign of splenetic annoyance, Goold left suddenly for Rome, just before Matthew Quinn and James Murray arrived in Melbourne. Such was his fury that he left instructions that they be refused the hospitality of his house. He had decided to spike their guns by getting two dioceses, Sandhurst and Ballarat, which he did, despite Matthew Quinn's urgent efforts to bring influence in Rome to delay any decision until his group could have its say.

As he aged, Goold's irascibility increased and his vision narrowed. He was annoyed by the appointment of Christopher Reynolds as Bishop of Adelaide in 1873: the previous two bishops, Shiel and Geoghegan, had been Melbourne priests, Reynolds was not. In the late 1870s and early 1880s the Irish junta was continually attempting to force the ailing Goold to accept a coadjutor—Irish, of course. Goold refused, and counter-attacked with attempts to break up clerical Irishry in Victoria with a policy of divide and rule. In 1882 he was telling All Hallows of his grave objection to receiving a majority of clergy from any part of Ireland—County Kerry had been his bane. In future, priests were to come from a variety of Irish counties, so as to prevent regional pushes and cliques. Goold succeeded in resisting the appointment of a coadjutor until just before his death in June 1886, in his seventy-fifth year.

However, it was Polding, as Archbishop, who was the major target for Irish pressure. The bishops wanted a synod, as a means of imposing their ideas and policy on the Australian church. Polding prevaricated. The bishops then secured a Roman directive to Polding that he convene a synod, telling him that if he could not preside, the senior suffragan could. Reluctantly, Polding made preliminary arrangements in 1868. Then, early in 1869, he saw a possible way of further postponing the synod. He suggested that it not be held until after the Vatican Council in 1870, as Council decisions might affect matters for discussion. Bishop James Quinn curtly reminded the Archbishop that he was under explicit Roman direction in the matter.

The synod was held in May 1869. It passed off harmoni-

ously, save on one issue. The uncompromising policy on
education which the Irish bishops had been pushing since
their arrival was acceptable to all, but their hard line on
mixed marriages, between Catholics and non-Catholics, was
not. The issue of mixed marriages was one on which the
Irish bishops reacted in terms of their Irish background;
they were vehemently unwilling that the Australian church
should continue in its former ways.

When Polding came to Australia, his problem had been
to get couples to convert liaisons into marriages. His view
was that a mixed marriage was better than none at all. By
the 1860s, with a generation of free immigration and
growing social stability, the problem of inducing couples to
marry rather than merely live together was fast vanishing,
while that of marriages between Catholics and non-Catholics
had grown large. Polding, although opposed to mixed
marriages, retained his old view, and adhered to his traditional practice of having mixed marriages celebrated in the
church with the priest wearing stole and surplice, as in
Catholic marriages.

James Murray regarded this as scandalous. He looked at
the situation in this way. In his own diocese he frequently
denounced mixed marriages, and would not allow them.
Those who sought such marriages merely went to Sydney.
Such people could thus 'defy our authority and people will
laugh at us for upholding the doctrine and laws of the
Church in reference to mixed marriages, which are so scan-
dalously trampled on and disregarded in Sydney.' Episcopal
authority was at stake. So were the doctrines and laws of the
church. Indeed, so was religion itself. Murray regarded the
total prohibition of mixed marriages as imperative. Only by
such a prohibition 'we may hope to root out of this land
that fatal indifference to *religion* which is the curse of this
country and which has crept in through mixed marriages
which have been so long tolerated.' With Moran's arrival,
and the decisions of the Plenary Councils of 1885 and 1895,
prohibition of mixed marriages became the general policy of
the Australian church, hammered home by all bishops,
Archbishops Moran and Carr in particular.

Here again, clearly revealed, were the redemptive intentions of the Irish bishops. They were seeking to tighten up

discipline so that the standards of religious performance and behaviour might conform to Irish standards. The objective was, as Murray put it, to make the people 'as good as they are at home'. To do this three things were necessary: Irish priests and religious teachers, Irish devotional practices, Irish episcopal authority and church discipline.

Priests and religious teachers, brothers and nuns, came from Ireland in rapidly increasing numbers to the dioceses of the Irish bishops. Those bishops returned to Ireland frequently seeking recruits. Devotions popular in Ireland, such as the Forty Hours' Adoration, novenas, devotions to the Sacred Heart, various male and female lay sodalities, extended rapidly in these dioceses and became a salient feature of religious observance. The proclamation of Papal Infallibility was received with joy as one which would 'inject new energy and vitality into the Church of God and confer incalculable blessings on the world.' Said Bishop Murray: 'We shall all be devoted children of the Church and more attached than ever to the Holy See which will cement us all more closely together and guide us safe through this world to our everlasting home. All scandalous divisions . . . will now disappear with the will of God and vanish like smoke.' Said Matthew Quinn for them all: 'we [he meant the Irish bishops] are the true sons of Rome.'

The vital question of who would succeed Polding was early in the minds, and planning, of the Irish bishops in Australia; they agreed that Dr Murray would be the most suitable. News of Vaughan's appointment in 1873 threw them into consternation and fury. Bishop Lanigan protested: 'Our flocks are so much Irish that you might as well send an English Metropolitan to a See in Ireland as to Sydney.' Lanigan, the two Quinns, Murray and Bishop O'Mahony of Armidale, feared that Vaughan's coming would gravely injure religion. For too long the Australian church had suffered from 'the intrigues of Friars and Monks'. Vaughan, they believed, would only continue 'the old rotten rule of the Benedictines'. The laity was dissatisfied. Vaughan's appointment would split the Catholic community, disintegrate solidarity, and destroy harmony. Conflict would probably occur between Vaughan and the suffragans, when unity was imperative in order to resist the secular education movement.

True, the Irish bishops were prepared to concede that almost any change was better than the existing state of church government, in which Polding had come under the influence of favourites. 'I believe Fr. Colletti is the practical Archbishop for the moment,' remarked James Quinn acidly; later he referred to 'two Italian priests of great cunning and duplicity who are now managing the old Archbishop to the great disgust of all parties.' Indeed, if Vaughan were honest, capable and energetic, they would support him. If he were not, 'I for one will show him no mercy', vowed Matthew Quinn. The Irish bishops had submitted to Polding because of his age and great service to the church. They would tolerate neither inefficiency nor the misuse of authority from Vaughan.

These were harsh words: the whole affair had become virtually an obsession with the Irish group of bishops. They felt frustrated, and very angry. 'What prudence is there in appointing one coadjutor who causes all these disturbances. Was not Propaganda told over and over that this would be the case?' They were hurt; they felt slighted. Lanigan reported that Vaughan's appointment 'is looked on by many as a slight on Irish Bishops and our Irish priests who are made to appear as if requiring an Englishman to be placed over them.' The bishops decided to petition Rome formally that Vaughan's appointment should not be given effect.

This was a very unusual and extreme course of action, and the Roman reply, rejecting the petition, was very stern. The stocks of the Irish bishops of Australia dropped sharply in Rome. They were soon to drop even further.

Vaughan quickly dispelled mistrust. In June 1874 Bishop Murray told Monsignor Kirby in Rome:

> We are all greatly pleased with Dr Vaughan. He is in our opinion the right man in the right place. Probably if the Pope travelled over the whole world, he could not have found a more suitable person for this important position. We have a fair chance now of doing something for the interests of religion and putting an end to all intriguing, dishonesty and treachery.

However, in 1875 an incident occurred which shattered this developing harmony. Allegations were made in Armidale that Bishop O'Mahony had been guilty of seriously lax behaviour unfitting him for office. The case was referred to Rome and Vaughan was requested to conduct an investigation on the spot. Vaughan found the charges unproven, but because the matter had become widely notorious he advised O'Mahony to go to Rome to clear himself personally, and not to return to Armidale as the publicity had made his position there untenable. (O'Mahony was ultimately exonerated and given a Canadian bishopric.)

The Irish bishops disagreed totally with Vaughan's advice. They believed that O'Mahony's going to Rome gave a public impression that he was guilty, and that were he not to return, it would confirm this. The bishops believed that O'Mahony was the victim of a conspiracy of fabrication by some Sydney and Armidale priests, and that Vaughan was their dupe, if not worse. What was the object of this conspiracy? It was, the bishops believed, an attempt to discredit them as a body, and to destroy Irish influence in Australian church life.

This was soon confirmed in their minds by rumours which reached them from Rome that the Irish bishops in Australia were so totally out of court that no Irish bishop would be appointed in future. As if to prove this, they learnt that Rome proposed to appoint Dr Cani, an Italian, to Rockhampton in north Queensland, and later, in 1879, another Italian, Dr Torreggiani, was appointed to the vacancy caused by O'Mahony's resignation from Armidale. Further rumours circulated that the Irish bishops were regarded as having insulted the Sacred Congregation of Roman Propaganda. The bishops were dismayed and deeply hurt. Matthew Quinn wrote to Kirby:

> Veneration for the Holy See is, as you know, a sacred tradition in Ireland and we all suck it in with our mother's milk. From the time I came to the use of reason, I have ever been willing to lay down my life for the interest and honour of the Sacred Congregation and I would deem it a great privilege to be called on to do so.

In this Quinn was utterly sincere: in sheer religious integrity and total dedication to the church, he, and the other Irish bishops, had few peers.

Why were they so gravely out of favour? All Quinn could think of, as a reason, was their protest against Vaughan's appointment. This was certainly part of the reason. Even more irritating to Rome were their actions in the O'Mahony case: they clamoured for his prompt vindication and immediate return to Armidale; they talked about asking for an Apostolic Delegate to examine the ecclesiastical affairs of Australia; they expressed impatience with delay; they protested O'Mahony's complete innocence and Vaughan's stupidity.

All this fuss and lobbying irked Rome, which for a long time had been sorely tried by Irish-English conflicts that the Italian mind found difficult to comprehend. Late in 1878 Propaganda sent Vaughan a most severe censure of the Irish bishops for the part they had taken in favour of O'Mahony. The suggestion was evident that Propaganda placed no faith in their statements, believing them to be a product of partisanship, rather than of rational judgement.

This unfortunate and protracted affair destroyed whatever chances there were of the growth of a warm human trust between Vaughan and his Irish bishops. It did not, however, injure their co-operation in the interests of religion. The politicking was far less important than the piety. Matthew Quinn's comment of 3 August 1877 is typical, both of his own true and fundamental religiosity and of the normal situation of his diocese: 'Here we are all well thank God & everything progressing favourably. The priests are everywhere working with a great zeal and the nuns spreading fast throughout the diocese & doing great good.' And what of the ordinary priest? In 1879 Bishop Martin Crane, of Sandhurst, referred to one of his as:

> a most excellent Priest, and a most zealous hard-working missionary. He has been labouring in this diocese some years . . . travelling almost continually in order to preach to the people, to hear their confessions and offer up for them, whenever he could erect an Altar, the Holy Sacrifice of the Mass . . . he has been since announcing the glad tidings of the Gospel to the poor aborigines [in Queensland] suffering amongst them many privations, having no object whatever in view, but God's Glory and the salvation of these poor people.

The interests of religion came first. In May 1879 Matthew Quinn called on Vaughan. Bishop Lanigan had asked Quinn to talk to the Archbishop with a view to getting a common episcopal policy to combat the extension of secular education. Vaughan promptly agreed to call a bishops' meeting Quinn asked why such meetings had not been held before. Vaughan replied that he was under the impression that the suffragan bishops had no confidence in him, and in such circumstances he thought it better to let each bishop work in his own way. Thereupon Quinn observed that 'cordiality was seldom had amongst all the Episcopal members of any church', and that, whatever their personal relations, united action on some matters was a religious duty—with which Vaughan agreed. After telling Vaughan that he had mishandled the O'Mahony case, Quinn left.

The outcome was a meeting which agreed on the Joint Pastoral of 1879, which Vaughan wrote. The meeting was completely harmonious, even to the extent of the suffragans' accepting the Archbishop's invitation to dine with him. They welcomed the explosion which followed the publication of the Joint Pastoral, for their Irish cast of mind stressed agitation as a means of securing progress. (Moran's approach was in strong contrast to this.) Matthew Quinn wrote in May 1880: 'Though the Government here has passed for the present a wicked law against us, the aggitation [*sic*] has done a wonderfully good work especially in Sydney Diocese.' Quinn was impressed, as was Vaughan, by the new energy displayed by the Catholic body.

However, Quinn's thinking—again, of Irish derivation—was intimately party political in a way which the outlook of Vaughan, or Polding, was not. For instance, Quinn, who had involved himself in the politics of his own electorate, was indignant at the behaviour of Catholic politicians. In his opinion there had been a majority of the Assembly in favour of denominational education before the Joint Pastoral. When put to the test, most Catholic members had betrayed their duty. Quinn's comment was filled with echoes of Irish political life: 'I hope we shall be able to turn the tables on all these traitors at no very distant day.' In the minds of the Irish bishops the education question was being set in the mould of battle; their terminology was that of enmity, conflict, power, victory. Bishop O'Connor, of Ballarat, expressed their mood in 1881 very clearly:

> So far thanks be to God we have been able by great sacrifices on the part of all, priests and people in fact at least to cope with our determined enemy the State. Politically too our power is being increased and each year sees the cause of Catholic Education versus the Godless system of the Government advancing slowly but surely to victory. It is hard to roll back this heavy stone from the sepulcre [*sic*] where our enemies foolishly hoped all our rights and liberties lay entombed for ever.

Again, Moran's approach was to be very different.

Vaughan and his Irish bishops were at one on education. The question of Irish interests and ambitions remained to divide them. Bishop James Quinn, of Brisbane, died in August 1881. Until the vacancy was filled, Vaughan appointed Dr Cani as administrator. (He had administered the diocese before in Quinn's absences.) Cani was an Italian, one of the twenty-five invited to Brisbane by Quinn in 1870, and the Irish reaction was immediate and extreme. From as far away as Adelaide, Bishop Reynolds stressed to Rome the strength of pro-Irish feeling, urging that Bishop Matthew Quinn be translated to Brisbane, which should be made an archepiscopal see. At the same time, Vaughan was suggesting to Propaganda that Brisbane be given to the German Benedictines. Eventually Robert Dunne, Quinn's Vicar-General and another former student of the Irish College, Rome, was appointed. Cani was given the see of Rockhampton.

That anyone other than an Irishman might gain an Australian bishopric enraged extreme Irish elements. An Ipswich Irish priest described Cani, privately, as 'a semi-lunatic and an unmitigated tyrant', whose appointment was 'an injustice to religion and a simple outrage on the very decencies of life'. When Cani died in 1898, Cardinal Moran wrote of him, also privately, as a most pious and humble man who had lived and died in poverty. He had given up his episcopal palace to the Sisters of Mercy, and rented a cottage for himself. There he lived alone, without a servant, subsisting on bread and milk, at times a little canned meat; he often rose about 3 a.m. to celebrate Mass an hour later.

Moran saw Cani clear and true—but Moran did not suffer from nationalist obsession. In 1882 the same Ipswich priest believed that there was an Anglo-Italian conspiracy to slander Irish priests and destroy the faith. He contended: 'It is very plain to any true Catholic that all Bishops and priests (not Irish) are quickly destroying the faith of our Irish people in this country.' This was no mere individual aberration. In July 1883 an anonymous pamphlet was published in Melbourne entitled *The Mystery Unveiled. Being An Exposure of the Agencies at Work for the World-Wide Defamation of the Catholic Irish Australian Clergy* . . . This alleged a nefarious Anglo-Italian plot, led by Vaughan and Cani, and backed by Propaganda in Rome, to 'wipe out' the Irish bishops and priests of Australia. Here was Irishry carried to the extreme of absurdity. Here, in this remote Irish realm, religion shrivelled to an absolute equation with Irish nationality: 'it is strange that there is no Irish priest to be found in the world fit to be Bishop of Rockhampton. It is to be hoped that Christ has a better opinion than his Vicar of the faithful Irish race and its priesthood.' Few inhabited that embattled Irish fastness where all outsiders—English, Italians, the papacy itself—were somehow enemies. But there were some Irish who did: to them the advancement of anyone else appeared as a racial insult. And even among the great majority of Irish, who had balance and perception, there continued to be considerable unease. English episcopal rule was a source of complaint until Vaughan's death.

When Cardinal Moran told Herbert Vaughan, in relation to the question of his brother's burial, that 'no one in Sydney would wish the matter spoken of', his report was substantially accurate. The appropriate panegyrics were spoken and then the name of Vaughan vanished, almost in some quarters as if it had never been. Moran himself may be exonerated from charges of deliberate neglect: he was often to mention and praise Vaughan's work for education. Others were less generous. Upon news of his death, the bishops met in Sydney to nominate three names from which Rome would select his successor.

The three names sent forward by the bishops were: Dr William J. Walsh, President of Maynooth College; Patrick

Francis Moran, Bishop of Ossory; and Dr James Murray, Bishop of Maitland. Murray's name was included solely for the purpose of excluding any Englishman, should neither Dr Walsh nor Dr Moran be willing to accept. The bishops agreed that there was not one priest of the Sydney diocese fit for the position, and noted that the priests themselves had not spoken of even one of their number as in any way qualified. The bishops defined what they required: an Irishman of ability.

Walsh was first on the bishops' list, but, apparently, they held little hope of persuading him to accept, so their efforts were concentrated on urging upon Rome the need to appoint Moran. When these nominations became known in Ireland, Cardinal McCabe, who was Archbishop of Dublin, was totally opposed to Walsh's going, as his work at Maynooth was too valuable, and so was Walsh himself. They made this bluntly known in Rome. McCabe favoured Dr Murray, on the grounds of his long Australian experience. His opinion of Moran may be inferred from his cryptic comment to Walsh: 'In *confidence* I think the owner of the second name [Moran] would scarcely suit.' However, McCabe was not aware at this stage that Murray's nomination was merely a device, and that the Australian bishops were pressing in Rome for Moran, particularly through Matthew Quinn, who was visiting the Vatican: indeed Quinn's name was also being mentioned in Rome in relation to the vacancy, but his poor health put him out of the question.

Moran was soon aware that, as he put it: 'The Australian Bishops were anxious to emphasise the Irish character of the Australian Church', by securing an Irish appointment—himself. He was not enthusiastic. Indeed, he specially asked Kirby in Rome to take no part whatever in promoting his appointment: the matter should be left to God's will. If there was no politicking, and he became the unaided selection of providence, he could 'be confident of the aid & blessing of Heaven in labouring for the Church in that distant see'. (There was however some English lobbying against him, or rather against any Irish appointment.) Personally, he expressed indifference, urging his own lack of strength, energy and administrative ability. He feared his own health was not strong enough. Yet he was resigned to God's will: 'for my own part I am quite indifferent as the field of labour that may be assigned to me for the few years of pilgrimage that remain.' When the Cardinal Prefect of Propaganda wrote to him asking if he would consent to go to Sydney, if appointed, he did not say yes, but answered that he had no will at all in the matter, being ready to abide by whatever decision the Holy See might make.

Nor was he much moved when, after three months, the appointment was made. In the interval he had been absorbed with problems in his own diocese and with the question of who should be Bishop of Cork. When news of the appointment reached him, he noted, with surprise, as some singular occurrence, that all the Australian bishops, save Torreggiani, were old friends of his, and were men of such zeal and prudence as to compensate for his own shortcomings.

Why did Moran express such indifference, to the degree of disinterest? Above all, he was pious, devout, and submissive to the will of God. In human terms, Sydney held few attractions for him. He was fifty-three, his health little more than fair. On a reasonable assessment, most of his life lay behind him. This life had been spent at the centre of affairs, in Rome and Ireland. What could the colonies offer in comparison? His ambitions, in so far as he had any, were focused on Dublin. Moran's had been one of the three names put forward to Rome to fill that see when Cardinal Cullen died in 1878. He had received only seven votes to McCabe's forty-three, but, as events were to show, Dublin exercised a strong attraction; he had thoughts of himself as successor to Cullen.

Successor to Cardinal Cullen. And this—but in Australia —is what, in some important ways, Moran became. He became a Cullen out of place and out of time, with Cullen as his model, with many of Cullen's attitudes and policies, and with something, perhaps much, of Cullen's power and stature. Moran, like Cullen, was to tower head and shoulders above his ecclesiastical colleagues. Feared or respected— these were the emotions they aroused—both men were inescapable in their dominance. Both exercised a profound influence on their religious worlds.

Patrick Francis Moran was born in Carlow on 16 September 1830, of farmers that had fallen in the world as a con-

VII Archbishop
     Moran
     circa 1884

VIII Cardinal Moran
     1905

IX Cardinal Moran
circa 1910

X Cardinal Moran
in his coffin,
16 August 1911

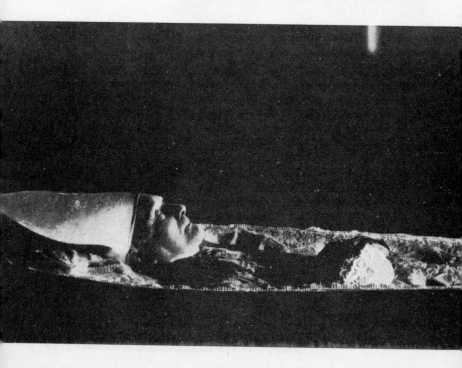

sequence of their involvement in the 1798 rebellion and the confiscations that followed. At the age of twelve (he was by then an orphan) he left Ireland for Rome in the custody of his uncle, Paul Cullen, who was Rector of the Irish College in Rome, to study for the priesthood at that College. 'Cardinal Cullen was more than a father to me', Moran acknowledged later; he admired his uncle, and wished to emulate him.

Moran stayed in Rome for twenty-four years, a period which shaped and consolidated his outlook. As a student at the Irish College, he acquired a reputation for brilliance. He received his doctorate in 1852 with acclamation from his examiners, among whom was the future Pope Leo XIII. He was ordained the following year. In 1856 he was made Vice-Rector of the Irish College, and also Professor of Hebrew at the Propaganda College. At the same time he was developing an interest in historical research, drawing first on archives in Rome, later from sources all over Europe. In 1861 he produced the first of some twenty works on various aspects of Irish history. This historical work was largely compilatory and antiquarian in interest, and marred by a tendency to stress what Moran judged edifying and to omit what he did not. But it was pioneering work, the product of prodigious industry, and it won for him an international reputation as an Irish scholar.

In 1866, the year in which Paul Cullen, Archbishop of Dublin since 1852, was made Cardinal, Moran went to Ireland as his secretary. Thus he arrived in Ireland just before the Fenian rebellion. This strengthened attitudes that he had formed during his personal experience of the Italian revolution of 1848, which had overthrown, for a time, the temporal sovereignty of the Pope. Such popular national and revolutionary movements as professed secrecy or violence, he held in deep detestation. In this, as in all else, he mirrored the outlook of Cullen, who confided frequently in him, a privilege which he extended to very few.

Cullen's influence over the Irish church was supreme: he *was* the Irish hierarchy from the 1850s until his death in 1878. He determined the character of that church, guided its policy, shaped its destiny, moulded its discipline, and was a central driving force behind constitutional political activity to press Ireland's claims. In this he was, in a sense, an opportunist. 'In political matters, he made it a rule to support every measure from whatever political party it came that he considered conducive to the interests of Ireland'—so Moran wrote of him: he might have written it of himself. And Moran, as did Cullen, linked religion and nationality. Not, however, in any crude sense. Cullen, it has been said, 'had, in fact, no political theories, only religious and ecclesiastical ones.' The same might have been said of his student Moran. Where Cullen's context was Irish, Moran's became Australian, and it was part of Moran's greatness that he could adapt his religious theories to a new national context in a way which few, if any, of his Australian hierarchical contemporaries could. Whatever might be thought of his Australian policies, he was—with astonishing adaptability for a man in his fifties, and indeed even into his eighties—attempting to make these policies truly Australian. And for all his Irishness, he was endeavouring to build a new Ireland —the religious nation of Australia—and not to recreate, on new and different soil, old Ireland once again. Most of his contemporaries, 'the Irish bishops', failed to make that distinction: old Ireland was the land of their hearts' and souls' earthly desire.

The parallels with Cullen did not end with Moran's considered, religion-oriented nationalism. Cullen had been entrusted by Rome with the task of tightening up ecclesiastical discipline in Ireland, centralising it, removing anomalies, and bringing it into subjection to Rome. Moran's Australian policies developed along similar lines.

As Cullen's secretary, he was drawn into, and became identified with, Cullen's policies. He handled much of the ecclesiastical diplomacy between Ireland and Rome. He was joint founding editor and a major contributor to the *Irish Ecclesiastical Record*, established by Cullen in 1864 as a link between Ireland and Rome. In 1872 Moran was appointed Bishop of Ossory, a diocese centred on Kilkenny, as a direct result of Cullen's patronage; the priests of the diocese scarcely knew him. Ossory at that time was the scene of a celebrated, spectacular and protracted challenge to episcopal authority by Father Robert O'Keefe, parish priest of Callan. From 1869 to 1875 O'Keefe was in rebellion against all such authority, and notably Cullen's, to the extent of mounting a long series of legal actions in the civil courts claiming libel and slander against Cullen and other clerics, for their use of ecclesiastical discipline against him. Moran was deeply involved in Cullen's case, and he had the difficult task of restoring tranquillity to the diocese which was the centre of the affair.

This task, that is, the defence of episcopal authority, of ecclesiastical discipline, and of Cullen himself, absorbed much of Moran's energies. In political matters, such as the Irish land agitation, he was cautious and constitutionalist, yet firm on occasion, for example, in insisting that tenant farmers be given just rentals. In politics he tended to be middle-of-the-road, with a penchant for seeing the influence of 'Fenianism' and 'Secret Societies' in any vigorous agitation. Cullen had the reputation among the more vehemently nationalist clergy and laity of being an ecclesiastical autocrat, reactionary and pro-English in politics; Moran was given credit—or rather discredit—for similar views. When Cullen died in 1878 the reaction against his rule extended to Moran. His Roman experience was useful to the Irish hierarchy, and they used him to negotiate various Irish affairs in Rome, but he was not popular, nor was he given much credit for ability or real importance.

For this, his personality was in some part to blame. Orphaned young, and living from the age of twelve in ecclesiastical institutions, Moran lacked warmth. He was reserved and shy, seldom even raising his eyes, never his voice. He had a habit of joining his hands in front of him, and rubbing them together softly. His whole demeanour spoke a stern, unruffled, ecclesiastical taciturnity. As Walter McDonald reminisced of him at Kilkenny: 'He was a Churchman born, very much respected, a good deal feared, but little loved.' Volatile personalities could not stomach him at all. Archbishop Croke, of Cashel, dismissed Moran contemptuously as 'some cold and colourless ecclesiastic'. True, the nationalist Croke had a hearty dislike of Moran's politics—or lack of them. But Cardinal McCabe, who, like Moran, fought very shy of popular politics, also had a low opinion of him. Simply on grounds of ability, Moran's reputation was not high. Cardinal Manning, in England, rated his ecclesiastical abilities as no more than ordinary.

In relation to Moran's appointment to Sydney, two things are evident. Australian religious affairs were regarded in Ireland as of minor importance, and nobody of consequence in Ireland was sorry to see Moran go. The appointment seemed an appropriate one: an ordinary man for an ordinary job.

Of course, in the eyes of Australian Catholics their ecclesiastical governance was no ordinary task, and so the man who came to undertake it could not be ordinary either. Moran arrived in Sydney in September 1884 to a tumultuous festive welcome, estimated to involve 100,000 people on harbour steamers gay with bunting, at the wharf, and lining the route to the Cathedral.

Moran's first public words were: 'Becoming today an Australian among Australians . . .' This sounded well, and Moran meant it; but most of those who welcomed the new Archbishop, welcomed the Irishman. As Bishop Lanigan wrote: 'I hope the Irish Archbishop of Sydney will give us an Irish Race in Australia living the traditions of their race, and proud of their attachment to Holy Church.' Lanigan thought in terms of Irish versus English. He believed that English Catholics were more contemptuous of Irishmen than were English Protestants. He had detected this contempt in the Vaughan era, believing it to have grown in Sydney to the extent of bringing Catholics to respect England more than Ireland, and even to respect 'English heresy', that is, Protestantism. Lanigan expected Moran to reverse this trend, and to create a situation in which 'feelings national and religious combine to work for the church's cause'. Or as Bishop Murray put it, the bishops under Moran's leadership would 'do the work of the Church and uphold the honour of old Ireland'.

With these sentiments Moran went a long way, but not all the way. Certainly he valued the Irishness he found. He reported on his arrival: 'I am happy to say that the schools are very efficient and full of fine lively children, as fond of the Faith and of Ireland as any children could be in the old land at home . . . Everywhere I have found real genuine Irish piety . . .' Certainly his tendency was to apply Irish religious policies to what he regarded as largely an Irish situation, but Irish religion was one thing, Irish nationalism was another. Moran did not intend to make himself leader of an aggressive Irish belligerence.

At fifty-four, Moran showed remarkable adaptability, within the framework of his essential character. His ways were those of peace and moderation, of integration; he sought to become an Australian, to adapt and conform to his Australian environment as far as he could. Lanigan recognised this when he remarked: 'There is about him enough of clear open speaking, but at the same time a sufficiency of moderation to avoid provoking opposition unnecessarily.'

Indeed his very moderation sometimes provoked criticism from Irish extremists. Despite his revival, in 1896, of the St Patrick's Day cult, he was no patron of drum-beating Irishry. Nor were his Irish heroes—the Venerable Oliver Plunkett, Cardinal Cullen, a galaxy of Irish saints and martyrs—the same heroes as those of his Irish laity, who celebrated the rebels of 1798, the Young Irelanders of 1848 —those whom Cullen had condemned as sowers of dissension. This difference of values was sharply illustrated by Moran's initial refusal, during the centenary celebrations of the 1798 rebellion, to allow the exhumed bodies of Michael Dwyer (hero of that time) and his wife to lie in the Cathedral, prior to reburial, with great Irish pageantry, in Waverley Cemetery. It was also typical of Moran that, in the face of bitter criticism, he should relent and even pronounce a eulogy. The self-description of the prominent layman E. W. O'Sullivan—Anglo-Celt—may also be applied to Moran; indeed he used the term himself.

Moran was, of course, not the first bishop to find that ultra-Irishism could create difficulties within society, and prejudice the mission of the church. In 1883 Bishop Goold was intensely annoyed by the Victorian activities of visiting agents of the Irish Land League, who aroused vigorous criticism from even the most tolerant Protestants. He remarked in a letter back to Ireland: 'I wish the home rule principle were strictly observed. Each one to mind his own business at home . . . Keep your red hot politicians in Ireland where they are much needed.' Goold's successor,

Archbishop Carr, was similarly embarrassed when the Irish politician John Dillon visited Melbourne: Carr's problem was—and it was also Moran's—how to show sufficient sympathy to conciliate the Irish-Australian laity, but not so much as to identify the church with such profane Irish politicians, or to arouse Protestant protest. The problem was rendered acute by the Parnell split in Ireland, leading to the rival factions canvassing Australian support. In March 1891 the Australian bishops unanimously decided, in view of the risk of 'serious dis-union in the ranks of our Irish Catholic People in Australia', not to support either of the rival groups. Later, when the Irish Parliamentary Party settled down under the leadership of John Redmond, Moran and the other Irish-Australian bishops gave this constitutionalist, mild Home Rule-ism their firm support.

Such was to become Moran's apparent dominance that it is easy to overlook this powerful clannish current of lay ultra-Irishism which tugged at him strongly, and to some extent drew him along with it, against his inclinations.

For, the essence of Moran's policy for Australian Catholicism was the pursuit of social integration. Moran was the great integrator, seeking to fit Catholics into a diverse community in which each element would accept all others on the basis of tolerance and respect. 'Discord being banished from us, how happy will be the result? Our citizens all united in harmony and concord, emulating one another in friendly rivalry in eagerness to promote the common good— who can doubt that a grand future must await such a land?' Moran saw Australian Catholic history as having passed through four periods: open persecution up to 1820; partial toleration up to 1850; nominal religious equality, 1850-80; and then, in his time, a period of comparative calm, in which sectarian prejudice was disappearing, and the church was emerging to 'exercise to the fullest measure a beneficent influence on the world around her, spreading abroad the light of truth and promoting the blessings of Christian civilisation throughout the length and breadth of this richest and fairest land.'

As a policy, this encountered serious difficulties. Moran sought to avoid sectarian strife, but his success was only partial. The pursuit of a radiant, enriching integration flew in the face of Australian facts. The basic fact was that on the fundamental matter of education, of cultural formation, the church had determined that Catholics should not become integrated into the majority of the Australian community. Fundamentally, this educational apartness remained, however much Catholic schools might conform to the educational procedures of the state. Because this avenue was closed, Moran's pursuit of integration necessarily took, in the main, another form: a blessing of the entry of Catholics into existing forms of political activity, particularly that form which reflected their dominant economic status, the Labor Party.

Moran did not create this political process. He recognised it, and encouraged it. However, this placed him, and Catholics generally, in a position of basic contradiction: they became committed to a political policy of social integration, and a cultural policy of non-integration. There was ample room for disharmony in this situation, which was questioned by some Catholics during Moran's lifetime. Yet, it was also a natural and perhaps necessary situation: the fact that, despite the basic contradiction, it lasted for half a century is witness to that. It was not until the 1940s and 1950s that the policy evolved in Moran's episcopate sundered into its conflicting components. Then, tension first appeared in the area of political integration, leading to the non-integrationist 'Movement', a political group arising from Catholic social principles. Later, in the 1950s and 1960s there was a cultural movement among Catholic intellectuals which stressed integration, arguing for the adoption of a philosophic outlook and an educational policy much more akin to that of the general community.

'The Movement' was an attempt to bring Catholic social and political thinking into line with the principles which lay behind Catholic educational policy. Recent moves towards cultural integration have been attempts to bring Catholic cultural attitudes into line with the conformist political policy evolved under Moran. Both 'The Movement' and Catholic cultural conformism have been attempts—stressing the opposite policies—to rid Catholic life of the radical inconsistency inherent since Moran's time.

To attribute any politico-social aims to Moran is to fall

short of the truth. He was a churchman of remarkable
dedication. He was neither a politician, nor a social leader;
neither of these fields, as such, interested him. He was a
religious leader who saw the clear relation to religion of
the world and its affairs. Or rather, vice versa. The church
would transform the world: it brought redemption, and
salvation, the things that really mattered, but also human
welfare and social progress: 'Even in matters that do not
come within her immediate sphere, her influence cannot be
but for good.'

Hardly had Moran arrived in Australia than he was summoned to Rome. The death of Cardinal McCabe in February
1885 created a political crisis, for the question of who
should fill the vacant archbishopric of Dublin became a
matter of major dispute between the English government
and Irish politicians. In Ireland, nationalists saw McCabe as
in the Cullen tradition—politically reactionary and subser-
vient to England. Given the importance of Dublin in
moulding Irish popular opinion and conducting political
negotiations, nationalists were determined to break the Cullen
tradition and install a nationalist archbishop; they believed
that William Walsh, President of Maynooth, would be ideal.
The English government was no less convinced of the
crucial nature of the Dublin appointment, Prime Minister
Gladstone's policy being one of attempting to use clerical
influence to pacify Ireland.

Gladstone knew Moran slightly, visited him in Ireland in
1877, and consulted him on some Irish legislation. He was
impressed by Moran's knowledge and by his mild and co-
operative political temper. The British government's agent
in Rome was instructed to oppose Walsh's appointment, and
press the Vatican for Moran, although his name was not
among the three forwarded from Dublin. Leo XIII, who
also knew Moran, was persuaded by the British case, and
summoned Moran to Rome. The Pope had decided to send
Walsh to Sydney.

In the meantime, the British politicking at the Vatican
became public knowledge. There was uproar in Irish
nationalist circles. Moran was denigrated as an English
pawn; the Irish demand for Walsh became noisily insistent;

under Irish pressure, the Pope changed his mind. Knowing nothing of this, Moran arrived in Rome. He was so confident that he was on his way to Dublin that, it seems, he had packed all his personal belongings. When Leo XIII explained the situation, Moran was deeply disappointed. It is true that he had written to his secretary from Adelaide, *en route* to Rome: 'So far as my own wishes are concerned, I am quite resolved to return to Sydney', but it seems likely that he had believed, until the Pope told him otherwise, that Providence had Irish designs for him, the inheritance of Cullen. Instead of Dublin, he received a Cardinal's hat.

These circumstances were not known in Australia, where it appeared that Moran's elevation to the Sacred College was a signal honour to the nation as well as to Moran. He returned, therefore, to an even more tumultuous welcome than his first. He was very conscious of the high dignity of his office: the new Cardinal was stately in bearing, aloof, every inch a prince of the church.

Moran's predilections were for a church identified, as far as was possible, with the dominant trends in the community and fitting harmoniously into the national life. For this, an appropriate degree of temporal status and dignity was necessary. The first projects which the new Archbishop put in hand in 1884 were an archepiscopal palace at Manly and a palace adjacent to the Cathedral. Benedictine monasticism had not lent itself to such undertakings: then the Cathedral had been the major concern. It remained a major concern with Moran but, in keeping with the environment with which he had been familiar in Rome and Ireland, he believed that other external evidence of the church's life also demanded due attention. Not only the dignity of the church buildings themselves, as centres of worship, but the dignity of the church's leaders required appropriate reflection in stateliness of stone. Moran's personal style of living was unpretentious, even frugal. But his imperial view of Catholicism in Australia demanded palaces as well as temples: it needed, in his view, the ecclesiastical trappings characteristic of European Christianity.

St Patrick's College, Manly, was evidence of this conception. When Moran wrote in 1885 that the College would be 'the finest Institution in the Australias', his comment was architectural, in terms of imposing building. Of course, in religious terms, St Patrick's meant much more—it was practical evidence of Moran's determination to have an ecclesiastical seminary in which Australians would be trained as priests. Unlike some other Irish bishops in Australia, he did not see Australia's clerical future in terms of exclusively Irish-born priests. To Moran, all that mattered was the need. Soon after his arrival he wrote: 'My great want is priests. I would require forty additional Priests for the work of this Diocese.' To some extent this want could be met from Ireland, but an Australian seminary was logical and necessary, although within a wider context. 'This will not of course,' explained Moran, 'interfere in any way with the Australian College in Rome, but will rather be a feeder for it.' The Australian College project did not materialise—Propaganda College became the substitute. But Moran's pattern of the ideal Australian priest endured—Australian-born, of Irish descent, partly Australian-trained, but with a final Roman patina.

Moran's swing to an Australian emphasis was in keeping with the trend of facts. In the 1870s about half of Australia's Catholics had been born in Ireland. Thirty years later this proportion was a fifth, and still dropping rapidly. Furthermore, this proportion was mainly confined to the older age groups. By the time of Moran's arrival, the priesthood, so dominantly Irish, was rapidly becoming alien to generations that had never seen, and would never see, the land of their fathers. This process of alienation long remained subdued by the extraordinary strength of Irish-Australian tradition, but even as early as the 1880s bishops were having to face the fact that difficulties over the absorption of Irish clerics were growing. On the subject of the appointment of bishops direct from Ireland, Lanigan had to report in 1885: 'There is amongst the priests a growing spirit of dislike to the appointment of men who are strangers to Australia.' And the priests to whom Lanigan referred were Irish born. If such was the trend in the green wood, what would it be in the dry—when the priests were not Irish, but Australian? The implied warning went unheeded, and the issue exploded in bitterness in the 1920s.

By the early 1880s, bishops were becoming increasingly

worried by the failure of some of their Irish clerical imports to gain social acceptance by the Australian Catholic community. This problem was not entirely new. In the 1850s there had been complaints from Australia that priests arriving from Ireland were sometimes 'very ignorant in polite education and in good manners', but such complaints had been mainly in reference to the impression such priests made on the Protestant community. Now many Catholics were taking offence. In 1883 Bishop Goold let it be known that some of the priests he was getting from Ireland were 'a little rough', appearing uncouth and unpolished in a Melbourne situation where 'the people here are very smart—especially the Colonial born'.

By the end of Moran's episcopate, the balance of Australian Catholic opinion was swinging, with increasing weight, against Irish priests, or at least against those Irish priests who did not measure up to the Catholic community's rising social standards. Archbishop Carr, an Irishman himself, did not hesitate to convey the situation in blunt detail to Irish seminary authorities in 1911:

> No student should be nominated for Melbourne who is not presentable above the average, cultured, a good English scholar, a good and correct speaker, and free from all brogue. In a word the students selected require to be . . . above the ordinary run of students. The condition of life here, the spread of education, the smartness of Colonial youth, cause a backward Priest to become a laughing stock when the Priests themselves least suspect or recognise it. Hence I beg of you to send us refined cultured Priests. Owing to the tradition in Ireland arising from the backward condition of the people, there is unfortunately a marked contrast between the manners, pronunciation, and general presentableness of the Manly students and those educated in any of our Irish Colleagues.

Carr and Moran sought, if they did not always find, an ecclesiastical policy which would keep pace with the rapidly changing character of the community. Other bishops, and their Irish successors, lacking such elasticity and perception, pursued a rigid Irishism even into the second half of the present century.

The Australian-born priesthood which Carr and Moran favoured was one aspect of the search for a general harmony and unity which was the pivot of their policies. This theme is most evident in Moran, even in his attitude to the matter on which harmony and unity did not exist—education. Looking from Ireland at the Australian educational legislation which excluded Catholic schools, Moran found it difficult to accept that such religious discrimination was possible in a liberal and enlightened nineteenth century. However, he had to deal with the situation, and, on his way to Australia in 1884, he had spent some time in London discussing the problem with Cardinal Manning, and had devoted a good deal of his shipboard time to thinking about it.

His policy decision reflected his whole social outlook—a practical acceptance of the existing conditions as the context in which he would work. This outlook reflected the change in papal policy from that of Pius IX to that of Leo XIII: Leo XIII proposed to show Catholics how to live in a liberal world without sacrificing their religious principles. It was an outlook shared by Carr in Melbourne: his principles and policy on the education question were at one with Moran's.

Moran's decision, seemingly an acceptance of things as they were, in fact placed the question of Catholic education on a much altered basis. He accepted the situation produced by the 1880 Act (and its equivalents in other States) as, if not final, at least likely to last for some considerable time. This contrasted with Vaughan's assumption—and that of the Irish suffragans—that the Catholic educational stand would be of short duration. Moreover, Moran, while continuing to seek state support, did so on altered grounds and with much less aggression. Previously, Catholic demands had been for state aid to denominational schools; Catholic education was conceived as a totality in which religion infused all learning, all subjects of study, there being no distinction between secular and religious. Moran demanded state support not for the teaching of religion, but for the teaching in Catholic schools of secular subjects. His education programme was to build a Catholic system of schools which would teach what the state taught—plus religion.

The rationale of this was practical, pragmatic, political. Moran believed that there was no hope of getting the state to aid the teaching of religion. To persist in agitation for this was futile and would produce needless strife: abandon it then, and recognise that the Catholic church alone would have to carry, permanently, the burden of teaching *religion*. Secular subjects were another matter. If Catholic schools taught these to a standard and content identical with the teaching of state schools, Catholics, he reasoned, would have an unanswerable case for state support of secular tuition in their schools. Accordingly the bishops sought and got inspection of Catholic schools by the state, which had the effect of imposing complete conformity on the Catholic system, and of conceding all educational initiative to the state.

Under this policy, Moran made a prodigious contribution to Catholic education. The figures for Sydney speak for themselves: in 1884 there were 102 schools; in 1911, 306; in 1884 there were 78 brothers, 252 nuns; in 1911, 220 brothers, 1,374 nuns; and the number of pupils more than doubled, from 11,000 to 24,477. These figures tell only part of Moran's achievement. They do not reveal the tremendous advances made in efficiency, improvements in curriculum, methods, organisation, teacher-training and the like. His policy envisaged a Catholic primary school in every parish. He was also conscious of the growing need for secondary education. The leadership was Moran's. In Melbourne Carr played a similar role; and elsewhere other bishops. Their lives became a succession of foundation-stone-laying and official openings. The expenditure was vast, reckoned at about a million pounds by Moran alone. All this growth was accompanied by a change, at least superficially, in relations with the states' educational authorities. The hostility of the 1860s and 1870s gave way to harmonious co-operation.

This was an enormous achievement. But Moran's educational policy, no less vigorously implemented by Carr, and soon becoming *the* policy of Australian bishops, enforced a separation between secular and religious subjects. The education system that Moran built contained secular instruction plus religious instruction. The conflict between this and the pre-Moran declarations of principles is evident. The 1862 Provincial Council had remarked that: 'Catholics do not believe that the education of a child is like a thing of mechanism that can be put together bit by bit—now a morsel of instruction on religion, and then of instruction in secular learning—separate parcels . . .' The Joint Pastoral of 1879 had stated that 'the secular and religious elements of education are inseparable'.

Moran's policy, in dividing secular from religious for the practical purpose of securing state aid, ran the danger of fostering, in the long term, a basic tension within the Catholic education system between secular and religious objectives. Moran's was a plausible pragmatic policy—plausible, but ineffective: it did not produce state aid. In order to achieve practicality, as he saw it, Moran retreated from the very principles on which a separate Catholic educational system had been founded. The consequences were enduring and profound. Moran's tactics on the education question failed: state aid was not forthcoming. And he had achieved in that pragmatic pursuit a degree of separation between that which the Joint Pastoral declared to be inseparable, the secular and religious elements of education. He contrived a rift in the religious and educational principles on which the Catholic system had been initially founded. But Moran never claimed to be an educational theorist; practicality was his criterion. Nor was his mind, in such matters, anything adventurous. When, in Ireland in 1883, most of the bishops favoured the introduction of compulsory education, he, as he always had been, was opposed to it.

The other major aspect of his handling of the education question was his sharp swing away from the direct denunciations and vigorous attacks on the state, characteristic of the Polding and Vaughan eras. From time to time, the old animus burst out. The 1895 Pastoral Letter of the Australian bishops referred to the 'poisonous founts' and 'blighting influence' of the 'Godless system of knowledge'. Much more typical was the approach outlined by Moran in October 1884 when he asked publicly:

What should be our Catholic position in regard to this delirium of the State in the matter of education? Our position should be one of calmness and patient endurance, and at the same time of energetic endeavour to enlighten those who combat

our views, as well as those who guide the helm of State . . .
our position should be to pursue the path we have hitherto
peaceably pursued in educating our people, and show that we
are in earnest in the work we have begun, and that we are
determined to persevere in it. We only claim from the State
that, when we have done a good day's work—work which the
State has the right to enjoin upon us—and have done it well,
we are justified in claiming a day's wages for the work we
have done.

Moran inclined to view the exclusion of Catholic schools
from state aid as a freakish mistake and confusion, which
would be put right if Catholics did not aggravate the unfortunate affair. As the Australian bishops put this approach
in 1895, Catholics might rely with confidence on 'the intelligence and justice which distinguish our fellow countrymen'.
Eschewing agitation, Moran preferred, in his efforts to end
the Catholic education grievance, to talk to those whom he
regarded as influential. In August 1885 he spent considerable
time seeking the co-operation of the Lord-Lieutenant of
Ireland, though how he believed this would assist is hard to
tell. What is remarkable about Moran's impingement on
Australian politics is not so much his support of labour, but
his failure to press the Catholic education grievance. This
failure became more and more noticeable as the years wore
on and the Cardinal's policy of patience yielded nothing.
Other bishops looked on this with dismay. In 1902 Archbishop Carr wrote from Melbourne to coadjutor Archbishop
Kelly in Sydney: 'the Cardinal influenced by your timorous
N.S.W. Catholic politicians has practically abandoned the
fight for justice.'

This education grievance, this confrontation with the
state so repugnant to Moran's disposition, was a legacy of
Benedictine rule. It is tempting to wonder if Moran regarded this inheritance as, at least in part, the outcome of
Benedictine mismanagement. Had not all their enterprises
turned sour, all that they touched gone wrong? Moran had
taken a leading interest in the cause of the canonisation of
Oliver Plunkett, seventeenth century Irish archbishop and
martyr. In 1883 the Benedictines at Downside arranged to
move the martyr's remains from Germany to England.
Moran told Kirby that a Benedictine who assisted at the

exhumation had informed him that the flesh had been found whole and quite incorrupt. But when the relics were opened at a solemn ceremony at Downside monastery, the flesh had crumbled into dust. Moran, whose piety drew much on signs and portents, had no need to ponder the implications of that incident; to him they were self-evident.

To the Benedictines, Moran's shortcomings were no less self-evident: they consisted largely of ignoring or suppressing the Benedictines' Australian achievements. Dom Birt's two-volume *Benedictine Pioneers in Australia,* published in 1911, was an attempt to magnify what Cardinal Moran had sedulously diminished in his *History of the Catholic Church in Australasia,* published in 1896. In 1903 Cardinal Gasquet, in a private letter, summed up—offensively—the Benedictine opinion: 'Moran is an aged Cuckoo, who having got possession of a Benedictine nest has always tried to ignore the work of his Benedictine predecessors . . .' Purged of its venom, the comment was accurate enough. Despite his historical research, Moran had a tendency to assume that Australian Catholic history really began with himself. What had gone before was less history than pre-history.

External harmony, internal unity: these were Moran's goals. In the external, secular world, these might be achieved by a willingness to compromise, a toning down of demands, and an appeal to public goodwill. In the world of the church, harmony and unity would be achieved by prayer, discipline and order.

This last took a variety of forms. For the laity it meant the introduction, under Moran's auspices, of numerous devotional organisations, such as the confraternity of the Holy Family (for *men,* not families) and the confraternity of the Sacred Heart and Living Rosary for women. Membership of these rose quickly to around two thousand for monthly devotions at the Cathedral. In addition there was the Temperance movement.

For the clergy, and the church generally, Synods and Plenary Councils were the means, as Moran explained in 1885, of laying 'the solid foundations of a united Australian Church'. Moran's Roman background gave him familiarity with, and a taste for, legal formularies as the basis of proper order. Attention to such matters was overdue, for the first principle of the previous Australian situation had been expansion rather than order and correct procedure. Moran valued law and authority. His was the Rome of the Syllabus of Errors, of Papal Infallibility: indeed, as Cullen's secretary at the Vatican Council in 1870, there is some suggestion that it had been Moran who had drafted the formula for the definition of Infallibility. Nevertheless, he was no blind devotee of authority as such. Hearing from Rome in August 1899 that the writings of a certain Italian priest had been placed on the Index, he remarked in reply: 'There are so many perverse writers now-a-days that those who write in a good spirit should be encouraged & even though there be mistakes, those mistakes may be corrected privately without public censure.' For those times, this was a remarkably liberal, and perceptive, view.

Indeed it was unity which Moran valued: authority would be a means to that end. From the outset he conceived of the church in Australia as Australian; a single entity, not a collection of colonial churches. His first Plenary Council, convened in December 1885, with eighteen members advised by fifty-two theologians, sought to impose uniformity of practice and discipline within the Australian church, and to introduce a new era of harmony and unity in which state distinctions would vanish. This was successfully accomplished amid scenes of remarkable public pageantry.

Thereafter, the Cardinal held frequent major assemblies in Sydney of all Australian bishops. In 1888 the occasion was that of Australia's centenary celebrations, which Moran also made the occasion of Catholic functions which tended to eclipse all others. He was able, during the celebrations, to devise a ceremony which assembled in the Cathedral dignitaries, ministers and important visitors from every state while Lord Carrington moved that St Mary's be advanced another stage towards completion. (This function exhibits, in microcosm, Moran's vision of the role of his church in Australian society.) Then there was a Second Plenary Council in 1895, a Third in 1905, and a National Catholic Congress in 1900, attended by 700 delegates, and other Congresses in 1904 and 1909. In between, Moran was travelling all over Australia, and to New Zealand, visiting, assessing, inspecting, consecrating bishops, opening buildings, everywhere supervising and dominant. Little wonder that his wishes determined development; that, like Cullen, he became *the* episcopacy.

Much of Moran's power over the Australian church lay in his remarkable administrative ability. His sheer tireless efficiency in dealing with administrative matters (he worked constantly, taking little recreation) gave him detailed control over day-to-day affairs. No less important was the fact that he had no rivals. Neither his ecclesiastical rank nor his imperious strength of will had any equal among his contemporaries. He came to Australia twenty years after the first Irish episcopal invasion of the mid-1860s. James Quinn was dead, his brother Matthew soon to die, the pioneer Goold ill and dying, the others old, or of little power of personality. One of Moran's major concerns was that of staffing the Australian church, not only with priests, but also with bishops. The appointees to bishoprics under Moran were men of unfailing piety and zeal, but not approaching his stature.

The only one who came near to it was Archbishop Carr of Melbourne. Carr was Bishop of Galway when appointed to Melbourne in 1886. Formerly he had been Vice-President of Maynooth. A large task confronted him in Melbourne. As Moran explained: 'The See has been practically vacant for a long time and an active energetic Bishop is quite necessary there.' Carr devoted himself to urgent practical affairs—churches and schools, and the completion of St Patrick's Cathedral. In these his achievement rivalled Moran's, and he also had a similar scholarly bent, in Carr's case towards theology and general church history, though he did not follow it to nearly the same extent. In matters of policy he was in general accord with Moran, though he became critical of the Cardinal's unwillingness to press Catholic claims with vigour and determination. After Moran's death he showed remarkable strength and adaptability in confronting new problems. A lesser man than Moran, perhaps, but nevertheless a man whose mind and will had edge and power, and whose warmness won him real affection in Melbourne. One of his Maynooth colleagues summed him up succinctly: 'He was not brilliant; steady, rather, and

sensible . . . He was built for administration and rule . . .
He was amiable, and even jolly; could enter into a quiet
joke or game; was even-tempered . . . He was a man of
blameless life: a priest and a gentleman.'

Although unrivalled, Moran gave an impression of being
jealous of his power. He neither shared nor delegated it.
Over subordinates he exercised his authority rigorously, and
constantly interfered, inspected and, when he thought appropriate, reprimanded sternly. His treatment of his coadjutor,
Michael Kelly, consecrated Archbishop in August 1901,
shows that Moran's use of authority could degenerate into
petty despotism: he loaded Kelly with work, issued him
with peremptory commands to go here or there immediately,
to perform this or that religious chore forthwith. His direc-
tives to Kelly were in a tone that presumed instant obedience;
he seldom consulted his coadjutor's wishes or convenience,
and he frequently found fault. When Kelly visited Ireland
in 1908 he was dependent for money on drafts Moran had
promised to send. His failure to do so reduced Kelly eventually to frantic appeals to which Moran made little haste
to respond.

Kelly, for whom Moran felt coldness which at times came
close to contempt, was a special case. Nevertheless, the
Cardinal was generally a harsh master, expecting much,
although no more than he would have expected of himself.
His example of hard work and self-denial did much to
make his strict demands tolerable. As in Ireland, Moran
expected nothing of the laity save obedience, which he
got without question neither in Australia, nor in Ireland.
Again, as in Ireland, he grouped around himself a handful
of priests whose salient characteristics were great piety,
loyalty, and uncritical willingness to promote the Cardinal's
policies; his secretary, Monsignor Denis O'Haran, was the
exemplar, albeit a somewhat unique personality, of this
minionship. This tendency to assemble near him a group
of 'insiders' bred, as a consequence, a group of clerical
outsiders', whose resentment was focused not so much on
Moran as on the 'insiders', notably O'Haran, whose
unpopularity grew steadily among his brother clerics. Nevertheless, Moran himself came under criticism for favouritism,

and indeed nepotism (he had many clerical cousins) in the making of clerical appointments.

Moran, then, was the centre and source of all power and initiative within the church. The devolution of authority and decision-making which had taken place under Vaughan stopped. It was typical of the Cardinal's attitude to such matters that he should, upon his arrival, immediately dispense with such committees as the Catholic School Board which Vaughan had established to assist in school organisation. He assumed all such responsibilities and functions himself.

Yet, to sum up Moran as an authoritarian would be a superficial distortion. The Cardinal's most striking characteristic was his piety, a strong Irish-flavoured and simple piety. This is the constant in his life. His piety explains much of his life and policy. Central to it was an optimistic faith in God and in the efficacy of prayer. However complex the situation, however adverse some circumstance might seem, Moran's tendency was to believe that good would eventually come from it. Not that he avoided decisions: on the contrary he took them firmly, without hesitation. However, having determined a course he tended to believe that if it was God's will it would prosper, if not, it would fail. And in either case, all would be for the best.

His piety, his conviction that the hand of God was active in the world, could be astonishingly literal—for example, on his first voyage to Australia, when a Protestant service held on the deck of the ship was doused by a freak wave. Moran saw no humour in this, but accepted it seriously as a judgement upon heretics. Such signs and portents of heavenly approval of his work, and that of his church, kept appearing to him throughout his life. He wrote during the 1885 Provincial Council:

> A singular thing happened at the little harbour which is on our ground at Manly. On the first day of the Synod, an immense shoal of Australian salmon came into our harbour. The fishing boats kept catching them for about a week & netted about 400 dozen of splendid fish . . . This I hope may be a harbinger of an abundant spiritual draught of fishes.

Ten years later, at the 1895 Synod, a similar phenomenon

occurred, which Moran again noted as a portent for fishers
of men. At the 1895 Synod there was a further manifestation, in the Cathedral, of divine approval: 'After the High
Mass when the Veni Creator Spiritus was intoned a little
dove came fluttering about the Cathedral & rested on the
Sanctuary.' The Cardinal interpreted parliamentary elections
in something of the same spirit. He reported to Monsignor
Kirby of the 1891 N.S.W. elections: 'It is pleasant however
to find that even on mere political grounds the Catholics
are holding their own & that their assailants are being pun-
ished by the loss of their seats in Parliament.' This piety
had a dash of puritanism in it, too. Walter McDonald
recalls the promulgation in Kilkenny, under Moran's episcopacy, of Synodal ordinances against improper dances.
Priests were obliged to admonish ladies that it was a mortal
sin to dance a waltz, in evening dress especially.

It would be easy to make light of this form of piety
if Moran had not been so transparently sincere in it, so
utterly conscious of God in the world, and so essentially
humble. He was not, fundamentally, a reflective man, nor
one much aware of the deeper, more agonised profundities
of the human spirit. He was a man for the task at hand—
building—and that he did with complete dedication and
remarkable success. Absorbed in doing, he seldom paused
to look for deficiencies, shortcomings, or errors. Partly, this
was because he was so busy. As he reported in 1892: 'Nearly
every week we have some ceremony connected with new
schools, or Churches, or Convents . . . All these things keep
us very busy & I fear that we sometimes forget to thank
God as we should for the bounty & mercy which he shows
to His people here.' Why should there be pause for assessment when the record of Moran's work was one of
continuous, successful expansion? In a letter of November
1891, the Cardinal made a comment which may be taken, in
an important sense, as descriptive of his whole Australian
career: 'Here everything is going on as pleasantly as we
could wish. There is great union & harmony among our
Bishops, clergy & people . . . The difficulty is to keep pace
with the everyday growing wants & developments of religion,
especially in the large cities.' That was, indeed, the great
difficulty. And what had been a major difficulty before—

dissension within the Catholic body—had virtually vanished. Moran's leadership brought internal unity and harmony to a degree unknown before.

Success, development, growth, harmony—this was Moran's story. This is how he saw it himself, without much reflection, but, when he did reflect, with humility. He confided to Kirby on the twenty-fifth anniversary of his episcopate, in 1897: 'It is a serious thing to look back on all that should have been done & was not done during these 25 years, and one is reminded that the day of reckoning & we trust of rest cannot be far distant.' The terms of this reflection bear notice: the Cardinal saw his shortcomings in what he had omitted to do. His disposition was not such as to readily entertain the thought that something he had done might have been mistaken. He was not a man to admit error. This characteristic was evident in his public life, where the tranquillity so notable within the church under his rule was often markedly absent.

Moran was a churchman. His public life was completely subordinate to his churchmanship, and reflected its nature. Thus, holding as he did a vision of a great national society quickened and enriched by religion, his view of public affairs was above politics, especially party politics, until he was forced to think in those terms. Similarly, with a vision of a national life which would be harmonious and unified, he held religious sectarianism as of no account, until it proved its destructive strength. Even when the facts hit hard against Moran's vision, he retained its essence.

Australia's air of freedom, and the warmness of the welcome extended to him by many Protestants, led Cardinal Moran to gravely underestimate the strength of militant Protestant antagonism towards Catholicism. And this, of course, fitted in with his hopeful vision of national harmony: he saw what he wished to see. From his arrival he was continually impressed by the friendliness of Protestants. His comment on a tour he made in 1886 of the southern areas of his diocese may be taken as typical: 'The Protestants everywhere united with the Catholics in their demonstrations of welcome . . . In a little town called Wallumla there were four triumphal arches. They informed me that all were

erected by the Protestants of that district.' Nor was it
unusual that when he preached in Brisbane, in December
1887, half the congregation was Protestant.

At the same time he was very conscious of hatred and
prejudice. He wrote in August 1886:

> Here we have nothing but battling away on every side. We are
> in the front of the army & we are surrounded by astute un-
> scrupulous enemies who renew their attacks every day. We
> give them a hard blow from time to time, but they are so
> numerous, so rich, so leagued with the infidel societies of
> England, & having such a hold of the Government Depart-
> ments here that we have to be always on the alert to ward off
> their attacks.

From time to time Moran noted 'outbursts of passion &
hatred from the anti-Catholic bigots'. 'We have to be on
our guard,' he wrote in 1889, 'not to give them a pretext
of combining all the various Protestant sects against us.'

Yet this is precisely what he did, by his decision to stand
as a candidate for the Federal Convention election in 1897.
Why? 'I expect it will go a great way towards breaking
down the Orange bigotry which at times is very intense in
some districts': so he noted privately at the time. That is,
he expected his candidature to destroy what it in fact roused
up. Why this grave miscalculation? Because of the intensity
of his vision of national harmony; because he seriously
undervalued the strength and extent of anti-Catholic
prejudice; because he seriously overvalued the power of
his own public stature and popularity to silence or disperse
such prejudice as might exist. The Cardinal seems to have
been flattered—and misled—by the fact that Protestants and
Jews were among the deputation that asked him to stand for
election. He did not have time to place the matter before
Rome. However, he consulted his bishops, and all were in
favour.

Moran's candidature sprang naturally from his concern
for the great issues of national character and destiny and
his policy of social integration. He was a nationalist, and
a federationist.

His basic disposition to accept English rule as praiseworthy,
and to work within it, had been well known before he left

Ireland, and English support for him in the Dublin vacancy had trumpeted that out for all to hear. In Australia, this tendency of Moran's was intensified, or, rather, given complete freedom to express itself in positive identification with the existing governmental arrangements. He visualised a strong Australia, independent, yet tied by strong bonds of interest to the Empire. This outlook, balancing Australian patriotism with imperial loyalty, showed itself soon after his arrival in his support for W. B. Dalley's sending of a New South Wales contingent to assist Britain in the Sudan campaign early in 1885. When preaching to the departing soldiers, Moran referred to the occasion as being the first time in history that an Australian flag would take its place on the battlefield of nations. Dalley himself took a similar pride in this, savouring the situation in which, after long years of accusations that Catholics were tainted with disloyalty, the first Australian force to serve the Empire at war had been sent on the initiative of 'a Paddy and a Holy Roman'. Cardinal Moran was later to give vigorous support to Deakin's policy of building an Australian navy. However, the Cardinal felt the need to justify his imperial attitudes when he visited Ireland in 1888. After cataloguing for an Irish audience the benefits of Australian society—'we enjoy legislative independence, we make our own laws, justice is impartially administered and the blessings of liberty are widespread among our people'—he concluded: 'Thus it is that for us the standard of the imperial rule is the symbol of peace. It is the shield of our strength, the aegis of our liberties.'

Patriotism—Australian patriotism—was a constant theme with Moran throughout his life. One of his arguments for a granting of Catholic educational claims was that to resist them was short-sighted on patriotic grounds, in terms of national unity and harmony. However, on one vital point his view of Australia's national destiny clashed with a major strand in Australian nationalism as it was evolving at that time.

The mission to Christianise China had long interested and attracted Moran. On his arrival in Australia, his enthusiasm took the form of visualising Australia as an Asian missionary base. He hoped to establish a college in Sydney to train priests for the Chinese missions. He saw the destiny of a united Australia as providing for 'this southern world a bulwark of civilisation and a home of freedom'; indeed it would become 'the centre of civilisation for all the nations of the East'. Specifically, he saw Catholics, particularly Australia's Catholic clergy, as bearers of what was a clear duty. He reasoned as follows: 'The Chinese represent an older civilisation than we have in Europe . . . if that civilisation could receive the impress of Christianity there is no doubt they would become one of the greatest powers and greatest peoples in the world.' Australia was 'a nation full of energy and life', almost at Asia's door. 'I trust,' the Cardinal told his clergy in 1888, 'that one of the fruits of Australia's faith shall be the spreading of the light of truth through those vast countries, and the gathering of those nations into the one saving fold.'

Moran's vision of Australia in Asia seems a commonplace now. In the 1880s it was three-quarters of a century before its time, seemingly absurd, and totally repugnant to an Australian national sentiment obsessed by the 'Yellow Peril' and rapidly evolving towards a 'White Australia' policy. Where Moran dreamed of a dynamic out-going Australia engaged in a holy, civilising mission in Asia, the bulk of Australian nationalists were busily engaged in fencing Australia off from Asia and in defending her against the expected Asian flood. Dubbed by the *Bulletin,* 'The Chow's Patron', Moran found himself the centre of public odium. This did not deflect him from his hopes and plans. When, late in 1909, he opened St Columba's College at Springwood, it was to be at first a preparatory college for clerical students going on to St Patrick's at Manly, but later a seminary for the Asian mission. Nothing came of this projected development. When priests went to China in 1918, under the name of St Columba, they came direct from Ireland.

Holding responsibility for the governance of a continental church, Moran's outlook did not fit into the system of separate states that he found in Australia. He thought in terms of one nation, and was saying so openly from 1885. In that year he referred to his projected St Patrick's College, Manly, as the future 'training place for the Catholic University of United Australia'. By the late 1880s he was expressing himself—and, generally, Catholic bishops and clergy—in favour of political federation. The fact was that Australian Catholicism was already operating as one, nationally, and he could see nothing but disadvantage in state divisions, religious or political. Nevertheless, when the federation of the Australian colonies first became a proposal attracting public interest in 1889-91, Moran's interest was detached: it was, after all, a political not a religious matter. When the first National Australasian Convention was held in 1891, Moran seemed less interested in its failure than in the edifying piety of John Murtagh Macrossen, a Queensland delegate, who died during proceedings.

However, in 1895 a state Premiers' conference agreed to provide for elections to a convention which would devise a federal form of government. This was followed in New South Wales by a Peoples' Federal Convention held at Bathurst, at which the Cardinal spoke in strong advocacy of federation, making a considerable public impression.

Moran's federal ideas were ordinary enough—moderate, conservative nationalism, a federation within the Empire. What was striking was that a cardinal should appear in such circumstances; Australia was not used to what was unexceptional in Irish public life. Those who saw behind the novelty saw that if the Cardinal's sentiments were excellent, they were also conventional. He added nothing new, saying merely what others had already said. Indeed, he said it even more vaguely: 'each State should enjoy the most complete freedom . . . while at the same time the Federal Government should be invested with full authority.' Admirable. But how was this ideal to be reached? Moran did not say. The *Bulletin*, with acid irreverence, answered for him: 'Ah, it'll come right, plaze God.' The sneer held more truth than was apparent to those who made it, for Moran's cast of mind did hand over much of the world's work to providence, and a salient feature of his idea of federation was that it should have religion as its basis.

Ideas about scotching bigotry apart, Moran sought election simply because he saw the immense value of federation to the Australian nation, and thought himself able to contribute to that achievement. From a negative angle, he did say that he looked upon federation as the only means of preventing one or other of the colonies going over to socialism (possibly a reference to the doctrinaire socialism then formally avowed by the Labor Party), but his dominant attitude was a positive enthusiasm for federation's benefits, and it is hard to believe that he would not have been a very useful delegate.

However, the reaction to Moran's candidature was a sectarian explosion. There was also a cleavage of opinion among Catholics: some feared it would arouse bigotry, others held that priests should keep out of politics. Ultra-Protestants saw in it proof of all their fears—that the papists were seeking political power, the rule of Rome, the death of liberty, Protestant blood. They believed that Moran was disloyal, acting under instructions from Rome. Their reaction is summed up by the *Protestant Banner*: 'The Cardinal says he is "going to put down anti-Catholic bigotry once and for ever." Never, while a drop of British blood runs in our veins!'

This was rabid extremism, but its context was a much wider Protestant dislike and distrust of Moran. The Cardinal was remarkably urbane, remaining always calm and unruffled, apparently superior to any situation. His manner was distant and courtly, accentuated by his remarkable erect posture: he 'held himself very straight—if anything inclining backwards'. This gave him an air of haughtiness, heightened by his radiation, in public, of an aura of dignity and impassivity. To some Protestants all this seemed false and hollow, the posturing of a pompous humbug. What grated on them even more was what appeared to them to be an attitude of arrogant contempt towards Protestantism. The *John Williams* affair, in mid-1895, indicates how deliberately offensive Moran could be. Two ships left the port of Sydney on the same day, one a Pacific islands trader, carrying a big cargo of rum, wine and tobacco, the other the London Missionary Society's vessel *John Williams*. In the *Herald*'s shipping news, their manifests were accidently transposed, an error for which the newspaper apologised, and promptly rectified. However, the Cardinal took the opportunity to make a derisive public reference to the *John Williams*'s 'spiritual cargo'. Unappreciative of the joke (if joke it was meant to be), the Missionary Society demanded that Moran withdraw and apologise. He did neither.

This kind of behaviour did not endear the Cardinal to Protestant opinion. However, only the extremist minority, under the provocation of his 1897 candidature, were prepared to express their hostility in organisational form. The Anglicans, for instance, refused to participate in a United Protestant Conference dedicated to the Cardinal's electoral defeat. A group of Protestant ministers arranged a day of public prayer to beseech God to spare the nation from the disaster of having a cardinal as one of those who would draw up its constitution. Public debate waxed furious, with almost all major newspapers strongly hostile to Moran.

Having nominated himself, the Cardinal did virtually nothing more. He issued a manifesto, and published his speeches on federation, but he did not campaign, or employ any electioneering devices.

Ten candidates were to be elected. Cardinal Moran polled fourteenth on a list of fifty. He responded as a good loser, congratulating the successful and thanking those who voted for him. Publicly he contended that his candidature had succeeded in its purposes—to arouse interest in federation as such (which may be conceded), and to destroy bigotry by attracting it from its secret hiding places. Privately, in a letter to the Irish College in Rome, he claimed that 'it has brought out the strength of the Church in bold relief & . . . I was particularly pleased to be defeated.' As the *Freeman's Journal* remarked: 'the figures for the election show that the vote for the Cardinal in no way represents the voting strength of the Catholic people in this colony.' Yet, his securing of over 40,000 votes was nothing paltry. But in addition the Cardinal had aroused, and to some extent created, a powerful anti-Catholic sectarianism in an organised form.

Tactically, the 1897 candidature episode seems to cut across Moran's general policy of seeking quiet, harmonious Catholic integration into the Australian community. It is not easy to explain the incident coherently. If Moran was pleased to be defeated, what point did he see in standing, as distinct from otherwise advocating federation? Certainly the peculiar difficulties of his official position are obvious. Like Archbishop Mannix later, he attempted to distinguish

between Moran the archbishop and Moran the private
citizen, a distinction too subtle for most electors, if indeed
it was a possible one at all. But, having decided to stand
in a public political election, he thereafter spurned the normal
methods of seeking support. He had called upon Jerusalem
to know the time of her visitation, but she would not. And
he? He would not enter the temple, there to cast out them
that sold and bought therein.

The confusion into which all this plunged Catholic thinking is reflected in the *Freeman's Journal* and in the *Catholic
Press*, a second Catholic paper which had been launched
(with strong clerical sponsorship) in November 1895. The
Catholic Press stated: 'we regard with horror anything like
a Catholic political organisation'. The *Freeman's Journal*
said: 'We have never advocated the organisation of the
Catholic vote for political purposes, nor do we do so now.'
These comments accorded with Catholic opinion generally,
at that time. Moran himself had remarked that he would
rather see good Protestants in parliament than bad Catholics.

At the same time, both Catholic papers saw a need for
political organisation among Catholics, bewailing its absence
when Moran was defeated. The *Press*'s formula to solve the
problem—'Catholics will vote for the Cardinal as the best
man, and in doing so they will be fulfilling as Catholics a
religious duty'—failed to work. While a vote for Moran
was a religious duty, the *Press* saw the United Protestant
Conference as aggressive ecclesiastical interference in Australia's non-sectarian politics. Cardinal Moran's candidature
raised the fundamental issue squarely. Thinking Catholics
deplored the prospect of Catholic political organisation: it
would amount to conceding, in some way, that the hopeful
trust they had in the increasingly friendly disposition of the
people of Australia towards the Catholic church had been
somehow misplaced. It went against their desire for acceptance, for integration. Against this, the Cardinal's electoral
fate suggested pointedly that unless Catholics adopted some
form of political organisation they would get nowhere with
what they regarded as matters of freedom and justice. From
1897 onwards the practical alternatives—political organisation or social rejection or inconsequence—were clear

enough, or at least rapidly clarifying. But Catholics did not want such a choice.

As to Moran's candidature, fundamentally this is not to be interpreted in political terms at all; the Cardinal was no politician. It occurred to him as a unique and, he thought, very favourable opportunity to call upon Australia publicly to endorse his policy of Catholic integration. Australian electors would demonstrate their acceptance of him as a symbol of their willingness to banish the past and welcome Catholics into the central areas of national endeavour. The Cardinal was sure they would. He did not believe that Australia harboured more than a dwindling residue of hostility towards the church. Nor did the bishops of Australia, assembled in Plenary Council in 1895—all of these 'free, energetic, and progressive people' were 'inspired by a common ambition to raise up a new nation' purged of prejudice and persecution. Lay leaders of Catholic opinion thought this too. Both Catholic newspapers were quite confident that the Cardinal would be elected. Why? Because they had faith in the Australian sense of fair play, belief that in this country the 'shibboleths of religious and race hatreds are only far-off echoes from a dead discredited past, without force or meaning.'

This was naive, perhaps. The fact remains that, however ill-conceived, miscalculated or badly managed, Moran's candidature in 1897 was his way of putting his vision of Australia to the test. Perhaps the test was fumbling and tentative, and obscure. But Australia had failed it. It had been weighed in Moran's balance and found wanting. Australian reality fell brutally short of his hopes, dreams, visions; and not only of Moran's—his idealist flights of harmonious, religious nation-dreaming had found reflections in the minds and hearts of bishops, clergy and laymen.

Nothing was ever to be quite the same again. The dreamtime was over. Moran's reign was soon to go sour. Certainly he retained his belief in Australia's destiny as a Christian society largely free from the errors of the old world, a potential base for the uplifting of Asia. But its context was to be narrowed and diminished. It was after Moran's 1897 candidature, his appeal to Australia as an integrated idea, that he turned, slowly and reluctantly, towards sectional, party politics. If the nation as a whole would not, perhaps a party would. Meanwhile the immediate sectarian backwash of his actions swirled in, thick, fast and evil-smelling.

Sectarian animus had existed since the first Australian settlement, welling up from time to time. Moran's candidature in 1897 set it simmering again. It boiled over in the O'Haran case of 1900. Moran had brought to Australia in 1884, as his secretary, Dr Denis O'Haran, then a young priest of twenty-eight and Vice-Rector of the Irish College, Rome. O'Haran was Moran's constant companion. He became diocesan factotum, administering Cathedral affairs, editing the *Australasian Catholic Record* which Moran established in 1895, going everywhere, doing everything. O'Haran was physically handsome. He had a great deal of real charm mingled with the less laudable characteristics of a considerable egoism (he gave away photographs of himself), a high opinion of the value of his ecclesiastical services, and a marked tendency towards emotionalism, particularly self-pity. Moran was, apparently, blind to O'Haran's shortcomings.

Towards the end of 1900, a book-maker named Arthur Coningham sought divorce from his wife on the grounds of her alleged misconduct with Dr O'Haran in the environs of St Mary's Cathedral. Coningham claimed custody of two of his three children (alleging that O'Haran was father of the other), and £5,000 damages. The court hearing was preceded and accompanied by all manner of explicitly sordid allegations, by charges of perjury and blackmail, by brawling outside the court between Catholic and Protestant factions, and by attacks on the sacrament of confession, on Catholic theology, and on the credibility of Catholic witnesses, including the Cardinal himself.

When the first jury disagreed and was discharged, the Reverend Dill Mackey took Coningham and his case under his anti-Roman wing, making the case a vehicle for organised ultra-Protestantism, establishing a fighting fund to solicit subscriptions from all those who wished 'to see the Romish church humiliated'. O'Haran's supporters, a motley and unscrupulous lot, organised a counter-conspiracy whose agents discovered that Coningham was being fed obsessively anti-O'Haran ammunition by a well-known Catholic priest, led the two Coninghams into perjury, and provided evidence of their close collusion. The activities of O'Haran's champions, no less than those of his opponents, point to the existence of an ugly and unprincipled religious underworld in which the labels Catholic and Protestant had no real religious meaning, but denoted merely rival politico-social power factions.

O'Haran was acquitted, to Catholic exultation. Moran regarded this as a triumph. It was no less a disaster. The O'Haran case was such that, whatever its outcome, all involved with it were degraded, subjected to indignity. Moreover, if Moran's dreams of harmony and unity, and an end to religious prejudice, had encountered strong adverse currents in 1897, they foundered and disappeared, almost without trace, in the O'Haran affair. Religious differences lost whatever chance they had of being embraced in some harmonious national resolution and became matters of political party and social faction.

The O'Haran case also had some internal ramifications. In 1889 Dr Higgins became Moran's auxiliary bishop. Their relations were excellent, but in 1898 Higgins was appointed to a Queensland bishopric. The Cardinal needed a replacement, and he wanted O'Haran. He had sought this before the Coningham case, but had been opposed by other Australian bishops. Moran could not see that the court case, though successfully fought, debarred O'Haran more effectively than before, and kept pushing for him in the face of a Roman refusal to consider this. Instead of O'Haran, he eventually took Michael Kelly as coadjutor. Until then his relations with Kelly had been amicable enough, but after his arrival, Kelly found himself treated by the Cardinal with coldness and arbitrary command. The Cardinal's attitude towards Kelly bore every mark of the sulkiness of a thwarted old man. Kelly represented the frustration of the Cardinal's will and the end of O'Haran's ambitions. The unfortunate and unpleasant personal relations that stemmed from this situation did not end with Moran's death. O'Haran, ousted by Kelly when he took over in 1911, continued, as parish priest of Darlinghurst until his death in 1931, to

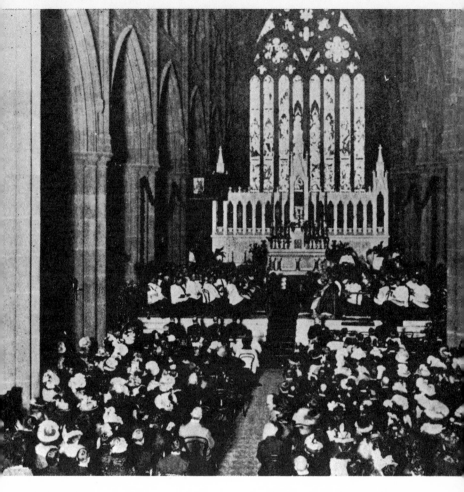

XI The laity at prayer: part of the congregation at the dedication of St Mary's Cathedral, 9 September 1900

XII Catholic education in the 1890s: the interior of St Brigid's new school at Marrickville, Sydney, in 1893

vent his bitterness in creating as much minor annoyance and difficulty for Kelly as he could.

Outside the church, the O'Haran affair spawned, in June 1901, the Australian Protestant Defence Association, organised to counter the growing influence of Rome in politics in New South Wales. Its leader was the dynamic demagogue, the Reverend Dill Mackey, an Irish Presbyterian minister, who stepped into John Dunmore Lang's place not only as pastor of Scots Church, but also as leader of the most determined anti-Catholic faction. The organisation soon spread interstate, and found an organ in the *Watchman,* whose object was, besides ultra-loyalty to the Empire, 'to preserve and defend the general interests of Protestantism against the encroachments of Roman Catholicism in matters religious, political, social and commercial.' Its first issue in February 1902 ran to 5,000 copies; in six months it had leapt to 13,000. Anti-Catholicism was on the march, its drumbeats not to grow feeble until the mid 1920s.

Moran was turning towards a party solution to Catholicism's problems in the early years of the century, but for a decade before that he had been sympathetic to workers' efforts to better their position. Again it must be emphasised that Moran's public life was subordinate to his churchmanship. If he was no politician, neither was he a partisan, save in the interests of religion. What were these interests? As he saw them, peace, harmony. In the context of the 1890s, when the colony was experiencing social struggle and turmoil, his sympathy for labour was the expression of his discernment that a major source of social disharmony was society's failure to recognise labour's just rights. This did not amount so much to a support for labour as such, as to support for redressing the balance of a society whose imbalance had led to strife. His aim was not the rule of labour, but a balanced harmonious society.

To Moran the great strike of 1890 testified to social imbalance and disharmony. His understanding of the issues at stake was in the most general terms. Briefly, his involvement amounted to this. He said the strikers' wage claims were just, and that his sympathies were with labour. He offered to act as a mediator in finding a solution acceptable to both parties. The employers, wanting, and eventually getting, complete victory, refused to accept this offer. The Cardinal thereupon vanished from the centre of strike affairs.

The importance of Moran's intervention lies entirely in his declaration of sympathy for the cause of labour. Despite the fact that this was nothing new in world terms—many bishops elsewhere, from the Pope down, had made similar statements—this, together with the similar attitude taken in Melbourne by Archbishop Carr, was of considerable importance in the Australian context. Hitherto, churchmen had supported capitalism, and ministers of the major non-Catholic denominations continued to do so. What was unique about Moran's attitude was that he did not do this. But it is an exaggeration to claim that he supported labour. When the Sydney Trades and Labor Council debated a motion to thank Moran for a public lecture on the rights and duties of labour, it was rejected sixty-four to thirty-three. J. C. Watson was opposed to thanking Moran because Moran had not taken sides. Watson was correct. What Moran had done was to set out the Christian principles which would produce a harmoniously balanced society; he was totally opposed to anything that looked like class war or social revolution.

Nor could it be claimed that Moran's pronouncements had either originality or clear practical application. As a socioeconomic thinker, he had little to offer beyond the promulgation of the teachings of Leo XIII, which were in very general terms. Left to himself, the Cardinal's thought consisted of unrealistic vaguenesses, pious sentiments, attempts to please everybody, and cautious platitudes. His proferred solution to the 1890 strike exhibits these characteristics clearly: 'I believe that the men will obtain what they have asked, and that, in granting the demands, the ship owners will hit upon some plan by which ruinous competition among themselves will be discontinued, and the companies, while honourably serving the public interest, will be able to pay, not only good wages, but good dividends.' Thus, all parties would be satisfied, all would happen for the best, in the best of possible industrial worlds. This kind of thinking is typical of Moran at his most optimistically utopian—somehow, everything would work out all right. When it did not—and every one of Moran's predictions was vitiated by facts—the Cardinal said nothing.

On more specific points, he tended to be evasive and cursorily superficial. Asked, in 1890, whether or not he approved of trade unionism, he replied: 'I am certainly not opposed to it so long as labour unions are kept free of abuses' (he meant socialism). He went on to announce: 'The present labour organisations are really only the old Catholic guilds under another name . . . formed to protect the workman from tyranny, and to secure to the workman just payment for his skill and labour'—an equation which was little better than nonsense. He and other bishops were soon disabused of such confusions. In 1895 the Bishops in Plenary Council, after a yearning look back at the Ages of Faith and at mediaeval guilds, conceded it 'necessary that the workers should combine amongst themselves for mutual aid', suggesting Catholic benefit societies under ecclesiastic patronage and direction, such as the Hibernians, as an appropriate form.

What, then, should be the relationship between religion and politics? Catholics received little precise instruction from the Cardinal. In 1890 he said:

> I am not frightened at all of the intermingling of religion and politics, because religion only requires that the citizens shall keep the Ten Commandments, and then adopt any political course they deem best in the interests of their country, and which corresponds best with the enlightened views of their own mind and their own conscience.

'Every care should be exercised,' Moran warned, 'to put the right man in the right place, and thus prevent the shaping of the destiny of this great country falling into the wrong hands.' Very true, but what did it mean in practice? Moran did not say—at least not in 1890. In 1905 he was still saying: 'our maxim in social matters is to keep the Ten Commandments and do what you please.' But by then he was prepared to reveal, at least by implication, his personal commitment to the Labor Party: 'keep the Ten Commandments and nationalise every bit of land as far as you please.'

Obviously, these kind of comments did not amount to even the beginings of analysis. Neither intellectual clarity, nor indeed intellectuality at all, was among Moran's strong points. When he spoke on other than very general social principles, his tendency was to confuse and obscure the issues at stake or dismiss them with some summary formula. In his celebrated expoundings of the social teaching of the Leo XIII, he set forth the principles, but he did not relate them to actual social practice in Australia. No doubt, ideally, this practical application was not the Cardinal's task, but that of those who knew the practical situation intimately. And most of his remarks are also associated with his tendency to see himself in a world context, prince of the church universal; his 1891 lecture on the rights and duties of labour, before a distinguished gathering, has the air of a set piece. Nevertheless, there is ample suggestion in what he did say that he was incapable of relating Catholic social principles to social practice in Australia. Immensely industrious, he had minimal intellectual rigour and little mental penetration. The social issue reveals this most clearly, but it is also evident in other ways, such as his efforts to diminish the reputation of J. H. Newman, the immense investment of time he put into arguing the case that Ireland had been given by the papacy the title of 'island of saints and scholars', and his historical scholarship generally.

Moran's histories are prodigious compilations. His enormous *History of the Catholic Church in Australasia*, 1003 pages, published in 1896, is a mass of undigested material, gathered by the Cardinal by virtue of his predelections for borrowing and seldom returning, and omitting anything he did not like. History, like life, was for edification. In both cases the scandalous, the unfortunate, should be removed from view: one should pretend that these distasteful things did not exist. Indeed, in a sense, for Moran they really did not exist, so trivial were they. He was at home with the great sweeping principles of Christian life, and with simple day-to-day piety, the ordinary life of religious observance within the devout soul. But he was remote from that great area of life that lies in between the individual soul and its Creator, the world of men and affairs. He did not really understand this area, nor did he weigh its problems as of great consequence in comparison with the relationship between the individual and God: 'keep the Ten Commandments and do what you please'.

This amounted not to social leadership, but to social drift, a surrender to whatever social currents might be strongest among the Catholic body, an uncritical acceptance of whatever most pleased it. Under Cardinal Moran, Catholics had no seriously considered leadership in social affairs. The Cardinal did not provide it; the laity was incapable of exercising it, or even of concluding that serious thought was necessary. The result was drift. And the natural drift was towards the Labor Party.

At first, Moran saw the Labor Party with the detachment characteristic of his political observations generally. In 1891 he noted with approval the appearance of *'the labour party* to protect the working man & to defend his rights in a constitutional manner.' He added: 'As Catholics we have not much interest in the elections'. (E. W. O'Sullivan saw it differently. He claimed that he was excluded from Dibbs's cabinet of 1891 because there were already two Catholics in it, and three might provoke a public outcry.) Moran's comment on the results of the 1891 election sums up his attitude throughout the 1890s and, to a somewhat lesser extent, later:

A new political party representing the labouring classes, has secured the return of several members. I don't think that there were ever so many Catholics returned, but in the balance of political parties, they can do but little than may improve the condition of our schools. In everything else all that we want is that they will leave us alone.

Moran wanted to be left alone to get on with the work of salvation, undistracted and unhindered by political or social battles.

This was to expect too much, but Moran's unwillingness to become involved persisted. Referring to the 1894 election he said: 'it does not give us much trouble. There is no religious principle at stake & we have many friends in both political parties, so that we take no part whatever in the political excitement.' By both political parties, he meant the free trade and protection groups, so his reference excluded labour, which did not, apparently, seem of great importance to him. Moran's tendency was to speak of 'Australian democracy' as something to which all parties aspired, a community, national affair, not the preserve of any party. In 1902 he was still repeating: 'So far from being allied to any particular party, the Catholic citizens were free to take whatever political course they thought best.'

However, they increasingly thought the best course was to support the Labor Party. The facts of economic and social life were driving Catholics into the Labor Party, though none too quickly and not without much misgiving. The career of E. W. O'Sullivan illustrates this. A New South Wales parliamentarian from 1885 to 1910, Catholic, radical, democratic, O'Sullivan did not join the Labor Party until 1910, just before he died. In the 1890s neither of the two Sydney Catholic newspapers were well disposed to the Labor Party. As to the episcopacy, Archbishop Carr in Melbourne was not disposed to make his sympathy for labour too public. He decided not to lecture, as Moran had done, on the labour question: 'already people are beginning to say that an Alliance has been formed between the Catholic body and the Labour Party. So it may be as well not to add to the fear which rumour excites in the minds of many.' In contrast to the sympathy exhibited by Moran and Carr, Bishop Dunne, of Brisbane, was so gravely perturbed by what he regarded, in 1895, as the threat to property posed by the rapid advance of the 'democratico-socialist party' that he was enquiring about means of transferring church investments and funds for holding in Ireland.

Cardinal Moran did not create the growing alignment of Catholics with the Labor Party that is evident from the turn of the century. He did, however, sympathise with it, justify it, and foster it. Part of his fostering was positive encouragement; part was negative, his rousing of sectarianism in 1897. Moran's standing for the Federal Convention produced a situation which urged Catholics into the Labor Party because his candidature led to a vigorous recrudescence of Orangeism as a political force. The 1901 elections saw this clearly demonstrated in Protestant tickets and in the Protestant Defence Association. Militant Protestantism favoured the non-labour parties. The Labor Party was by

1901, in Catholic eyes, the only party not patently tainted by bigotry.

It was this, together with the obvious facts of economics and social class, that led Catholics into the Labor Party from the early years of the century, and led also to their embarking on a process of justifying what they were doing. In 1902 the Cardinal was claiming that the church and the Labor Party shared a common aim in their seeking to elevate the masses of people: 'They are coadjutors in the great work.' In 1905 the *Freeman's Journal* was claiming that: 'It would be unfair and unjust to assign to the Labour Party those false maxims that imply the name of Communism.' This problem, which became something of an obsession with thinking Catholics in 1905, was resolved by nearly all of them in the Labor Party's favour, a resolution best illustrated perhaps by the Australian Catholic Truth Society's pamphlet, *Socialism,* written by a Melbourne priest, Dr E. J. Kelly, and first published in 1905. The argument of this pamphlet strongly suggests that the principles and spirit of Leo XIII's *Rerum Novarum* were neither understood nor influential among even the doctors of the Australian church. Dr Kelly's *Socialism* was confused, erroneous and superficial, at times in blunt conflict with papal teaching, lacking consideration of the materialism basic to the Marxist position, and riddled with fundamental historical, philosophical and theological misunderstandings. Like many of his coreligionists, Dr Kelly seems to have allowed the fact that Catholics were gravitating towards the Labor Party, and his sympathy for social reform, to dictate his intellectual assessment of socialism.

The question of the nature of the Labor Party's socialism had arisen in 1905 as a result of the claim by a Catholic delegate to the Political Labor League's conference of that year that the Party was socialist in a sense condemned by the church; and because the politician George Reid set out to prove that Labor was revolutionary socialist. Catholics looked to Cardinal Moran for guidance. In February 1905 he made his opinion clear: that the Labor Party was not socialist in any condemned sense, nor did he believe that such socialism would ever take root in Australia. In this, Moran was not alone. Carr, in Melbourne, and Delany, in Hobart, supported him publicly. The 1905 Joint Pastoral of the Australian Bishops confirmed this by implication, giving a blessing to 'socialism' defined as the effort 'to redress the wrongs and to alleviate the miseries of the labouring poor'.

In following years, Moran reiterated this judgement. 'Our Labour Party does not cherish any vague theories, any ambiguous and high sounding formulae. Its object is precise reforms, and concrete measures in favour of the toiling masses.' Indeed, as he grew older, he became, if anything, more radical. He envisaged the solution to the 1909 Newcastle coal strike (in which he offered to mediate) as nationalisation.

However, Moran's pronouncements did not rid some Catholics of their misgivings. Some priests continued to be firmly convinced that Labor *was* socialist in the condemned sense, or that its danger of becoming socialist was so great as to warrant Catholics repudiating it. This view was strong in Queensland. In Victoria, Bishop Higgins, of Ballarat, entertained a similar distrust, remarking in a letter to Ireland in 1910: 'Our present government is labour and disposed in some things to follow the bad example of your French socialists.' And, generally, not a few Catholics, even active Labor Party supporters, were uneasy about an alignment which linked them with labour elements which were militantly socialist or irreligious.

This feeling surfaced in 1910, the year in which an alignment between Catholics and the Labor Party particularly in New South Wales, became obvious in Labor victories in both Federal and New South Wales state elections. In May 1910 Joseph McCabe, ex-priest and prominent publicist of rationalism and evolution, arrived in Australia for a lecture tour. To Marxian socialists, McCabe came as 'the preacher of that Historic materialism on which all Socialist philosophy rests'. The entertaining of McCabe at Parliament House, in Melbourne, by a number of Labor members including Fisher, the Prime Minister, drew a vigorous public protest from a Tasmanian parish priest, who implied that Labor must consider the feelings of its Catholic supporters or suffer. Further instances of Labor support for McCabe led to further Catholic protest which prompted Labor counterattacks alleging that Catholics were sectarian political blackmailers who cared nothing for Australia as a whole, only for themselves. Meanwhile McCabe's attacks on the rule of the church in Spain had set off a major sectarian controversy.

The McCabe visit made a number of important matters clear. One was that Moran's policy of harmonious integration of Catholics into the general Australian community had failed completely. The 1910 controversy over Catholicism in Spain, and generally over church-state relations, showed that the envenomed bitterness and hysterical frenzy that marked the extreme elements of the Protestant attack were accompanied by a moderate but widespread general hostility to the reactionary ecclesiasticism, infringement of religious liberty, and attempts to frustrate enlightened democracy alleged to be characteristic of the Catholic church. Moran had totally failed to persuade Australians to accept his image of the church as the friend of peace, progress and enlightenment. In 1910 he and Kelly were forced to lead a defence of the church, a defence which was, at its worst, arbitrary, ill-considered, distraught and haughty.

So far as the Catholic-Labor alignment was concerned, the McCabe affair revealed its true nature—that its benefits would be to Labor, not to Catholics. In so far as they were workers, Catholics would gain with other workers from Labor's efforts, but as Catholics they would gain nothing. The 1910 disputes clearly showed that there was an extremist and irreligious element within Labor, and that the Party was intractable to Catholic demands. Not that this was any revelation—Labor leaders, such as W. M. Hughes, had been saying this for some time. And the 1910 affair also showed that Catholic members of parliament were not prepared to speak out on Catholic grievances.

At the same time, it was apparent that Catholics were virtually prisoners of the political situation. If Labor was not good, the non-labour parties were definitely worse. Given that Catholics, at this stage, were not prepared to consider a political party of their own, alliance with Labor was the lesser of two evils, and one quickly consecrated by a tendency to make a virtue of necessity. But it had nothing to offer Catholics as Catholics, as the more perceptive quickly saw. Bishop Dunne, of Broken Hill, wrote to Archbishop Kelly in 1911: 'I am afraid the Labour Party as such will not do much to relieve us from disabilities.' Alignment with the Labor Party was essentially the result not of the operation of Catholic principle (though this played some part), but more importantly of economic logic, and drift—social and intellectual drift.

Nor in 1910 could Catholic observers escape the unpalatable conclusion that a large section of Australian opinion required them to refrain from voting or thinking as Catholics. The assertion of any Catholic viewpoint was branded as selfishly sectarian, in so far as it was specifically Catholic and critical of the *status quo*. Such viewpoints were denounced as un-Australian. As the *Freeman's Journal* put it in August 1910: 'it has seemed to be the mission of the daily press to mispresent and distort Catholic sayings and doings as in some wise alien and hostile to Australia's common citizenship.'

The conclusion to be drawn was that Catholics were socially acceptable so long as they did not behave publicly as Catholics. Some Catholics, and particularly politicians involved in the *status quo,* accepted this conclusion passively, and confined their Catholicism to their personal lives. The Catholic-Labor alignment expressed, and continued to express, the need and determination of Catholics to conform, and to be involved in 'Australia's common citizenship'. But the alignment was never total, and was often strained, because Catholics, as Catholics, were never wholly welcome within Labor. In the face of this refusal to admit their individuality and the value of their contribution to national life, some Catholics tended, by way of compensation, to proclaim their virtues to themselves, to retreat into the comfort of the ghetto, leaving the world to its own contemptible devices.

Meanwhile, throughout Moran's reign of nearly thirty years, a slow process of erosion continued to undermine religious belief. Moran, and Catholics as a whole, had despite frequent denunciation paid it little real attention. The furore provoked by McCabe showed that, along with other Australian Christians, Catholics were more influenced by the Catholic-Protestant division than by the threat posed by materialism and irreligion. Few Catholics were fully alert to the gravity of novel and more insidious threats: the forces of Catholicism were securely dug in, grouped, in the main, to cope with the expected onslaughts of the traditional foe, Protestantism. Appreciation of the need to obviate inter-Christian strife, in the face of common and very dangerous enemies, was rare. Both Catholics and Protestants accused each other's churches of breeding atheism, materialism and rationalism. Both ascribed these evils to a revolt of generous and capable minds from a sterile bigotry. From these continuing, bitter exchanges only the infidel—acknowledged to be generous, capable, intelligent—emerged with honour.

Moran's policy on education, his whole integrationist social outlook, and his pragmatism, had caused him to underestimate the growth and vigour of secularism and rationalism, of intellectual alienation generally. The Modernist crisis, that movement within European Catholic intellectual life which sought to adapt dogma to modern rationalist thought (condemned by Pius X in 1907), roused the Cardinal to form, in 1908, a Council of Vigilance of the priests of the archdiocese. The Council's investigations convinced the Cardinal 'that we had reason to be thankful here in Australia as well as in Ireland that the wave of Scepticism and infidelity, which caused such havoc to the faith in other Countries, had not reached us. Our own Catholic people were not in any way imbued with the recent errors.' Outside the church, of course, matters were different, and in the University of Sydney, in particular, indifferentism, rationalism and materialism were rife. 'Our young men attending there were in danger of being infected by serious error', warned the Cardinal. Within the fold, however, he was convinced that all was well.

And, as to Modernism, so it was: Catholic life in Australia provided a too intellectually thin, too alien a ground to give root to such a subtle, thoughtful heresy. Australian Catholic 'philosophic' problems were rudimentary, concomitants of a building, expanding, missionary church. To distil these problems into one, religious action had come almost to preclude religious thought. This was a natural tendency in a pioneering church, yet the real pioneers—

those who had preceded Moran—had escaped it to a considerable extent, because they had been faced not only by big practical problems, but also by big intellectual and ideological issues—religious freedom, authority within the church, Irish-English conflicts, the question of religious education.

Under Moran, these issues seemed, on the whole, to have been settled, and a high degree of stability of character achieved. If, as it seemed, there was little to question, or think about, in the nature of the Australian church, and its aims, the only problems left for important attention were practical ones. And practical problems (religious ministry and education for all Catholics, the improvement of Catholics' social and economic position) required practical solutions, that is, action. The taking of practical measures was the theme of Catholicism, clerical and lay, as it evolved under Moran. Thought, intellectual activity—the ascertainment of principles and facts, their relating and analysis, the drawing of prudent, logical conclusions, in all, rational judgement—fell into the background, there to become shrouded in suspicion and contempt. Thus grew a gap between thought and action, with action dominant: what was valuable was what worked, or seemed to work, there and then. Moran was a great builder, and so were the men, clergy and laity of his time. But (to adopt Moran's literalism) even God, in the days of creation, when He made heaven and earth, paused, looked upon what He had done, and found it good. Reflection, that lucid looking upon what had been done, was rare indeed in Moran's days. The tenor of the Australian church, as Moran left it in 1911, was one of mindless pragmatism.

Even in that, the broad national horizons which Moran had once scanned had shrunk to the dimensions of his own backyard. The Cardinal's great and noble dream of Australia as one nation, religious and free, had been deflated and crushed, reduced to the confines of political party. His bid to gain for Catholics full and complete social acceptance had been repulsed to such effect that, by the end of his life, they had been driven into tighter, more exclusive confessional camps than ever before. Instead of, as in Moran's vision, enjoying in tranquil equality the fruits of

Australian freedom, Catholics were bivouacked on the out-
skirts of a hostile civilisation.

Moran died, at the age of eighty-one, in August 1911.
Four months later, Bishop James Dunne wrote to Archbishop
Kelly: 'The need of some Catholic Federation or Defence
Society seems to be generally felt. If well organised . . .
Catholics would begin to be a power in the State and in
the Commonwealth.' The Cardinal had outlived his time,
the time of hopes of harmony, of soft words and gentle
entreaty. These failing, a new era had already begun, the
era of organisation, pressure, confrontation.

And Moran? Is there any one key to this singular man,
this enigma, now one thing, now another, now expansive,
now small and petty, now powerful, now weak? His
episcopacy—what happened between 1884 and 1911—has
a firm feel of solidarity, of a stabilising, of a settling down,
of integrity. But with Moran himself, for all the intimations
of greatness, there is a hint of something insubstantial, a
trace of hollowness, of unreality. The question cannot be
escaped—was this a man acting a part, an actor filling a
role that fitted him, almost, as a glove? What part would
such a man act? The answer, too, is inescapable—that of
a great churchman. His adaptability to his new Australian
circumstances has been noted. Was it adaptability? Or
was it that he had constructed for himself an image of
episcopal greatness, to which he sought to aspire? Was it
that on leaving an Ireland in which he had been rated
ordinary, he had decided that he would mould for himself
a new personality in the new world, take upon himself the
mantle of greatness?

Whatever the cause, Moran seems not quite to fit himself,
to both rattle within, and protrude outside, his essential
being. He was both larger—and smaller—than life.

5

Dr Mannix 1911-1925

Confrontation, challenge, conflict: Daniel Mannix was this policy personified. For half a century, from 1912 to 1962, Mannix, as Archbishop of Melbourne, faced Australia with Catholic principles as he saw them, often amid a blaze of controversy. Here was another Catholicism, that which aggressively accepted a role as a standing scandal in the eyes of the world. Moran's search for peaceful harmony gave way to Mannix's rigorous pursuit of principle. Assertion replaced amiability as the Catholic mode of social behaviour. In 1914 Mannix summed up his enduring social credo, and implied a hard judgement on what had passed:

> Strife among Christians is painful and distressing; but worse still, peace bought by the barter of principles or of conscious conviction. The man who would say that for peace he is prepared to compromise, to give way on this or that article of his creed, shows that in reality he has no convictions, no principle to give away.

Peace—or principle? By the early years of the century, this was the unhappy, invidious choice with which Catholics were presented. It was an agonising, profitless dilemma: to choose either path meant endangering the other. Each course had much to commend it, and much to condemn it. Moran had chosen the path of peace. Principle had suffered, and peace had not been attained. Mannix chose principle. Peace vanished, turmoil took its place. And principle was still not realised in practice.

Mannix personified the assertive Catholic approach. However, he was not responsible for the appearance of the new wave of aggressive Catholicism. Its emergence preceded his arrival. A sharp re-orientation of Catholic public attitudes is discernible from 1910 to 1911. In 1910 Archbishop Carr was foreshadowing the formation of a Catholic social-political organisation. Early in 1911 Archbishop Kelly was reported as telling a Hibernian's Conference: 'The Catholics of today . . . were fighting in a corner.' Before 1911, as the *Catholic Press* observed: 'it would have been almost impossible in Victoria or elsewhere to fill a small room for the purpose of discussing a fighting Catholic policy. It was insisted even in Catholic circles that we ought to be quiet, lest that worse should come of an untimely demonstration.'

This pacific, retiring approach, which had taken deep root among Catholic members of the Labor Party, persisted. Typical of its continuance was the attitude taken on the education question by the Catholic J. H. Scullin, a future Labor Prime Minister. In 1915 Scullin refused to support the deletion of Labor's secular education plank, and the substitution of one that recognised Catholic claims; he argued that this would be to introduce divisive religious controversy into party political matters. However, alongside this secularist conformity there was developing, from 1911, a very different frame of Catholic mind which was assertively Catholic. This development was symbolised by, and expressed in, the Catholic Federation, formed in Melbourne in December 1911, and quickly spreading to all states in a phenomenal growth (about 100,000 members within two years) Dr Mannix remarked later of the Federation's formation: 'It came at a time when, perhaps, there was danger that the Catholic body should settle down into patient, if not contented, servitude.'

Catholicism—the Christian religion generally—as a social force contains dualistic tendencies, both conservative and revolutionary elements. It contains both a tendency to accept the world, to conform to and integrate with its environment, and a tendency to reject the world, to confront its environment. The occurrence of a swing towards confrontation may be explained in terms of a growing feeling among active Catholics that the policy of integration had failed. That this occurred from 1911 appears to be related to Moran's death, and to the bitter disappointment felt by many Catholics at the failure of Labor governments, first elected in 1910, to make any attempt to remedy Catholic grievances—specifically, education. That Melbourne should see the birth of this movement in organised form reflects its distance from Moran's immediate sway, and Archbishop Carr's disenchantment, from the early years of the century, with the Cardinal's basic social attitudes. Carr had come to believe that Moran's policy of pacifism, enlivened by bursts of moral pressure, was futile, and that only a fighting organisation would yield results.

The Catholic Federation was formed at a meeting, in December 1911, of delegates from various Victorian Catholic societies, sodalities and confraternities, the Hibernian Benefit Society being the most significant. It had Archbishop Carr's warm approval, and indeed the movement towards its formation seems to have derived from suggestions he had made in the previous year. The organisation was patterned on similar federations in America, England and Germany. It was non-political in any party sense. Its purpose was to achieve organised Catholic unity 'for the purpose of advancing the religious, civil and social interests of Catholics throughout Australia.'

> Our Church is one. Our Faith is one. Our aims are the same —the good of man, the salvation of the race. Why should we not be one in organisation? Why should not Catholics march to their glorious goal of human betterment with the ordered steps of a disciplined regiment, rather than with the hustling and jostling of a disorganised multitude? . . . *People of one mind must unite their strength or go under.*

So read the Federation's manifesto. But what had decisively prompted the Federation's formation was the education grievance. The Federation began with educational justice as the flag at its masthead, with state aid its major concern and focus for agitation. There were other objectives: a Catholic daily newspaper, circulation of Catholic literature, prohibition of corrupting publications, and the tightening up of divorce laws. But education was its *raison d'être*. The Federation was formed in New South Wales in April 1913, with Archbishop Kelly's blessing, P. S. Cleary as first President and that outspoken priest, Dr Maurice O'Reilly, then President of St Stanislaus College, Bathurst, as its most spectacular public advocate. The Federation's organisers had seen that 'the success of the movement must largely depend on the clergy'. This was true, so far as initial organisation went, and the clergy did not fail the Federation. The laity, however, did, as time was to show.

Dr Mannix arrived in Melbourne, as coadjutor to Archbishop Carr, in March 1913. He was then forty-nine. His aggressive disposition and concern for education chimed in exactly with the new departure in Catholic affairs which the Federation represented. Mannix found a congenial Catholic atmosphere. The new movement within Catholicism found a congenial leader.

Daniel Mannix was born in Charleville, County Cork, in March 1864, the son of a reasonably well-off farmer. He studied—brilliantly—for the priesthood at Maynooth and was ordained in 1890s. The following year he was appointed to the junior chair of philosophy at the Dunboyne Establishment, associated with Maynooth. In 1894 he became professor of theology, and in 1903 President of Maynooth.

At Maynooth, Mannix revealed that intense interest in practical social questions which was characteristic of his life. As first secretary of the Maynooth Union of priests, Mannix was responsible for swinging the emphasis of clerical discussion away from theoretical, 'academic' questions, towards the political, semi-political and economic questions of the day. He urged that priests, in the true interests of religion, should concern themselves with such urgent, practical matters as the co-operative movement, housing for the poor, and the nursing of the sick; he was himself prominent in the temperance movement.

Mannix's Maynooth presidency was no sinecure. The College was passing through a period of some strain, as it was faced with new demands for scholarship and changing circumstances in Irish life. Mannix played a major role in securing the incorporation of Maynooth into the Irish university system, with the establishment of the National University of Ireland in 1908. He was also centrally involved in the fierce controversies of the O'Hickey case. Dr O'Hickey was professor of Irish at the College. He was a strident promoter of compulsory Irish, and in this he met the resistance of Mannix, and of the College authorities generally. O'Hickey's response was such that, in 1909, he was deprived of his professorship for insubordination and disloyalty to the College. Mannix's handling of this affair (it was alleged that he had long been in personal feud with Dr O'Hickey) and his opposition to Irish as a compulsory language requirement brought him odium throughout Ireland among the dedicated nationalist elements. Nor was his rule within the College much liked. He saw his role as that of restoring a tighter discipline and a greater respect for authority—not a popular task—and the stern measures he took to achieve this pushed the College into resentment, and almost into rebellion. His promotion to regret, although no one questioned his remarkable personal qualities and abilities.

Mannix had a high reputation in Ireland for his activities in regard to educational questions, and considerable experience of the politics of church-state relations on those questions. The bishops of the Irish church were aware of the central position that education occupied in the Australian Catholic scene. Cardinal Logue, Primate of Ireland, remarked at Dr Mannix's consecration as Archbishop:

> There were some things that required special care, and in Australia one of the things which was their most important concern was the education of the young. The question of education was a great question at the present day, and his Eminence didn't believe that within the four seas of Ireland or the British Empire an ecclesiastic [existed] who was better prepared and qualified to assist in the great work.

One of Cardinal Moran's achievements, or at least a characteristic of his reign, had been the development in Ireland of a much intensified regard for Australia as a province of the Irish church. Irish ecclesiastical concern for the future of Catholicism in Australia had been sharply accentuated because of his death in 1911. The Cardinal had dominated and moulded Australian Catholicism for nearly thirty years. His death threw the future into uncertainty, particularly as Archbishop Carr had never sought dynamic influence, and was ageing; and there was, in Ireland, little confidence in the governing ability of the Cardinal's successor, Archbishop Kelly: 'In Ireland he was credited with great piety, but a small share of wisdom', a Dublin nun had told Moran in 1907.

The circumstances, and the speeches made at his consecration, suggest that Archbishop Mannix's appointment was
seen in Ireland in terms of providing a potential successor
to the position of dominance vacated by Cardinal Moran;
that is, the provision within the Australian church of a
strong force of formation and leadership. Mannix would
succeed to the Cardinal's position of influence, but not to
his policies. Archbishop Carr had sought Mannix as
coadjutor in 1908, and by then Carr was firmly convinced
that Moran's policies were mistaken.

The theme of the speech-making on Mannix's arrival
in Melbourne was the fight for educational justice. The
new Archbishop described the existing situation as 'the one
great stain upon the statute books of this free and progressive land' and as 'a crying public wrong'—which he
pledged himself to attempt to right. The *Advocate* held that
Mannix's arrival heralded 'an epoch making stage' in the
education fight, seeing Mannix and the Catholic Federation
in natural liaison: 'We have a new fighting force amongst
us.' So evident was this potential liaison that the Melbourne
Argus referred to it editorially, appealing to Mannix to
accept the secular education system in the interests of social
harmony. In March 1917 Dr Mannix said of himself that
'he did not come to Australia to court . . . popularity. He
had come for a purpose, and, according to his own conscience
he was working for the attainment of that purpose.' That
purpose seems to have been, generally, to stiffen the public
attitudes and demands of Australian Catholicism, and,
particularly, to exert pressure on the state to recognise
Catholic educational claims. Within a year of his arrival,
his policy had acquired for him a press reputation as the
'most belligerent and provocative' Catholic prelate in
Australia.

In 1929 an Italian artist, fascinated by Mannix's face
and head, remarked that one portrait of him would be
quite inadequate; at least ten portraits would be necessary:
'he is always different . . . it was necessary to choose some
particular frame of mind and just barely to suggest the
others. The difficulty lay in choosing the frame of mind.'
The impression the new Archbishop created among the
general public (or at least, that created for him by the

press) may have been that of belligerence and provocation.
Among the Melbourne laity his reputation was for charm,
geniality, and firm assertive leadership. He felt at home,
and the laity felt at home with him. Accord existed,
particularly on the education question, which was his
paramount concern from the beginning of his Australian
career to its end. Just after Dr Mannix's arrival, the Bishop
of Sale observed to a friend: 'In his public addresses he is
moving with caution yet getting splendid work in on the
enemy when there is an opening.' Who was this enemy? It
was the secular state, unmoved by Catholic educational
claims. 'Enemy' is no loose usage. Just how bitterly
Catholics appraised the Federal government of Joseph Cook
may be judged from this description in the *Catholic Press*:
'Their spirit is still the spirit of the old Penal times when
the Irish were kept in chains, and Catholics remained true
to the faith at the risk of the triangles and the lash.'

Dr Mannix did not cause this increasingly belligerent
souring in the temper of Australian Catholicism, but it was
in accord with his own temperament and convictions. He
fostered it, gave it leadership, and became its major spokesman. He was indeed, as was said at his welcome, 'a new
energy, a new light, and a new force'. Yet, it would be
a mistake to see Dr Mannix as alone in expressing this new
militant spirit. His denunciations of the terrible trio of
educational injustice, freemasonry and mixed marriages were
little, if at all, more forthright and blistering than those
of some other bishops, Kelly in particular. And when war
broke out in August 1914, Mannix was by no means alone
in his refusal to desist from scathing social criticism.

Little of the rabid patriotic enthusiasm which seized the
general community can be detected in the Catholic reaction
to the outbreak of war—sorrow, misgivings as to Australia's
involvement, then a hardening acceptance of unpleasant
duty. Archbishop Kelly approached closest to the patriotic
stereotype then prevalent among public figures. His commitment was totally sincere: he believed strongly in the
ennobling influence of the martial spirit and of discipline; he
believed that death in battle for a just cause brought the
glory of self-sacrifice. He became a senior Army chaplain,
appearing on patriotic platforms and at recruiting meetings,

though his activities waned as the war raised divisive issues.

Nevertheless, Kelly, and all the more vocal bishops, continued unabated and unabashed their onslaught on educational injustice. Archbishop Kelly's initial pledge of Catholic support for the war effort was couched in stinging terms: 'whether our schools are treated fairly or not, we will do our duty'. While Mannix contended that educational injustice to Catholics branded Australian society as one of slavery, not of freedom, Kelly likened the situation to that under the Irish penal laws of the eighteenth century. Men were dying for freedom while oppression disfigured their homeland: what did Kelly denounce in his sermon at High Mass, in May 1915, for Australian soldiers killed in battle? —educational injustice. Even Archbishop Mannix said nothing to rival the scalding comments of Bishop Gallagher of Goulburn to the boys of St Patrick's College, in December 1914:

> Remember that you live under a Government which, whatever party be in power, is the narrowest, the most bigoted, the most intolerant, so far as Catholic institutions are concerned that now exists in Australia; that, perhaps, exists in the civilised world. Join the Catholic Federation, have the courage to fight for your rights by all constitutional means.

Such comments were, in themselves, provocative enough at any time. Catholic educational claims had always tended to re-arouse the bitter resistance so characteristic of the controversies of the 1870s—which was why Cardinal Moran had not pressed them too forcefully. The outbreak of war created a situation in which these Catholic claims were vastly more unpopular and offensive. Archbishop Mannix announced, in October 1914, that 'a paramount and dominating issue for us is whether our Catholic schools are to retain their Christian character, and whether Australia is, as the years go by, to become more and more a Christian land, or more and more a pagan land.' What Mannix saw as a paramount and dominating issue seemed, to the non-Catholic community, at best an irrelevancy or a tiresome annoyance—the *Argus* dismissed Catholic educational claims as trivial—and at worst a dangerous evil; the old charge that Catholic schools bred disloyalty revived sharply with the war.

For the non-Catholic community, the paramount and dominating issue was the successful pursuit of the war. In a war situation verging on hysteria, the non-Catholic community was doubly affronted by what had long been depicted to them by the press and politicians as a narrow and unreasonable sectional demand. Many, even Catholics, held that to introduce the contentious Catholic education question in a time of war was a form of disloyalty, for it showed blindness or indifference to matters of national honour and even survival, and hampered a united war effort. Mannix, it seems, thought differently. To him the war presented a favourable climate in which to insist on Catholic claims. Some remarks he made in February 1916 suggest that he had adapted the old Irish rebel adage of 'England's difficulty is Ireland's opportunity' to the situation of Australian Catholicism: 'Even when great issues were at stake—perhaps just because they were at stake—a militant minority might be tempted to use its opportunity. At all events a majority that is tyrannical . . . cannot always feel at ease when in a crisis they have to invoke the aid of a minority that feels aggrieved.'

Catholic talk about educational injustice was bad enough. Much worse was Catholic action to remedy it. It was his willingness to take vigorous and determined action that marked off Archbishop Mannix from his episcopal colleagues. Who were these colleagues? In 1914 the Australian church had twenty-two bishops and archbishops. Most of these men took little part in public affairs. Those who did attract public attention, besides Archbishops Carr and Mannix in Melbourne, were Michael Kelly, Archbishop of Sydney, and, to a lesser extent, James Duhig, Archbishop of Brisbane, and Patrick Clune, Archbishop of Perth.

James Duhig's episcopacy was in the Moran tradition: the knighthood conferred upon him in 1959 represented, in a personal symbol, the goal of his endeavours for the church —a harmonious linking of church and state. He was also in the tradition of the first Bishop of Brisbane, Dr Quinn, in his substantial acquisitions of church property, and his wide business and investment interests. And like Quinn, his special work was building, particularly in Catholic education. Duhig's first bishopric was that of Rockhampton, which he occupied in 1905 at the age of thirty-four—the youngest Catholic bishop in the world. In 1912 he became coadjutor to Archbishop Dunne in Brisbane, taking over the see in 1917 when Dunne died. Duhig was, as a bishop, essentially ordinary. A good man, with a love for books, and great zeal for the church, immensely popular in Queensland, his reputation as 'James the builder' sums him up—a man of outstanding practical achievement, but otherwise of little distinction. He had no relish for the tense, fighting atmosphere in which the church lived in the First World War; his natural inclinations were towards the avoidance of conflict, of politics, of arousing animosity. Nevertheless, his duties as a churchman, and his Irish sympathies, occasionally made him the centre of controversy at this time.

Archbishop Clune's public reputation sprang from two circumstances: his consistent advocacy of conscription, in which he was alone among Catholic prelates, and his involvement in 1920 as a peacemaker in the hostilities between England and Ireland. But these things were, basically, aberrations in Clune's career, which was devoted to reducing the crushing debt he inherited in Perth when he took over the diocese in 1911, and to the tasks common to every other Australian bishop of building churches and, always, schools. Clune was no controversialist. A happy, hearty man of great earnestness and zeal, with a lively sense of humour, his greatest talent, outside his remarkable preaching abilities (he was a Redemptorist missionary of wide experience), was for making friends.

And then there was, of course, Michael Kelly, Archbishop of Sydney from 1911 to 1940. Kelly was a man of extraordinary piety but, as Irish opinion had accurately divined, of no great ability. He faced the problems of this time honestly and courageously, but his understanding and vision were limited and ordinary, and his personality lacked human warmth. Besides the dynamic brilliance of Mannix he seemed a dull, phlegmatic and pompous figure. Yet Kelly, with his caution, with his puritan piety, with his adamantine faith and unbendable, holy will, stood rock firm against the world. Its storms and furies expended themselves upon him.

When they passed, he stood square where he had been before. His was a sound policy for anchoring in gales, be they of the devil's or the world's making. When it came to steering the barque of Peter into uncharted seas . . . but Kelly then was old, and he had never been a navigator.

Michael Kelly was born in Ireland in 1850, ordained priest in 1872. The first years of his priestly life were spent at the House of Missions in Enniscorthy, going out on missions in which the preaching of temperance loomed largest, becoming a cause that dominated Kelly's life and absorbed most of his energies. He was associated with Father Cullen, S.J., founder of the Pioneer Total Abstinence Association, and was a central figure in the temperance crusades that were such a feature of Irish religious life from the 1870s.

In 1891 Kelly was appointed Rector *pro tem.* of the Irish College in Rome. (His mother bore his departure from Ireland with fortitude: 'Thank God, my Mother was religiously brave. She said: "May God's will be accomplished" and giving me her blessing she said: "May God grant you a long, a happy and a holy life." ') His appointment to the Irish College was an attempt by the Irish bishops to rescue the College from the slackness into which Monsignor Kirby's ill health and great age (he was nearly ninety) had allowed affairs to drift. As a disciplinarian, Kelly, who tended towards the arbitrary and the petty, was not popular, but he did a great deal to restore a proper order, and financial solvency, to the College. His main problem was, however, to get the Irish bishops vitally interested in the College's affairs.

When Kirby died early in 1895, Kelly was confirmed in the Rectorship which he held until his appointment as coadjutor to Cardinal Moran in June 1901. He was an efficient administrator, but not on any close terms with any of the Irish bishops. Nor was he adept, as Kirby had been, at Vatican politics. But his governance of the College, if undistinguished, was firm. He was firm too in his Irish refusal to attend a solemn Te Deum in Rome on the occasion of the Diamond Jubilee of Queen Victoria in June 1897—his reason was England's misrule of Ireland.

And he took a similar stand towards pro-English demonstrations during the Boer War.

In Sydney, Kelly lived very much in Moran's shadow, carrying out the Cardinal's dictates with a patient, suffering humility, in no way false. Kelly's piety, his ingrained respect for authority, his lack of originality, enjoined him to accept Moran's rule as exercised over him personally. When Moran died and Kelly succeeded him he had nothing new to offer, by way of policy, save a much heavier accentuation on the piety characteristic of Moran.

Kelly's piety merits consideration, as central to his episcopal rule, and as typifying a form of religious life then common in Australia. His piety was narrow, austere, and rigidly disciplined. Its emphasis was on mortification: 'Die to thyself in this life.' Kelly applied this maxim to every aspect of his life, to small things of daily occurrence and routine. 'Reject fancies regarding arrangement of books, ornaments, etc., as leading to forgetfulness of God and spiritual blindness', he instructed himself. He must 'Subdue the enemies of God, of my soul, in my heart following Christ as Leader, attack them, persist until they are beaten down or captured. They are pride, anger, gluttony, avarice.' This was no mere rhetoric. The Archbishop felt himself sorely menaced by these enemies. 'Greediness of the belly', for instance, troubled him intensely: he fought against his desire to eat too much, to take second helpings. 'Plain food taken regularly, sparingly, modestly, religiously': this was the ideal. And anger also troubled him. He must correct his curtness in speech, his brusqueness in manner: 'According to the example of my divine Saviour I should be meek and humble of heart, affable, merciful, mortified, cautious.' And, astonishingly (Satan has his own congruities), Kelly yearned for riches and worldly honour. From these he turned to follow Christ: 'I should follow Him now in renunciation of worldly desires—riches, pleasures, honours and in choosing poverty—spiritual and actual —with humiliations and contempt.'

The result was a spirituality of intense, at times tormented, self-questioning, in long hours of meditation. 'Why my present lethargy, my thoughtlessness and unbelief, living without the fear of God and all happiness and along with this infinite loss knowing the doom of dwelling with devouring fire and everlasting burnings? Why?' 'H. Mass— the renewal of the death and sacrifice of Xt for the salvation of the world—my attention is distracted by other thoughts, my feelings are indevout, my ministry is very much a routine function.'

Kelly was constantly at war with the devil. He saw him clearly, in his mind's eye, 'the evil one', 'seated on a throne of fire, enveloped in smoke, horrible in figure and threatening in aspect.' Milton was one of his favourite authors, particularly in *Paradise Lost,* and he shared that sombre puritan vision on a wide variety of subjects—virtue, pain, sin, merit, pride, passion. His daily meditations show a deep and agonised spiritual life moving in intense personal patterns. Here was a man at war, against self, against pride, against temptation. Here was a man painfully conscious that, at the centre of himself, the eternal war between God and Lucifer was taking place, with his soul as the prize.

Yet, none of this showed: externally the Archbishop appeared as unruffled, maddeningly calm, imperviously aloof. Why? It was partly temperament, but it was also because Kelly was listening to the discipline preached by his inner self: 'In conversation guard every sense esp. the tongue, be friendly but not free with any one, show no displeasure or surprise in any way at anything. Resist motions of aversion or of sympathy, suppress impatience, and haste.' He did not always succeed in living up to his own rigorous code, but his constant attempt to do so, the merciless discipline of the self, came across to others as a colourless evisceration of personality, as chill remoteness and inhumanity. And even this response of dislike by other men fitted Kelly's spiritual plan. He craved popularity, and, seeing this craving as a stumbling block to salvation, sought to destroy it. He actively and deliberately sought 'dishonour among men'. There was ample to be found. He embraced opprobrium, pursued contempt.

In this deeply personal spiritual life there is little glimpse of the daily affairs of men, except in so far as these are, in general, 'vanities and trifles', distractions from holy living. As the Archbishop noted in January 1916, the 'Fascination of earthly things [was] to be resisted in thought and deed'.

The implication of this in relation to Kelly's episcopal leadership is obvious. 'My interests in this world must be secondary and subordinate regarding the Kingdom of God.' He had set his face against 'Inordinate application to affairs external and to occupations of subordinate nature by which attention to God is prevented even during prayer.' To Kelly, the affairs of the world were secondary and subordinate and his entire episcopacy reflects that emphasis. Those involved in the world found him firm in that great truth, but of little help in that multiplicity of problems which beset church and churchmen as living in society.

Kelly's social principles were to moderate a little under the pressure of Australian radicalism, but they were not transformed. Basically he was conservative and hierarchical: 'honour the priest, obey your prelates, humble yourself in all things—have confidence in God.' And from St Paul: 'Let every soul be subject to the higher powers . . .' He was a devotee of Edmund Burke, subscribing to his general conservative outlook, and accepting his particular judgements on law, authority and good government. Aphorisms from Burke held great appeal for him: 'Rather hope for small and safe concessions from the legal power, than boundless objects from trouble and confusion.' He regarded the separation of church and state as intrinsically wicked. He had a high regard for industry and frugality; work was a penance which must be accepted gladly as an aid in resisting concupiscence and preventing temptations. Injustice ought not to exist, but if it did it should be endured in a penitential spirit. At a time of rapid social change, Kelly's disposition was opposed to change, on which he sought to act as a brake, not to channel and direct.

Even in this, Kelly was hampered by the public impression he made. His sense of episcopal dignity often appeared to others as stiff pomposity, and his stilted habit of referring to himself in the episcopal plural 'we' seemed ludicrous, and was much guyed. Even within the church he had a reputation for insensitivity and tactlessness, which resulted in much needless alienation, and the growth of resentment. Such was the Kelly men knew. Their knowledge was small and shallow. Their world was not Kelly's.

Instead of seeing the decorous shelving of the education question, the first months of the war saw a Catholic campaign more intense and aggressive than any since the 1870s, a campaign whose spirit and objectives clashed sharply with the surge of patriotic feeling, and the tide of wider worries released by the war. In October 1914 the Catholic Federation of Victoria began a campaign, in conjunction with the Victorian state elections, for educational rights. The Federation was strongest in Victoria (where it had about 40,000 members) and its campaign was under the active patronage and encouragement of Dr Mannix. This drew national Catholic attention: 'all Catholic eyes are at present on Victoria where for the first time in our history, the anti-Catholic candidate is being really fought by Catholics at the polls, and where even a Labour ticket, wildly flourished, will not save him.' A similar effort had been made by the New South Wales Federation, which had been rebuffed by W. A. Holman as a move to secure 'sectarian domination' of the Labor Party.

The Victorian campaign led to a tremendous rumpus—dragging on into 1916—during which Dr Mannix made very clear what he regarded as the proper relationship between politics and religion: 'There should be no conflict between conscience and the programme of any political party'—and Labor's secular education plank violated Catholic conscience. 'The cause of the Catholic Church is the cause of God and justice, and it cannot be swept aside by any caucus or any party', Mannix declared, warning the Labor Party that if it persisted in its refusal to countenance Catholic educational claims, and to bind its members to accept this refusal, Catholics would withdraw their support.

In May 1915 he went much further, electrifying Victorian political life with a blunt warning:

> The Catholic Church was an organisation which in the past, whenever religion was threatened or conscience violated, had supported, and, if need be, selected, candidates for Parliament, and he could tell the Political Labour Conference that in similar circumstances in the future it would do the same thing again.

Here, frontally, was the threat of a Catholic party. By the

time of Mannix's arrival, Archbishop Carr was thoroughly disillusioned with the Labor Party. He had wanted to give Labor's general social policy his public support, but he refused to identify himself with a party so hostile to Catholic principle. He therefore echoed Mannix's threat: 'There would be created in this State an independent Labour Party which would in the end acquire power and sovereignty.' The nucleus for this was to hand in the Catholic Federation, the hope of militant Catholics, and the horror of militant Protestants.

Swiftly this threat moved towards actuality. In September 1915 a Victorian Catholic Workers' Association was formed, with episcopal approval, for the explicit purpose of working within the Labor Party to secure educational justice. The Labor Party retaliated by expelling members of the Catholic Federation. Mannix came back with reiterated warnings: 'The Catholic Workers' Union was trying to come to the rescue of the Labor Party from within, and if it failed it would have to fight the party from outside.' (Broadly, the Archbishop's tactics were based on the belief that it should be possible for Catholics to secure a balance of political power.) As the dispute continued into 1916, Dr Mannix attributed the Labor Party's growing internal difficulties to its failure to drop its secular education plank. If this was, as a sole explanation, wishful thinking, the Archbishop's strictures and declarations of Catholic intentions cannot have endeared him to Labor leaders, a factor to be born in mind when considering later the anti-Mannix campaign led by W. M. Hughes. In Sydney, Archbishop Kelly made no threats, but attacked the Labor Party on its educational platform. He was also very critical of the failure of Catholic parliamentarians to champion Catholic interests.

Early in 1916 Dr Mannix announced a change already apparent in Catholic Federation policy.

The Federation was, I believe, moderate and sanguine enough to hope that the education question could be settled by reasoning with the politicians . . . That suited the politicians admirably, and they were lavish with soft words and sympathy . . . But the Federation soon came to realise that votes are the only things that move politicians . . . To reason with the average politician, unless you vote against him also, is about as useful as throwing confetti at a rhinoceros.

In New South Wales Dr Maurice O'Reilly had advanced this conclusion much more crudely in 1913: 'We are going to sell ourselves to the highest bidder.' To which the *Daily Telegraph* had then made the predictable retort: 'The Catholic citizens of this State are about to attempt to set up a sectarian domination over the rest of the community and subordinate all civil politics to ecclesiastical rule.'

Dr Mannix's political vigour was received by the public in various ways, anger and delight being two obvious extremes. However, these reactions had one thing in common—astonishment. Not since Cardinal Moran's candidature in 1897 had a Catholic prelate engaged so directly in politics, and the Cardinal's candidature had not been nearly as aggressive or as redolent of potential Catholic political organisation as Dr Mannix's intervention. However, what astonished Dr Mannix was that his activities were regarded as unusual. Within clerical circles at least, he was known, by May 1915, to have expressed surprise at the Australian clergy not having much influence in politics. Obviously he regarded this as unsatisfactory and proposed to remedy it as far as he could.

Dr Mannix was ordained in 1890, and thus his priesthood began at, and continued through, a time of deep clerical involvement and influence in Irish politics. The widespread rejection of the Papal Rescript in 1887, and the Parnell divorce of 1891, convinced the leaders of the Irish church that they were losing the leadership of the Irish people to turbulent and irreligious politicians. Dr Mannix's career in the Irish church was situated in the midst of clerical efforts to regain control over national life. The contrast between this and the Australian situation of clerical non-involvement, was, no doubt, heightened for Dr Mannix by his belief that the Australian church was, of its nature, Irish. In part it was, but its Irish derivation was mainly of a period prior to that of Dr Mannix's experience, and in Australia it was set in a secular environment. Something of the Archbishop's surprise, even bewilderment, is apparent in his comment of April 1917:

I do not remember that up to the time I came to Australia I ever took part in controversy of any sort or description. The reason for the change that has come in my habit of life must be that in the old countries I had never come into close official contact with people like some of those I have met since I came to Australia.

A more fundamental reason for the change would seem to be the Archbishop's pursuance of assertive Irish clerical policies in an environment fundamentally unsympathetic or hostile. He saw clearly the blindness of a secular community alien to religious values. He saw its failure to act from spiritual or moral motives. But he did not appreciate the degree of venom and hatred with which that community would strike back at him.

Mannix said precisely what he thought, however offensive it might appear to non-Catholics. 'The age of persecution, we are asked to believe, is over. Catholics are not any longer flogged for not attending non-Catholic worship. True, but they are still fined, and fined heavily, for not sending their children to non-Catholic schools.' This was the negative side of his social crusade, the destruction of injustice. The positive side—the creation of justice—was no less threatening to established society. 'Catholics might justly hope to secure, without fear or favour, their due and proportionate share of the good things that Australia has to offer', Mannix insisted, claiming that Catholics, comprising one-quarter of the population, held not one-tenth of the wealth, influence and positions that they ought to have. And, in all things a practical actionist, he set out to do what he could to redress this situation—which endeavour was a salient element in his educational policy.

At the top of his educational structure he placed a keenly perceptive evaluation of university education and Catholic intellectual life. In his inaugural address in March 1913 he stated: 'The progress and development of Australia is essentially bound up with the University.' He foresaw the 'greatest danger if Catholics were to stand aloof from the universities', for this would deprive the Catholic community of learning and culture, of leaders, and of vital influence on the future history of Australia. So he embarked forthwith on the campaign which led to the laying of the foundation stone of Newman College, in the University of Melbourne, in June 1916 and to its opening in March 1918. And he embarked too on that general encouragement of intellectual life which was such a notable feature of his episcopacy. His support, in 1917, of the Catholic monthly review *Australia,* with its programme of Christian social reform, and his fostering of Father Hackett's establishment of a Central Catholic Library in Melbourne in 1924, were indicative of the value he placed on a free and lively Catholic intellectual life.

How positive was Mannix's attitude in this may be discerned from a contrast with the situation in Sydney. Both Moran and Kelly were suspicious of the University of Sydney, believing that it endangered the souls of Catholic students. Moran's relations with St John's College had not been good: it was, after all, a construction of the Benedictines. 'He has . . . a heavy cross & crown of thorns with *St John's* College—*its fellows & Rector',* sighed Bishop Reynolds in commiseration with Moran in 1885. The reference was to the College's unwillingness to surrender itself to Moran's complete control. This friction came to a head when a relatively minor incident, construed by Moran as a slight, caused him to walk out of a Fellows' meeting, never to return. However, other factors, not the least of which was the low output from Catholic schools of aspirants to university education, were probably more important in the College's steady decline in scholarship, student numbers and general prestige, notable at this time. Under Archbishop Kelly, Dr Maurice O'Reilly, of the Vincentian Order, was made Rector. His stormy political activities did the College no good, nor could he and the Archbishop get on together. Their disagreements had led, by the early 1920s, to a situation of mutually frustrating hostility, neatly illustrated by the Archbishop's presenting himself at the College, with stiff formality, as College Visitor bent on exercising his authority, only to find the Rector deliberately absent.

As the war extended into 1915, so did the education campaign, spread by the Catholic Federation to all states. Its tenor jarred discordantly against the trumpets of war. 'There is no subject of greater importance to a State than national

THE BARGAINERS.

"Oh! Australia, my country my heart bleeds for you."

XIII Cartoon comment on the public statements of Archbishops Kelly and Mannix: *Daily Telegraph*, 9 May 1918

XIV A Protestant Federation leaflet issued during the 1922 N.S.W. election campaign

education', the *Catholic Press* announced in the face of claims that the survival of civilisation was at stake: 'The struggle for the schools is a struggle of life against death'—but the struggle which obsessed the general public was war against Germany. While the patriots were shouting that Australians must band together to win the war, Catholic spokesmen were insisting that Catholics must band together to secure their rights. The president of the Catholic Federation, P. S. Cleary, announced that Catholics must fight—fight until the Sisters and Brothers obtained some recompense from the state for the great public service they rendered by bringing up educated, valiant and patriotic Australians. But pressure from the Catholic Federation on the New South Wales Labor Party had yielded nothing except some minor concessions (for instance, a grant of £2,000 towards Catholic hospitals) and a continual howl of sectarianism.

Both Federal and state governments sought the co-operation of the church in fostering recruiting. Even those bishops who co-operated most actively, such as Archbishop Kelly (Holman wrote to him personally), were viewing government policy on war matters with increasing disquiet. The 'War Census' Act of July 1915 compelled registration of Australian resources, both of wealth and of manpower. This provoked considerable annoyance and some alarm in clerical circles: annoyance because it required all clergy to state their income and the value of their property, and was thus regarded as an intrusion into the church's affairs, and alarm, because it raised the suspicion that taxation or conscription of church property or clerical persons might be coming. The anti-clerical history of European governments in the nineteenth century had made the clergy very sensitive indeed to any hint of state interference. Archbishop Duhig feared that the 'War Census' Act, emanating as it did from a Labor government, might be the thin end of a wedge of socialistic legislation aimed at confiscation of Catholic property. Dr Mannix shared this general suspicion. In France priests served as ordinary conscripts in the front line. Clearly Mannix had the continental religious situation very much in mind in his criticism of the 'pestilent and godless' refusal of the Labor Party to accept Catholic principles. 'The

Catholics of Australia know how the very same principles which are now being sown by certain politicians here had almost destroyed religion and morality in France, and other countries.'

Dr Mannix's reference was to freemasonry, a threat which loomed large in his mind. 'Already in this democratic country of ours, Freemasonry had planted itself on the neck of the nation. It was a huge tumour growing upon the life and blood of the whole of the country.' And Dr Mannix pointed out that on W. M. Hughes's own admission, free-masonry was rampantly parasitic in the Labor Party. He suggested to the Catholic Federation that it prepare a list of freemasons for use at election times. Archbishop Kelly was no less convinced of the prevalent malignity of free-masonry; he considered that it was responsible for the refusal of the University of Sydney to permit the extension of University lectures to the College of the Sacred Heart nuns at Elizabeth Bay.

A variety of other government activities, both state and Federal, strengthened Catholics' misgivings. German Catholic priests were interned. Kelly protested: 'They are just as much Australians as we are. Some have been here for twenty years or so.' The equation, however understandable, was very dangerous: increasingly the public was accepting what the Archbishop said as true—that the Irish Catholics were just as much Australians as the Germans, that is, not Australians at all. More and more Catholics were awakening to a pressure which insisted that they were, basically, a foreign community. Also W. M. Hughes, who became Prime Minister in October 1915, did not attract Catholic trust. As Attorney-General earlier in that year, his legislation on marriage had come under strong Catholic condemnation as encouraging easier divorce.

The New South Wales Premier, W. A. Holman, was even more unacceptable, being continually accused of anti-Catholic animus. As early as 1914 the *Catholic Press* had begun characterising him as a trickster, and was upbraiding Catholics in his ministry for allowing him to get away with it. Yet Holman's extraordinary personal gifts and political brilliance continued to dazzle many men, including Arch-bishop Kelly, with whom Holman made it his business to ingratiate himself. Kelly responded with a kind of ponderous friendliness, solicitous of Holman's health and apologetic in a minimising, embarrassed way, about the issues that divided them. Thus, in 1915, he wrote to Holman: 'I had proposed to write to you this evening intimating my views in publishing a pastoral letter on the Schools . . . It is not to shape or propose any political action but to focus Catholic opinion and to instruct the well-meaning public.' Here was action of the kind described by Mannix as confetti thrown at a rhinoceros. The laity, and particularly the Catholic Federation, was, however, using ammunition that stung. By the end of 1915 tempers in the New South Wales cabinet had risen to the point of discussing how the Catholic annoyance might be ended by setting Catholics at each other's throats. The education issue apart, there was another issue of great importance. In so far as Catholic lay opinion was working class—and it predominantly was—it was increasingly critical of the failure of Labor governments to stop war profiteering and rises in the cost of living; in general, critical of their drift away from working-class policies.

So, all in all, by 1916 relations between the Catholic church and Australian governments, and between Catholics and non-Catholics, were, to say the least, unsympathetic. Increasingly, the loyalty of Catholics was coming under public question. In June 1915 the *Sydney Morning Herald* insinuated that the papacy favoured the German cause. Accusations that Catholics were shirking their obligations to join the army and help the war effort became so prevalent that they could not be ignored. One of the most vigorous denials came from Dr Mannix, a denial coupled with a scathing counter-attack. Despite, he said, the fact that Catholics lacked freedom for their religion and schools, despite the anti-papal and anti-Irish material featured by the press, despite the domination of the army by bigoted freemasons, Catholics had, nevertheless, joined the army in full proportional strength.

Mannix infuriated patriotic elements because he consistently refused to accept the war as the yardstick by which everything in Australia must be measured. He was forever dragging in social and moral issues, such as abortion: 'It was well known that there were medical men in Australia who were putting more lives out of existence in a year than one of those big German guns could do during the whole war. Yet for these and other crimes there was to be no shame, no humility, no humiliation.' And Mannix's references to the war effort were irreverent, with cheeky jibes at the God of the patriots: 'there have been found a few irresponsible persons to question the loyalty of the Catholic body. If the Catholics would only do the fighting, these people would undertake to look after the division of the spoils—among themselves of course.' 'The Catholic schools . . . have been singled out as breeding grounds of disloyalty. Probably the nuns have not been enlisting in sufficient numbers.' Archbishop Carr was insisting that the Pope wanted men to pray for peace, not for victory. Mannix, as well as hammering this point, was critical of the conduct of the war, seeing the lust to destroy Germany utterly as unjust, seeing England as too arrogant to deserve victory, and Gallipoli as a blunder. His plea was 'for a wider, nobler, better-informed patriotism here in Australia'—beginning with fair play for the Catholic church, 'the one institution that by her religious system, of which her schools are an essential part, opposes any effective bulwark against the two enemies of your policy, class warfare and racial decay.'

The simmering cauldron of antagonism was set boiling by the Irish rebellion of Easter 1916. In Australia the issues this raised were not only Irish issues—the proportion of Irish-born persons living in Australia was about three per cent—but also Catholic issues. Ireland, and its treatment by England, became the symbol for many Australian Catholics of their own oppressed position.

When war broke out, Home Rule for Ireland was regarded in Australia as virtually certain. In 1913, for instance, many Irish-Australian organisations were making arrangements to send representatives to the anticipated opening of an Irish Parliament in Dublin. In fact, Australian Irishry prior to 1916 was neither aggressive nor particularly strong. Of 185,000 Catholics in Sydney and its suburbs, only 4,685 attended the 1914 St Patrick's Day celebrations, which were, by this time, teetering on the verge of collapse through lack of patronage. As to 'loyalty', even as late as March 1916 the St Patrick's Day procession in Melbourne halted outside the Federal Parliament House while 'God Save the King' was played. The Home Rule solution to the Irish problem suited the Australian-Irish admirably. Ireland would be, like Australia, free within the British Empire. The Australian-Irish could thus reconcile, without difficulty, their old and their new loyalties: they could be loyal to Ireland, Australia and the Empire, all at once, without any conflict.

The Irish rebellion in April 1916 altered this radically by posing loyalty to Ireland and loyalty to the Empire as alternatives. Irishmen, aided by Germany, had taken up arms against Britain, which was fighting Germany with Australian aid. Small wonder that Irish-Australians reacted to the rebellion with almost unanimous condemnation— including Dr Mannix, who described the rebellion as 'truly deplorable', 'lamentable', and referred to its leaders as 'misguided'. However, Dr Mannix, like Archbishop Kelly, was quick to blame the rebellion on British provocation, particularly Britain's failure to repress the Ulster Unionists led by Sir Edward Carson, who had threatened to rebel if Home Rule was implemented. The execution of the leaders of the rebellion, followed by a protracted period of martial law, violence, mass arrests and deportations, rapidly turned Irish-Australian opinion sour. English policy, contrasting with the lenient treatment of Ulster Unionists and South African rebels, was seen as discriminating against the Irish, a calculated and vicious affront and humiliation, bitter repayment for Irish, and Irish-Australian, loyalty to England and to England's war.

The real significance of the Easter rebellion in Dublin was not that it alienated the Australian-Irish from the British government, but that it seemed to them to show that government to be ruthlessly and vindictively alienated from the Irish. Archbishops Kelly and Duhig, no less than Dr Mannix (though in less strident and less scarifying terms), attacked British policy in Ireland: What was the war being fought for? Where were the rights of small nations now? Where was freedom? Where was humanity? Soon, a majority of Australian-Irish were condemning both the rebellion and the retaliatory measures taken by British authority. To Australia's jingoes, and even to those of less extreme patriotism—including some Catholics—any criticism of England, in the circumstances, seemed arrantly disloyal, seditious. Many Irish-Australians, and some politicians, notably W. A. Holman, keenly appreciated the explosive Australian potential of the Irish situation, and sought to avoid the emergence of a division of loyalty by pressing the British government to grant Home Rule immediately. They failed.

The months following the rebellion seethed with bitter emotions. In September, Dr Mannix spoke out on the key question. 'Irishmen,' he said, 'are as loyal to the Empire to which, fortunately or unfortunately, they belong, as self-respecting people could be under the circumstances.' At last what had been whispered, hinted—and evaded—was emerging into the open. Taxed by the *Argus* with disloyalty and with condoning rebellion, Dr Mannix spelt out what he understood by loyalty: ' . . . if he could not be loyal to the Commonwealth and to the Empire without forgetting his own people in Dublin and Ireland, then he was no longer loyal to the Empire. The hypothesis was, of course, absurd.' Absurd to Dr Mannix perhaps, but entirely logical to those who regarded Ireland as rebelliously treacherous. Dr Mannix held that 'Catholics could be loyal to the Commonwealth and loyal to their own people'. Others, however, did not.

An over-simplification may clarify the contrast. Dr Mannix's loyalties were, in this order, Catholicism, Ireland, Australia, the Empire and Britain—and he regarded Britain as having been disloyal to Ireland on its failure to implement a Home Rule Act which had already been passed. The loyalties of, say, W. M. Hughes, were (if one is to except his considerable loyalty to himself) first the Empire and/ or Britain, and second Australia. If these contrasting loyalties were to be brought into direct conflict, what would happen? To Archbishop Mannix, Catholicism and Ireland were the dominant realities, the focal points of his loyalties. Hughes cared nothing for Catholicism, and although he was in England, and in consultation with the British government at the time of the Irish rebellion, and though he had been asked from Australia to intercede on Ireland's behalf, he had done nothing, said nothing, to mitigate English repression, let alone to suggest that Home Rule be implemented.

On Mannix's loyalties, another comment needs to be made. Archbishop Carr died in May 1917. Over 100,000 people filed past his body as it lay in front of the High Altar of St Patrick's Cathedral. His greatest achievement had been in building Catholic schools. 'His best books were written in the hearts of the children,' said Mannix. And Mannix also said, in panegyric: 'People thought it strange that, as he [Carr] grew older, he became, as they said, more aggressive.' Carr, retiring, gentle, patient, tactful, calm, his religious life deep and sensitive, a man of prayer, had in his later years savoured the ashes of his illusions. He had trusted parliament and politicians to give Catholics educational justice: trust in others was at the centre of his character. His heart hardened as he saw, with approaching death, that his trust had been misplaced; that those who complimented him on his moderation ignored the claims he urged so moderately. He died, nearly eighty, thwarted, disillusioned, beaten by his own gentlemanly reticence, by his naivete in the shrewd ways of the world—and he died in total, outspoken support for the policy of vigorous, assertive belligerence adopted by his coadjutor. Mannix said of Carr, at his death:

> When he came to Melbourne he had great faith in the justice and the fairness of the Australian people. He came with the generous hope that if, in season and out of season, the Catholic claims were stated clearly and moderately, public opinion would revolt against the manifest injustice done to Catholics . . . in his last years, he was forced to recognise that mere appeals to reason and justice were unavailing, and that other measures —more crude perhaps, but more effective in the conduct of public affairs—should be resorted to.

Mannix himself hoped for great things from Australia. By 1916 there was little to suggest that his hopes, like Carr's trust, had been correctly placed.

This is by way of explanation: the fact was that within the Catholic hierarchy Mannix and Carr were foremost in their determination to take a hard line. When news of the Dublin insurrection reached Australia, Archbishop Kelly had invited Archbishops Carr and Mannix to sign a cable from the Australian bishops to John Redmond, leader of the

Irish Parliamentary Party at Westminster, 'deploring and condemning German-managed Irish rising' as 'anti-patriotic, irrational, wickedly irreligious'. They refused. Carr thought 'it might be regarded as slaying the slain to express united condemnation of the action of the insurgents', and said they believed such an action might cause embarrassment to the Irish bishops, whose actions and attitudes they did not know. This opinion, however, did not deter Kelly.

Nor was the Irish rebellion a signal for Catholics to cease their activity. On the contrary. A Dublin Relief Fund to aid distress in the devastated city was set up at meetings throughout Australia, to the fury of loyalists. The Catholic Federation embarked on a new membership campaign. The education controversy flared up again in mid-1916. When the government closed Lutheran schools, Dr Mannix warned that a similar fate might at any time overtake Catholic schools on the plea that they were disloyal, or a menace to the state. As the tide of questioning of Irish Catholic loyalty grew daily stronger, so did Mannix's statements grow more provocative. 'Catholics,' he said, 'should be on the side of the Pope. They should look forward to and pray for peace.' This sounded like neutrality, at best; and at the Orange Lodge celebrations of July 1916 the first calls for Mannix's deportation were made. Meanwhile, under this pressure, Catholics were, in general, becoming ultra-sensitive, their ranks closing prior to battle.

Conscription was a culminating point. When W. M. Hughes announced, on 30 August 1916, that a referendum would be held to decide this matter, a flock of existing divisions and dissatisfactions, fears and hatreds, with all the bitter and violent emotions they had spawned and fed, came home to roost on that single issue.

The entirety of the conscription issue falls outside the scope of this history, but its religious aspects fall within it. Given Dr Mannix's vigorous opposition to conscription, an obvious question is—did conscription raise religious or moral issues in itself? It did. But these were glimpsed only faintly, if at all, and there was division of Catholic opinion. Conscription had been discussed, as a moral question, as early as September 1915, by a group of leading Sydney clergy. They could come to no conclusion. Dr Mannix's references to this point were general and equivocal: 'conscription is a hateful thing, and is almost certain to bring evil in its train.' Archbishop Kelly, apparently, did not think it a moral question, for he declared: 'every Catholic was free to express his own personal opinion and act up to it. The priest had no opinions to offer on that subject.' Archbishop Duhig was sufficiently perturbed as to solicit advice from the Apostolic Delegate, Archbishop Cerretti. The Delegate, in a reply that was made public, stated that the church did not have the right to intervene in the conscription campaign and, in consequence, Catholics should vote as their consciences dictated: the question of conscription did not affect the church as a church. Bishop Phelan of Sale came out publicly on the same ground of church neutrality.

At first glance it might seem that Dr Mannix emphatically disagreed with this view. He had said:

> I claim the right, and I mean to exercise the right to give my views for what they are worth, on conscription or on any other public question to all those who care to listen or to read. We all have the right, perhaps sometimes the duty, to contribute our quota to the formation of that public opinion which, in the last resort, is the sovereign power in a democratic country like Australia.

What he was maintaining was that his episcopal office was no bar to the expression of opinion to which he was entitled as a citizen. This raised the point that it was a little much to expect the public to separate his views from the office he held, and also that the occasions he used to publicise his views, to vast crowds, were usually official occasions, openings and foundation-stone layings. Against this it must be noted that Archbishop Clune made his opinion clear, in favour of conscription; that Archbishop Duhig's personal view was that 'we are not prepared to bleed our country white, in order to make the reputation of an ambitious politician'; that Bishop Phelan stated his personal opposition to conscription, and his contempt for the attitude of the Protestant churches where 'Loyalty to the Crown or Imperial patriotism, as it is called, seems to form an essential part of the religious worship.' However, the point to be made is that no Catholic ecclesiastic regarded the conscription issue as a moral one in its own right. Rather, they regarded it as one of practical politics, of social and national outlook, of personal judgement.

But it did have serious implications for the church. These became a dominating matter in the clergy's eyes early in 1917, after the first conscription referendum but before the second. New Zealand had begun to enforce its Conscription Act in November 1916. Already in Australia, the mobilisation scheme which preceded the first referendum had thrown the position of the clergy into some doubt; some Army authorities wanted to oblige the clergy to prove that they were entitled to exemptions, a matter which Archbishop Kelly took up with the Minister of Defence. The implementation of conscription in New Zealand led to grave alarm: priests were called up and had to argue their case for exemption before a magistrate.

Immediately, latent clerical hostility in Australia was crystallised. From then on, if they had not done so before, most Australian priests regarded conscription as a direct threat to the church. In November 1917 Archbishop Kelly protested to W. M. Hughes against the exclusion from ecclesiastical immunity, in the projected conscription arrangements, of seminarians and brothers. He told Hughes that this would upset schools and clerical supplies and consequently excite deep-seated and general Catholic opposition. If Hughes had not agreed—which he did by return mail—to extend immunity to seminarians and brothers, several New South Wales bishops, consulted by Kelly, believed that the bishops should appeal publicly to the people to defeat conscription. Even so, Hughes's reputation was so low in clerical circles that his assurance was not enough. Many clerics believed that no reliance could be placed on promises of exemption after a conscription act had been passed. The remedy was obvious: defeat conscription.

The hardening of clerical attitudes in 1917 was also a product of the venoms of the first referendum campaign. Archbishop Kelly, for one, was appalled at the divisive furies that had been unleashed. 'The question of conscription was not one to divide the people about', he complained. He went on to criticise jingoes and super-patriots. 'Those who went in for war were not Christians. Those who would

press people beyond their wish to go were not true demo-
crats.' Kelly attacked the government as 'the enemies of
freedom of conscience, of civic liberty, as long as they kept
Catholic schools at a disadvantage.' In Sydney, the general
clerical feeling was that the government was under 'bitter
Orange and Masonic influence'. It was widely believed that
Hughes had actively fostered the flood of anti-Catholic
propaganda then prevalent.

Nevertheless, the fact remains that the element of opposition to conscription led by Dr Mannix was essentially the
product of pre-existing hostilities and divisions. It applied
very practical emotions and logic to the situation. The
Catholic Press summed up one theme when it queried:
'Surely it is reasonable that before Irishmen and their sons
in Australia are conscripted, we should ask the Imperial
Government why this force [in Ireland] of at least 70,000
men are not sent to the front, and Ireland granted the
freedom which is enjoyed by other parts of the Empire.'
Then there was Hughes, the traitor to Labor. Was not
conscription merely a device he was using for his own
personal ends, to endear himself to the English Tories who
had persecuted Ireland? And there were questions of national
interest, and of fact. Men were needed at home to develop
Australia: Mannix did not invent this argument, it had been
a strong conviction and often repeated observation in
Catholic circles since the outbreak of war. Moreover,
Mannix's comment that 'Australia has done her full share,
and more' reflected an opinion common among Catholics.

But these arguments, however strongly and sincerely
held, sprang from and bolstered attitudes formed before
the particular issue of conscription arose. In brief, they
derived from a deep conviction, formed in the long struggle
over education, and driven home sharply by what had
happened in Ireland, that the dominant forces in Australian
society sought to exclude or demean Catholics. In fighting
conscription, Dr Mannix led a crusade against those dominant forces, a crusade whose supporters saw conscription
as a summation and symbol of a history of manifold
oppressions. Conscription seemed to them the programme
of the ascendancy party in microcosm.

It is obvious why Dr Mannix commanded the support

he did: because he expressed what many Catholics felt—
a sense of oppression, of injustice. He was the spokesman
of a group who felt isolated from, and penalised by, Australian society. As to his own personal motives, certainly
he saw himself as a spokesman for the Catholic people: he
openly claimed this. It must be an interesting point for
speculation whether or not Dr Mannix saw in the conscription split of the Labor Party perhaps a providential means
of securing that more Catholic, more Christian Labor Party
he so ardently desired. Of the twenty-four Federal members
who defected from Labor over conscription, twenty-one were
Protestants, and Catholics were much more important in
the Labor Party after the split.

Archbishop Mannix was the most spectacular figure on
the anti-conscription side, but the vast majority of Catholic
bishops and clergy opposed conscription, some quite out-
spokenly. Mannix had a Sydney counterpart in Dr Maurice
O'Reilly, Rector of St John's College. By the end of 1917
O'Reilly's public reputation for 'disloyalty' rivalled Mannix's.
He attracted the fairly general support of the Sydney clergy,
and the detestation of Catholics of wealth and position.
Dr Herbert Moran summed up O'Reilly as 'one of the
enfants terribles of the Australian Catholicism. A great
clerical egoist, he was also a man of charm and culture,
gifted, witty, but loving the limelight.'

Where most priests differed from Drs Mannix and O'Reilly
was not in their attitude on conscription, but in tactics.
Their problem was not usually whether they opposed conscription or not—mostly they did—but whether it was
appropriate that they should say so publicly. A group of
Sydney priests discussed precisely that question. One
consideration restraining some priests was the simple fact
that someone—Mannix in particular—was already doing
the job admirably. Another influential factor was the spirited
public reaction to Dr Mannix's stand, and the vexed question
of whether his activity was doing more harm than good to
the church.

The lay Catholic reaction was another matter. Mannix's
anti-conscription campaign soon made public the division in
social attitudes between the small group of 'upper class'
Catholics, men of some wealth and social position who

occupied places within established society, and the great majority of Catholics who were workers or in the lower middle class, and who felt alienated from society. 'Upper class' Catholic criticism of Archbishop Mannix came to a head in November 1917 with a series of newspaper letters from Mr Justice Heydon of Sydney, maintaining that the Archbishop had taken up a position alien to Australian sentiment, and disassociating himself, as a Catholic, from Mannix's statements. Mannix hit back, with untypical pettiness, by referring to Heydon as 'a second or third class judge', who 'could not have got as many to listen to him as would have filled a lolly shop'.

In response to this, a number of prominent Catholic professional men, mainly in law or medicine, also publicly declared themselves against Mannix's views. Sir Thomas Hughes may be taken as typical in his accusation that the Archbishop was setting race against race, class against class, was fanning old world quarrels, was attempting to set up an Irish republican organisation in Australia, and was, indeed, disloyal. Such protests as those by Hughes and Heydon point to the socio-economic basis of the conscription split. As members of the establishment, these Catholics accepted its attitudes and values and were grievously embarrassed when a leader of their church directly challenged these attitudes. Appeals were made to the Apostolic Delegate to have Mannix silenced. Incidents occurred of such Catholics walking out of Mass in protest against some priest's anti-conscriptionist attitudes, or even of standing up during sermons to contradict preachers. There were, of course, others who refused to associate socially with those who had criticised Mannix.

It would be untrue to say that conscription split the Catholic community—Catholic members of the establishment were too few to constitute a split. However, conscription did create a discernible and important rift, bred a good deal of anti-clericalism among Catholics of wealth and position, and demonstrated that social and economic factors could disrupt, as well as unite, the Catholic body. The conscription controversy showed that the natural lay leaders of the Catholic laity were far removed, by their socio-economic position and cast of mind, from those they might have led—led in such matters as the education crusade.

It was Dr Mannix's tactics that made him famous, combined with, and perhaps overshadowed by, the circumstances of the conscription campaign. He was the only major public figure in the anti-conscription forces, and as such came under concentrated conscriptionist fire, particularly from W. M. Hughes. The Prime Minister's direct attacks substantially increased the Archbishop's public stature in the eyes of both friend and foe. More importantly, Catholic circumstances called for leadership, for a hero, and Dr Mannix was well fitted for that role. He dared to say what others thought. He had a calm, deliberate, yet forceful and pungent style. He rarely spoke at much length. His remarks were not, like Archbishop Kelly's, buried in a sea of words. (Of Kelly, Herbert Moran remarked with unkind truth that his addresses 'touched always on all subjects without illuminating them'.) What Mannix had to say was astringently sharp and unavoidable, with an edge of taunting sarcasm which evoked a laughter tinged with relish. His giant meetings (up to 100,000 people, few of whom heard what he said) were enormous public attractions, circuses. And his democratic inclinations, pro-worker, anti-capitalist, drew the Catholic working class to him. The Archbishop seems to have enjoyed his chosen task, even at times to have been carried away by the momentum of his own cutting wit. The taste of action, of public influence, and of adulation, appears to have been not without its sweetness.

But what most established Dr Mannix's fame was the unexpected defeat of the first conscription referendum in October 1916. Analysis of the results suggests that his influence was not a deciding factor: Victoria, with the greatest proportion of Catholics, voted in favour of conscription; South Australia, with a much smaller Catholic proportion, rejected conscription. However, Dr Mannix and the Irish Catholic opposition were the most spectacular and publicity-catching element in the anti-conscription campaign; and the immediate, but erroneous, public assumption was that Dr Mannix was responsible for conscription's defeat. It was bad enough that conscription—which had been equated with loyalty and patriotism—had been defeated: that it had been defeated by priestcraft was intolerable. Obviously, to many Protestants, Catholicism, as led by Dr Mannix, stood revealed for what it was: a dangerous and subversive power.

From the end of 1916, an unprecedented storm of sectarianism swept across Australia, identifying Catholicism with disloyalty, with tyranny, with German money and power. Dr Mannix stood firm, 'unchanged and unrepentant' as he put it himself, against this blast, symbolising Catholicism not only for its opponents but for most of its adherents. One of the major issues of the second referendum may be said to be Dr Mannix, representing Catholicism. He was, as he said, 'made a sort of lightning conductor for all the abuse of the State of Victoria'. He drew to himself, and to the Catholic church, all the hostility which had been accumulating around Catholic activity and opinions over the previous several years—since 1911, or earlier. The emotions generated by the Catholic education campaign, by Catholic organisation, by Catholic political pressures, by Catholic reactions to the Irish rebellion, had all exploded when touched by the spark of conscription. When his most extreme opponents demanded the deportation of Dr Mannix (and sometimes also Archbishop Kelly), they were in fact demanding the deportation of Catholicism; for Dr Mannix symbolised, more than any other man, those features of Catholicism which they hated most: its demand for educational justice, its political potential, its uncompromising moral rigour, and its refusal to keep quiet.

What was fundamentally at issue at this time, so far as Catholicism was involved, was not conscription, but the place of Catholics within Australian society. This fundamental issue was, as always, closely related to the question of state recognition of Catholic educational claims. Throughout the whole conscription crisis it is remarkable how constantly Archbishop Mannix kept returning to this matter. So did his opponents: they claimed that Dr Mannix was using German money to build his Catholic schools and churches. The Archbishop treated this accusation as a joke. He was reported to have told an audience:

> One man, thinking of the money needed to erect the Catholic
> schools and churches . . . had said, 'Ah, these Catholics, and
> especially Dr Mannix, have plenty of German money at the
> present time.' (Laughter) Well, if they had, he hoped it would
> keep coming. He could engage to make use . . . of a good deal
> more German money if it came their way.

This sort of levity infuriated loyalists, especially when
coupled with the thrust that, over education, Catholics 'were
being robbed right and left, and everybody knew it'.

Nor would Archbishop Kelly, in the middle of the conscription campaign, allow the public to forget education.
For instance, in July 1917 he created a sensation with his
claim that Fort Street school was 'doing the devil's work . . .
by driving true religion out'. Kelly's views on secular education were very decided. He noted, privately, in September
1918, that:

> sin and filth are the result of one cause; and that cause is
> everyday Godlessness such as our public schools are largely
> responsible for. This system is responsible for a want of
> vital Christianity, of a lack of faith and religion that pene-
> trates the human fibre and makes God and morality a factor
> in every deed. Deprived of this, youth has nothing to fall
> back on when the hour of temptation comes; and when he
> falls, nothing to keep him from the bottom of the pit.

Kelly did not regard the war as in any way diminishing his
admonitory duties as a churchman. 'Do I warn all committed
to my charge as a Bishop of the devouring fire and everlasting
burnings reserved for sinners?' he asked himself. And
Mannix, in the midst of the conscription controversy,
asserted that birth control—race suicide he called it—was
a greater enemy to Australia than either Germany or
Austria.

'For the Catholic, all peace is now gone': the sectarian
aftermath of the conscription campaigns was of a kind
symbolised neatly by the formation in Brisbane in January
1917 of an organisation called the League of Loyalty to the
Empire and for the Protection of Civil and Religious Rights,
which spread quickly to other states. Only the major features
of the sectarian war deserve attention.

It was particularly intense in Queensland where T. J.
Ryan had been a Catholic Labor Premier since 1915.

Allegations that the government was priest-ridden, favoured
Catholics, and was disloyal came thick and fast, particularly
after Ryan had declared his opposition to conscription.

Mannix continued to provide grist for sectarian mills.
His celebrated comment of January 1917 that 'as a matter
of fact, this was a trade war—simply an ordinary trade
war', sent his critics into a paroxysm of rage. Was this
disloyalty? What is usually overlooked is that the Archbishop argued out this interpretation, that it was quite a
common one among other commentators, and that it was an
interpretation for which there was, in fact, a good case.

And there were other focuses for sectarian eruptions. At
the end of 1918 a fierce tussle developed in New South
Wales between church and state over the refusal of the
health authorities to allow Catholic chaplains to visit dying
influenza victims in the Quarantine Station. Dr Maurice
O'Reilly, speaking in the Sydney Town Hall, promised the
government that Catholics would remember when the next
election came. Archbishop Kelly presented himself at the
gates of the North Head Quarantine Station, demanding
admittance, and was turned away. Catholic protest meetings
were held throughout Australia, the Catholic community
seething with indignation at what was taken to be an attempt
by the state to deprive Catholic souls of their last sacramental consolations. Indeed, it was a common clerical and
lay view that the limitation of church services imposed by
health authorities in the 1918-19 influenza epidemic was a
disguised attempt to erode the independence of the church,
and convert it into a department of the state.

The Father Jerger case, in 1920, seemed to Catholics to
raise similar principles. Father Jerger was a German
Passionist priest interned in 1916 after complaints against
the pro-German content of his sermons at Marrickville.
When, in July 1920, it became known that the government
intended to deport him, some Catholics boasted publicly that
he would be rescued and set free. Throughout Australia,
Catholic demonstrations proclaimed Jerger a religious martyr
to a persecuting state, and demanded that he be released.
This provoked counter-demonstrations insisting that he be
deported—which he was, but not before much drama,
threats of a seamen's strike, a comic-opera attempt of rescue

at sea, and a veritable maelstrom of abuse and counter-abuse.

But what really sustained, embittered and protracted the sectarian war of 1916-25 was the situation in Ireland. This period saw the 1916 rebellion and its aftermath, leading to the Irish war for independence against Britain, the Anglo-Irish Treaty of December 1921 and the Civil War in Ireland 1922-3. These events, particularly the terrible inhumanities of the Anglo-Irish war of 1919-21, with its Black and Tans, its assassinations, murders, and destruction, cast a deep shadow over the affairs of the Catholic community in Australia. As Archbishop Mannix had said: 'the Ireland that England was to do justice to was not merely the Ireland at home, but also that Ireland of men and women who were scattered to the ends of the earth.'

Archbishop Mannix, of course, was in the forefront of protest against British policy in Ireland. Other bishops were less forthcoming on this painful subject. Nevertheless, when, in 1918, Archbishop Kelly canvassed the Australian hierarchy about making joint public protest against the introduction of conscription into Ireland, only Archbishop Duhig was against this as he thought it was unnecessary, and calculated to arouse bitter feeling in Australia. As to Archbishop Kelly, his temperament and convictions were against clerical involvement in such contentious affairs. Particularly in 1920 and 1921, he devoted much time and energy to an attempt to restrain and discipline such priests as the irrepressible Maurice O'Reilly, Dr Tuomey and Father M. D. Forrest, M.S.C., who were free and fierce in their public denunciations of British policy in Ireland. Kelly's reasoning was that priests must minister to all men, and that: 'By political utterance and party propaganda on the part of any priest many are alienated from the Sacraments, even in death itself, to our knowledge.' Thus, he admonished a Wollongong priest advertised to lecture on Irish Questions: 'Attend to the teaching of the Catechism, parochial instructions in matters of faith and good works, the Confessional, the Schools, the house visitation, and regularly priestly study.' Kelly's general view of the public role of the clergy was: 'The relations of a priest towards the world are truly illustrated by a ship afloat. She must be in the waters yet the waters must not be in her.' In mid-1923 he sent a memorandum to Catholic newspapers, cautioning them against 'Doctrinal, Controversial, Contentious party political and sectional contributions by the Clergy.'

Yet, despite even these firm principles, the whirlpool of public disputation sucked Kelly towards it. He found himself publicly linked with disloyalty and violence no less than was Mannix. He was misrepresented, as far afield as the London *Times,* as having said at the St Patrick's Day sports in 1919: 'I do not mind blood, I do not mind slaughter, I do not mind revolution, as long as we get what we wish to accomplish in the cause of right.' In fact, what Kelly had done was to explicitly condemn that proposition. Kelly visited Ireland himself in 1920. He had an interview with Lloyd George. When he returned, certainly he denounced violence, but he was also bluntly and very severely critical of English rule, on which he placed the responsibility for the violence that was occurring.

Kelly's belief in non-involvement was not shared by other bishops. Archbishop Mannix's activities in 1920-1 illustrate this in a spectacular fashion. In March 1920 he paraded in Melbourne's St Patrick's Day procession with fourteen Catholic Victoria Cross winners as a guard of honour—a manoeuvre that stunned his critics into a brief silence and was savoured by his friends. In May 1920 he left to visit Ireland and Rome, on what was to prove a sensational trip. First came a triumphal progress across the United States of America, with a series of wildly enthusiastic Irish meetings, culminating in his appearance in New York with the President of the Irish Republic, Eamon De Valera. Then in July Mannix left for Ireland. His ship was intercepted by British destroyers off the Irish coast and Mannix was presented with a prohibition, under the British Defence of the Realm Act, against landing in Ireland, or visiting Liverpool, Manchester or Glasgow, all cities with large Irish populations. The Archbishop refused to leave the ship until an officer placed a hand on his shoulder, which he took as arrest. He was transferred to a destroyer and landed in England. 'Since the Jutland battle,' jibed Mannix, 'the British navy has not scored a success comparable to the capture of the Archbishop of Melbourne without the loss of a single British sailor.' There was uproar in Australia. Dr Spence, Archbishop of Adelaide, who was visiting Ireland, summed up the popular Catholic reaction. Dr Mannix was

the greatest democratic prelate and greatest democrat in the world today. The treatment of Dr Mannix by the Government was an insult of the greatest magnitude, the first time since the Penal days that any minion of law had put his hand upon a bishop, and told him that he was practically a prisoner.

Archbishop Mannix did not return to Australia until August 1921. The St Patrick's Day procession of that year illustrates the situation in Melbourne during his absence. The City Council insisted that a Union Jack be carried at the head of the procession. After the procession ended, Bishop Phelan of Sale was reported as having told the assemblage: 'He was proud of the fact that no Irishman could be got to carry the Union Jack. No Irish Australian would carry it either. (Applause) When they got a man to carry it they had to pay him 15/- for the service. (Laughter and applause).' It was payment well earned, for when the flag was unfurled, two men rushed upon the bearer, one striking him and the other attempting to seize the flag, before police intervened. Thereafter, as it was born along, it was hissed and hooted. 'The Union Jack stood for unparalleled crimes in Ireland', said Bishop Phelan. Two months later, at the Sydney Orange Lodge demonstration, Sir Thomas Henly, M.L.A., declared: 'The foundation of disloyalty today was in the Roman Catholic Church. It was too late to fight disloyalty in Ireland, but it must be fought here.'

In 1922 the Melbourne City Council prohibited the holding of a St Patrick's Day procession, a decision which was ignored by the procession's organisers and later held invalid in law. This was the last major occasion on which the Irish issue, in any spectacular form, came to the forefront of Catholic affairs. The reason was simple—events in Ireland itself swiftly killed Irish-Australian enthusiasm for the Irish cause. For after the establishment of the Irish Free State in December 1921 had led to a bitter civil war between Free Staters and Republicans, which dribbled on in the sabotage of the Irish Republican Army, even after the war ended in 1923, the question was—what was the Irish cause? The civil war which ravaged Ireland in 1922 and 1923 dismayed and baffled Irish-Australian opinion. In January 1922 Archbishop Clune of Perth asked an Irish friend: 'Don't you get practically all you would have as a Republic?' 'The bickerings and recriminations' which followed the Anglo-Irish Treaty 'made us sick', the Archbishop reported. By November 1922 Bishop O'Farrell, of Bathurst, was writing to Ireland:

> You can form no idea of the depression and humiliation in the sentiments of the Irish-Australians at the state of things in Ireland. If tomorrow there was complete peace in Ireland she will start her role as a nation under the severe handicap of loss of that sentiment & sympathy she had in Australia anyhow. I don't think anything will restore that.

The attitudes of the hierarchy mirrored the reactions of the laity. With one exception—Mannix, and he with reservations—they opted out of the Irish civil war issue. Nearly all of them were, personally, against the Republicans. A few tried to speak well of both sides: Bishop Carroll of Lismore said that 'both sides are animated by high ideals'. Only one, Mannix, was prepared to support the Republican case.

Envoys from the Irish Republican forces visited Australia early in 1923. Mannix welcomed them, but not so his clergy. In Sydney about ten priests gave them support. By the time they reached Brisbane, their reception had so embittered them that they attacked the Australian bishops as a body, particularly Duhig. In Australia, Irish republicanism was blamed for the civil war, which was inexplicable, repugnant and embarrassing to those who believed that the title Irish Free State described the actuality. 'No one wants to speak of the Irish question out here', reported Bishop O'Farrell. 'When will sanity and humour return!' asked Bishop Barry of Tasmania, in 1924.

Archbishop Mannix remained firm, a committed Republican of De Valera's stamp. He visited Ireland again in 1925. He was critical of the Free State government, and his reception was not generally enthusiastic. He had turned his ire against partition, the division of Ireland into North and South.

By 1927 disillusionment in Australia had reached even those who had been most committed. Maurice O'Reilly wrote in February: 'As to poor old Ireland and how she stands, like most Irishmen abroad, I can hardly pretend to be interested. Possible, I had idealised too much and have thus made more painful than needs be the inevitable disillusion.' The dream had tarnished, vanished. 'I am completely disillusioned,' wrote Bishop Barry in August 1927. 'This is not the Ireland of my youth and my dreams.' So passed an era: Barry was pronouncing a belated epitaph. Irish realities had destroyed the grand dreams of her sons, at home and abroad. Those abroad had little choice now but to be about their own, if adopted, business.

What of politics? The conscription split allowed Catholics, as individuals, greater scope within the Labor Party, but much more important in determining the character of the party in the years immediately following 1916 were left-wing and also entrenched party machine influences. Labor's 1921 Socialisation Objective, however acceptable it may have been to individual Catholics, was not the outcome of any Catholic policy; the Labor Party remained impervious to such policies, however prominent in its ranks Catholics might be.

If no party would accept Catholic policies, the solution was simple—a separate Catholic party. This idea had been floating about for some time. The fact that proportional representation was to operate at the 1920 New South Wales election seemed to make it a practical possibility. This new electoral machinery offered, on the basis of Catholics being 25 per cent of the population, the chance to return to Parliament a number of Catholics committed to Catholic policies. It was conceivable that such a group might secure a balance of power, and thus be able to extort its demands.

The move towards a Catholic party came from within the Catholic Federation, in which Catholics with sensitive consciences were prominent—sensitive in particular to the development of strong left-wing currents in the labour movement, especially after the 1917 Russian Revolution: P. S. Cleary, the Federation's President, was well known for his anti-socialist pamphleteering. But this was not any Labor splinter group; it was a movement among Catholics outside the Labor Party, and close to Archbishop Kelly.

The Federation did not want a Catholic party, but an Australian party. 'Catholic' had a sectional ring, whereas the Federation believed that what it sought would bring general social good. The first name proposed was the Social Unity Party. Its constitution had a labour bias well beyond that of the usual balance of Catholic social principles. But the idea of such a party was opposed by some Federation branches, and by many individual Catholics—those who were Labor supporters, and those who were wary of introducing religion into politics. However, the key Federationists, and Kelly, thought they should proceed, at least as an experiment. The core of their reasoning is set out in the relevant resolution of the Catholic Federation:

> That for the future Catholics be run for the State Parliament, as a separate and independent body, because (a) public opinion will thereby be educated more effectually and more quickly; (b) it will be the best way of dissipating the bigotry now directed against us; (c) it will finally result in Catholic ideals and claims having direct representation in the country's Legislatures.

So, in October 1919 the Catholic Federation in New South Wales gave birth to the Democratic Party, with a platform reflecting the Federation's objectives, especially state aid.

The Democratic Party went to the 1920 New South Wales elections with the enthusiastic support of both Catholic newspapers and the Catholic Federation. The party demonstrated its political naivete and inexperience. It had insufficient funds, and unknown candidates who either did not understand their platform, or disagreed about its interpretation or application. Above all, the fate of the Democratic Party clearly demonstrated the apathy of Catholics. The party stood candidates in nine electorates, in which there were about 115,000 Catholic voters. These candidates secured a total of about 16,000; that is, one in every six or seven Catholics voted Democratic. The rest voted Labor, and Labor was returned with more than half its members Catholics. There were five Catholics in the new Labor cabinet. The *Freeman's Journal* observed: 'Although Catholics are not asking favours or looking for miracles, they expect a complete change in the official attitude of Labor towards our Catholic Schools and our Catholic Charities.' Neither miracles, nor favours, nor change of any kind, were forthcoming, and the journal was left to bemoan the supineness of Catholic politicians, who preferred, in politics, to ignore their religious affiliations.

One thing the Democratic Party did achieve, and that precisely the opposite of its intentions: it provoked a spectacular eruption of Protestant bigotry, and gave rise to organised Protestant political activity on an unparalleled scale. The appearance of a Catholic party was construed as a dangerous threat to Protestant interests, and throughout Australia Protestant organisations sprang up with the aim not merely of preventing the election of Catholic governments, but of ensuring the election of Protestant governments. The first and most effective of these organisations was the New South Wales Protestant Federation, formed in 1919. This Federation, and its imitators in other states, sought to influence politics by backing Protestant candidates in existing parties.

Such was the situation, when, in July 1920, the usual stock-in-trade of anti-Catholic organisations (disloyalty, Ireland, Mannix, popish plots) received an enormous and long-continuing gratuity in the Sister Ligouri case. In that month, Sister Mary Ligouri, a young nun of the Presentation Order, ran away from a convent in Wagga Wagga in her night attire, seeking shelter nearby with what proved to be a militantly Protestant family: they promptly informed the Protestant Federation and Orange Lodge in Sydney. Sister Ligouri appears to have been emotionally distraught, under illusions of persecution, and ignorant of the normal machinery available to persons wishing to leave the religious life. Unaware of her whereabouts (the Protestant family did not disclose her presence), Bishop Dwyer of Wagga Wagga asked the police to locate her. They did, and the Wagga government medical officer (a Catholic) said, after examination, that she was of unsound mind. Sister Ligouri spent five days at the Reception House, and was then declared sane. Thereupon, she sued Bishop Dwyer for £5,000 damages, alleging wrongful and malicious arrest; the Orange Lodge meeting her legal expenses.

A year passed before the case was heard, a year in which the Ligouri case, inflated with scurrilities and embellished with malignant rumour and invention, divided the community in a way similar to that of the O'Haran case twenty years before. And, as in the O'Haran case, the Ligouri case hearing, in July 1921, did little good to anyone involved. Protesants believed that the Ligouri affair testified to the iniquities of convent life; Catholics believed that they were being persecuted. The *Sydney Morning Herald* reported that the scenes outside the court, the size of the crowd, its temper, the frequent scuffles, 'were perhaps unprecedented in the history of the law courts of this State'; and this was a reflection of a public interest and feeling which were general throughout Australia: tempers ran no less hot in Melbourne or Brisbane. Inside the court, the prosecution interrogated the Mother Superior of the convent on the prevalence of insanity, of nuns escaping, mortifications and so on. Bishop Dwyer faced allegations of disloyalty, his remarks in criticism of English rule in Ireland being quoted against him. As in the O'Haran case, the prosecution sought to try not the specific case, but the Catholic church. The verdict for Bishop Dwyer was received by a sea of people outside the court with an uproar of cheers and hisses which were echoed around Australia.

Nor was the affair yet dead. Three months later, Sister Ligouri, now Miss Bridget Partridge, was kidnapped and bundled into a car after a violent affray, in which, as was later revealed, both Protestant and Catholic parties were armed with revolvers. Rumours circulated that the abduction had been engineered, and carried out, by priests. In fact it had been the work of Miss Partridge's brother and some friends, who had sought to persuade her to leave the home of the Congregationist minister with whom she was staying, and return to some Catholic environment. She refused.

Thus it was that, drawing on such sources of contention, politics and public affairs between 1920 and 1922 reached a pitch of sectarian bitterness perhaps never excelled. Protestant bodies petitioned the Federal government to refuse

Archbishop Mannix re-entry into Australia. The Anglican Archbishop of Perth said that the Pope was the bitter foe of England. The Protestant Federation slogan for the 1922 New South Wales elections was 'Who shall rule Australia— the people or the priests?'

The answer the electorate gave was, neither: in the New South Wales elections of March 1922 Protestants of a militant kind gained control of the government. Their programme was obvious from the questions the Protestant Federation sent to candidates during the campaign: no aid whatever to any kind of denominational institutions, rigid government inspection of such institutions (including, for example, convents), the freeing of the public service from 'sectarian influence' (that is, a purge of Catholics), and legislation making the promulgation of the *Ne Temere* decree illegal. It was no consolation to Catholics that the 1922 elections also saw the election of one Democratic Party candidate, Dr Cyril J. Fallon, for Eastern Suburbs: this indicated strong personal, rather than party, support.

The key figures in the National government which took office in 1922 were, in addition to the Premier, Sir George Fuller, prominent members of the Protestant Federation. J. T. Ness, M.L.A., was its President. The Minister of Justice, T. J. Ley, was an active member. From the first the sectarian atmosphere was tense. Rumours of all kinds circulated freely. A member produced in the House some books used in Catholic schools. In one was a picture showing St Patrick and St Bridget offering Australia to the Virgin Mary. 'What right have they to offer Australia to the Virgin Mary?' he asked. 'What is wrong with King George?' A Bill to impose rating on school playgrounds was rejected by the Upper House in December 1924. Archbishop Kelly did nothing to placate militant Protestant feeling. 'The other schools,' he said in October 1923, 'did not attempt to make the children obedient and law abiding. The other schools were making Australia a pagan nation. They allowed the marriage tie to be broken up and the family scattered.'

The government took its first—and last—major step against the Catholic position in 1924. It brought forward legislation to amend the Marriage Act so as to prohibit the promulgation of the church's *Ne Temere* decree. This papal decree, which had come into force in 1908, had angered militant Protestants ever since. Its effect was this: Before the decree, mixed marriages (between a Catholic and a non-Catholic), even those before a civil registrar, were accepted by the church as valid (though sternly condemned and prohibited); that is, the parties were truly man and wife, before God and the church. Now, with the decree, they were not. The decree set out that no marriage, between Catholics themselves, or between a Catholic and a non-Catholic, was real and valid before God and church unless it was contracted in the presence of a Catholic pastor. According to the Protestant Federation, this defied the power of the state, which recognised such civil and Protestant marriages as fully valid, and it also allowed priests to insult and harass parties to such marriages. The legislation was designed to forbid such reflections and interference by priests, and to assert the overriding power of the state in the sphere of marriage legislation.

In the face of the government's intentions, Archbishop Kelly stated that: 'if the State becomes a persecuting State and interferes with our religion and sacraments, then we say "We obey God before man".' Retorted J. T. Ness: 'if the priests intend to obey Church laws and defy State made laws, then we will extend the gaols of N.S.W. to accommodate them.' Said Kelly: 'Let the priests go to prison, rather than go contrary to the marriage laws of the Catholic Church. This law [*Ne Temere*] will stand against public opinion, Government, or anything else.' And the Archbishop made explicit his personal determination to suffer imprisonment rather than submit to the state on the *Ne Temere* issue.

The New South Wales Legislative Assembly passed the government's legislation in October 1924, but the Upper House rejected it by twenty-nine votes to twenty-seven, liberals siding with Catholics in the division. Sectarian feeling was already so intense that there was little room for worsening. The Protestant Federation demanded that the government make new appointments to the Legislative Council, and flood it with Protestants. But some Protestant opinion, notably Anglican, sided with Catholics against the government, on the ground that the laws of God, as inter-

preted by His church, must be upheld against the laws of
the state.

Determined to have its way, the government called
parliament together in March 1925 for a session whose
only business was the legislation to prohibit *Ne Temere*.
This time the legislation was amended by the Upper House
in such a way as to destroy its intention and power. Faced
with this, the government saw its best course in the pretence
that it had achieved what it wanted. It was not to have
further opportunities. The Nationalist government was defeated in 1925. (So was Dr Fallon.) By this time, the
Catholic Federation, and the Democratic Party, had faded
away.

'It is all over now,' said Archbishop Kelly in March 1925.
'Let us go ahead building our schools, and with the marriage
laws of our Church.' It was indeed all over, a period of
fifteen years crammed with dramatic incidents and passionate
emotion. No community could live for long with such
intensity. Thereafter, for thirty years, until 1954, peace
reigned, in the main the peace of exhaustion.

6

Problems of Identity and Politics 1925-1967

In 1838 Ullathorne had predicted that Australia would become an Irish mission. By this he meant that Irish priests would dominate the Australian ministry. Numerically, his prediction was true until the 1930s, when the number of Irish-born priests began to drop below half the Australian total. But what of the character of the Australian church? In that the clergy was one element; there were also the religious brothers and nuns, and the laity.

Cardinal Moran's arrival in 1884 may be taken as marking the achievement of an Irish dominance, to the degree of virtual monopoly, of the priesthood and church policy in Australia. Yet, even at this time, the other elements of the church exhibited no such Irish-born monopoly. For many years, the religious orders of brothers and nuns—the Marist Brothers is a good example—had been recruiting Australian-born members. The Sisters of St Joseph was an order entirely Australian, with nearly a thousand members by the time of Mother Mary's death in 1909. And the laity? When Moran came, about one-third of Catholics were Irish born. By 1901 the Irish-born represented about 5 per cent of Australia's total population of 3.7 million; that is, the general situation was that four in every five Catholics had been born in Australia.

By the time of the First World War, this situation of an Irish clergy ruling an Australian laity was coming under serious challenge—but not from the laity itself. Lay passivity had a number of related causes, aside from the important one of mere apathy. Occupying, predominantly, a low economic and social status in the community, Catholics were preoccupied with improving their position in the world. This preoccupation left little room for attention to the church's internal affairs, particularly as the construction of the education system was such a vast undertaking as to blot out almost all else. Moreover, such was the nature of the Catholic lay community that it had not yet produced any educated, intellectual section which might have pondered and questioned matters within the church. Then, of course, the cultural formation given in Catholic schools had been strongly Irish, as was the flavour of the clerical establishment. And a Catholicism which occupied a position of inferiority in the community, and was frequently under attack, was not likely to engage in much self-questioning.

Only among the clergy was there the education, inclination and opportunity to evaluate the church's internal affairs. Obviously, the church itself, in both ministry and teaching, has absorbed much of the intellectual ability and cultural energy of Australian Catholicism. It was Australian-born priests who questioned Irish clerical dominance.

Cardinal Moran had established St Patrick's College, Manly, in order to foster the growth of an Australian clergy. The College opened in 1889, and by 1914 it had produced 160 priests, out of an Australian total of about 800, the rest being nearly all Irish. Moran had given St Patrick's, his brain-child, strong support, and so did Archbishop Kelly. In 1913 Kelly proposed that the College be made a national seminary, receiving students not only from the Sydney diocese, but from all over Australia.

Kelly's proposal encountered strong opposition from most of the other bishops, on two major grounds: their wish to retain a predominantly Irish clergy, and their unwillingness to allow Sydney territorial possession of the national seminary. The reaction of Bishop Shiel, of Rockhampton, in letters to Ireland in 1914-5, reveals the temper of a majority of the bishops.

Manly . . . has been formed into a National College under the management of the Bishops of Australia and we are supposed to give it all the help we can. Very few of the Bishops, I think notwithstanding, will be anxious to cut off their supply from the Irish Colleges.

There are three or four young fellows who are just starting in Sydney—I am reluctant to increase the local product but what can I do?

This reluctance among bishops to 'increase the local product' was no secret, and was resented, not unnaturally, by the local product themselves, that is, priests who had studied at Manly. Few of these held responsible positions; only Monsignor Terence McGuire, Vicar-General of Lismore diocese, represented their numbers at any senior level of the governance of the church, and that was of little comparative importance.

However, at St Patrick's Silver Jubilee in 1914 a group of priests who were products of the College formed the Manly Union, under Monsignor McGuire's presidency. The Union's general objectives were to stress the Australian character of the church, and its need for an Australian priesthood (and hierarchy); specifically it wanted the College made national in its functions, and developed into 'the Great National Ecclesiastical University of the Commonwealth'. The Union also decided to publish an annual magazine, *Manly*.

Monsignor McGuire was an outspoken President. He told the hierarchy and clergy present at the Jubilee celebrations that, in the new Australian priesthood he envisaged, Irish, English and Scots blood would mingle, uniting 'a love of purity, a love of country, a love of God', characteristic of the Irish, with 'the strength and justice of the English, the strength and prudence of the Scotch'.

> Say not that the Irish priests have served Australia in the past, and can serve her in the future . . . You have first right in your own country . . . Does anyone sneer or smile when I appeal to Australian tradition? . . . The mission of the Church in Australia is no longer to save the Irish exile, but to convert the Australian race. In the first, the Church relied principally on the Irish priest. In the second, she must rely principally on the Australian priest.

This was not at all pleasing to many of the Irish clergy. The Manly Union was soon defending itself against the charge that it was fostering division and faction among the priesthood in Australia, that it was rampantly, disloyally and irreligiously anti-Irish. There was already ample suggestion abroad, in clerical circles, that Australians lacked this or that quality essential to the priesthood. Thus, the usual tension between old and new clerical generations was exacerbated by a growing Australian-Irish hostility. But, initially, there could be little more than tension and hostility: Irish control of the hierarchy, and of all higher levels of clerical authority, was absolute. The first Manly graduate to become a bishop was Matthew Brodie, in 1916—but his bishopric was the New Zealand diocese of Christchurch. The Australian laity showed no interest in the issue.

The policy adopted by the majority of the bishops was a very simple one—do nothing. The proposals for the establishment of a national seminary at Manly languished, and the project atrophied simply because bishops outside Sydney would not supply students, or at least not enough of them. Largely this was because they wished to maintain an Irish clergy, but this was not the only reason. Localism, and the pressure of other affairs, were important contributing factors. Despite Cardinal Moran's ideals and influence, regionalism remained strong within the Australian church. Bishops were kept apart from each other by busy lives and great distances. They tended to place their local problems and needs first, and these were always urgent and absorbing, particularly in regard to education.

Much has been made, and properly so, of the tremendous educational achievement of Australian Catholicism. To say that the education system was the church's only great achievement is patently false. The salvation of souls apart, the church's enormous network of services in charity, in the care of the sick, aged and handicapped, is a contribution to national life of such magnitude, yet so quietly efficient and so integrated into the general community as to be commonly overlooked. (This aspect of the church's life and work has a massive history in its own right, too vast and complex to be more than acknowledged here.) Nevertheless it is true that the education system was a unique feature of Australian Catholicism, and that its creation entailed demands which, inevitably, could be met only at the cost of ignoring, neglecting, or, usually, giving only perfunctory attention to other demands and problems. The cost of the education system was not merely financial. Among those matters which received little attention was national planning of church development as a whole. Such was the pressure of the educational situation that only urgent

XV Archbishop
Mannix in 1912

XVI Archbishop
Kelly speaking
at St John's
College 1939

XVII Archbishop Duhig of Brisbane, Archbishop Bernadini, the Apostolic Delegate, and Archbishop Mannix of Melbourne, at St Patrick's College, Manly, 8 April 1934

XVIII Cardinal Gilroy returns to St Mary's Cathedral as Cardinal Archbishop, 1946

problems could claim the bishops' attention. And the situation of the priesthood did not seem an urgent problem. A supply of capable, zealous priests was easily obtainable from Irish seminaries. These priests were, as Irishmen, personally congenial to the Irish-born hierarchy of Australia; they understood each other, their view of the church was the same. And they were much cheaper to obtain. A priest could be educated in Ireland at the cost of his board, lodging and training, but to build up a supply of Australian priests required an enormous and initially unproductive outlay in expensive buildings and teaching staff. While a ready supply from Ireland existed, and showed every sign of long continuing, why invest enormous energy, resources and money (urgently needed in other areas) in attempting to create a local supply?

The answer of those priests associated with the Manly Union was simple, clear and sharp: 'the more close the union between our Australian priests and our Australian people, the stronger will be the influence of that priest-hood . . . We look forward to an Australian priesthood educated in accordance with Australian ideals and Australian characteristics, the pride and safeguard of the nation.' In essence, the Australian argument against the Irish priesthood was identical with that used by the Irish against the Bene-dictines. Just as the Irish argued that a predominantly Irish laity needed a predominantly Irish priesthood, so Australian priests were now arguing that a predominantly Australian laity needed an Australian priesthood.

This was the basic, central argument used by Manly Union priests from 1914 to 1930—the year which may be taken as beginning the period of their success. However, they also proferred a wide range of associated arguments. These priests had a strong sense of missionary obligation towards Australia, and applied themselves to working out what its major religious problems were. Unanimously they concluded that the major single problem was irreligion and indifference. 'It must be acknowledged that Australia is largely a pagan country.' This being so, Australian Catholic-ism's main duty was to convert secularists, an emphasis reflected in *Manly* and also in the *Austral Light,* the official monthly magazine of the Melbourne Archdiocese, from 1900 to 1920.

This conclusion led those who held it into strong criticism of the Irish clerical outlook, which, they maintained, was blind to Australia's real religious problems. They were critical of seminary teaching which, they contended, stressed a discipline in conflict with Australian aspirations towards liberty and democracy. But the real Irish blindness was in confining clerical activity either to ministering to the converted, the Catholic community, or to attacking the traditional enemy, Protestantism. The Manly critics saw the Irish priests comfortably attending to a Catholic ghetto, with occasional forays to massacre Protestant straw men, while the real enemy—secularism—unhindered, laid Australia waste. Their argument again paralleled that which the Irish had used against the Benedictines—failure to meet the real needs of pastoral religion.

The Manly activists were also convinced that the close involvement of Australian Catholicism in Ireland's political cause was detrimental to the church's religious interests. This feeling became intense between 1919 and 1923. The reasoning behind it was as follows: Catholicism had become confused with Irish national feeling, and passions aroused by political affairs had extended to involve the religious. Catholicism ought not to have any national identification, and certainly not one alien to any land in which it existed. And it was alien in its present incidentals, the Manly priests thought. For the Australian priest, as for the majority of the Australian people, the Union Jack had never meant other than freedom and prosperity. Agreed, it had meant something very different for the Irish, but that was their business, not Australia's. The Manly priests contended that Irish priests were unfitted by their detestation of England to minister effectively to a people whose loyalties were broadly English, or, at least, who saw no direct reason to hate England. They also suggested that the Irish priests' concern with Irish problems was a distraction from their priestly duties, and took them away from what should be their first concern—Australia's religious problems. The positive side of all this was the argument that an Australian priesthood would heal the grave sectarian wounds inflicted since 1916, break down the prejudice the Irish had aroused from political, not religious, causes, and inaugurate a new era of harmony and conversion. An Australian priesthood, so it was said, could rely, in a way that the Irish priesthood could not, on the Australian characteristics of democracy and fair play.

By 1920-1 the Australian movement among the priesthood had acquired a sharp impatient edge: the local echoes of the Anglo-Irish war rapidly widened the breach between the Irish clergy in Australia and the Australian-born, who were thoroughly sick of Ireland and its politics. Monsignor McGuire's candour, always notable, came closer and closer to the bone. *Manly* openly avowed itself propagandist. And the focus of the Australian campaign became, more and more obviously, the hierarchy.

From the beginning of the Manly Union agitation, there had been a strong feeling that the hierarchy had a duty to encourage an Australian priesthood. Given that by the early 1920s there was no sign of hierarchical response, that Manly was still no nearer being a national seminary than it had been in 1914, and that Australian Catholicism's embroilment in Irish political affairs seemed to be getting worse, not better, the Manly feeling towards the hierarchy had grown acutely critical. There was a feeling abroad among the promoters of Australianism that the hierarchy were not merely doing nothing, but worse, were deliberately obstructing the Manly campaign in a determination to retain Irish ascendancy in the Australian church. There were suggestions (once again reminiscent of the Irish campaign against the Benedictines) that the Catholic faith in Australia was being endangered by an allegedly deliberate obstruction by the hierarchy of Australian vocations to the priesthood: this was tendered as at least part of the explanation of the paucity of Australian vocations.

That such extreme conclusions were not entirely irrational is suggested by the openly expressed conviction of many of the bishops that it was only Irishism that kept the Australian faith alive. As late as March 1924, Archbishop Mannix's words illustrate this exactly: 'The more deeply they [his Australian Catholic audience] breathed the Irish atmosphere the stronger and more vigorous would be the Australian faith. When an Irishman began to forget his country, or the country of his fathers, almost invariably his hold on religion also began to weaken.' And the strong and undisguised preference of some few bishops for Irish priests, to the exclusion of the Australian-born, cannot be said to have died completely until Bishop Norton of Bathurst died in 1963.

In 1922 an event occurred which brought the conflict into the open. Archbishop Kelly was seventy-two. In February it was announced that, as the *Daily Telegraph* put it: 'Contrary to the expectation of a large section of the Roman Catholic community, another Irish cleric has been appointed to one of the highest positions the Church has to offer in the Commonwealth.' This Irish cleric was Dr Michael Sheehan, Vice-President of Maynooth, a distinguished scholar well known for his work in classics and in the Gaelic language, and author of a standard text on *Apologetics and Catholic Doctrine*. The position that Dr Sheehan, then aged fifty-two, was to fill was that of coadjutor Archbishop of Sydney, with right of succession.

To the advocates of an Australian priesthood, this appointment direct from Ireland seemed both a frontal rebuff and a most serious reverse. It suggested that the hierarchy had not been moved in any way by the arguments they had presented, and it opened the prospect of at least another twenty years of Irish episcopal rule in the major, primatial, Australian see. What was to be done? Up to this time the Australian priesthood agitation had taken place largely, though not entirely, within clerical confines. Now, in March 1922, Father J. M. Cusack, one of the Manly group, made the issue public.

Father Cusack had already attracted the unfavourable attention of Sydney's ecclesiastical authorities for his outspoken views on the Australian *v.* Irish priests issue in 1919. Even then Archbishop Kelly's advisors were perturbed by the spirit of unrest prevalent among the clergy. They discussed its causes: Was it modernism? Should it be recognised by having an Australian representative on the Bishops' Council? But nothing was done. Upon Dr Sheehan's appointment in 1922, Father Cusack wrote to the Catholic press—significantly, the Melbourne Catholic press—in appreciation of the new Archbishop's fine qualities, but expressing regret that the principle 'Australia for the Australians' had been ignored, and that the widespread hope if not for the selection of a native-born successor to the primatial see, at least for a priest with long experience in Australia, had not reached fruition. Father Cusack promptly found himself transferred to a country parish remote from Sydney, but the clerical agitation was now public knowledge. As time was to prove, Archbishop Kelly, by virtue of sheer longevity, was to defeat not only Father Cusack and the Manly Union, but also Archbishop Sheehan. He did not die until March 1940, aged ninety. By that time Sheehan had been gone nearly three years. A man of retiring, scholarly disposition, who shunned the public eye, he had resigned the coadjutorship in July 1937, to return to Ireland. His resignation led to the appointment of another coadjutor, Archbishop Norman Thomas Gilroy.

Father Cusack's public comment in 1922, representing as it did a discontent of growing proportions among Australian-born priests, was not the only factor pressing the hierarchy to reconsider its position. The Manly Union group were strong supporters of the Australian Catholic Federation, as something Australian, and the Catholic Federation had an Australian priesthood among its objectives. This was of minor importance. Of much greater significance was the fact that the Manly priests looked for their strongest support to Rome, represented in Australia by the Apostolic Delegation, which had been established in April 1914, and was situated in Sydney.

The first Apostolic Delegate, Archbishop Cerretti, arrived in February 1915. The following year the Delegate delighted the assemblage at the Manly College prize-giving by remarking: 'Australia for the Australians', and by saying that he was sure Australian-born bishops would soon come. This was in line with the evolution of Roman policy on a native-born clergy, clarified in 1919 in a papal encyclical: 'the native Priest, inasmuch as he is one with his countrymen in birth, in character, in feelings, in interests, has a peculiar power of introducing the faith into their minds.' Such Roman ammunition contributed much heavy reinforcement to the Manly campaign.

Though they reflected official Vatican policy, Archbishop
Cerretti's remarks also had another context—the Delegation's general policy of building up for itself an ambassadorial
prestige and initiative in which it would not necessarily
be identified with the local hierarchy, but rather occupy
a position of friendly, involved independence. The introduction of a papal representative raised, at least potentially,
delicate problems of relationship between that representative
and the local hierarchy. Delegate and hierarchy need not
always see eye to eye—what then? When a new delegate,
Archbishop Cattaneo, was appointed at the end of 1917,
the Rector of the Irish College in Rome warned Archbishop
Kelly that the delegate was coming with ideas critical of
the existing situation in Australia: 'he has swallowed some
ideas given him by some bouncing Australian students at
Propaganda'; to wit: 'he thinks of the Irish as a secondary
race there [in Australia]', and he—the Delegate—believed
that the bishops should more actively foster an Australian
clergy. But, in fact, the conflicts latent in this difference of
opinion, and in others, were largely avoided. Certainly the
impingement of differing ideas and jurisdictions led to
tensions of various kinds in the years that followed, over
such matters as the smallness of collections for the Propagation of the Faith, and in general over the Delegation's
occasional inclinations to intervene decisively in Australian
affairs; Archbishop Mannix, in particular, was a point of
firm resistance to such tendencies. Nevertheless relations
were, in general, very harmonious.

However, it seems likely that the Delegation's exposition
of Vatican policy was one of the factors which led the
Australian hierarchy to refer to Rome, in 1923, the question
of whether or not St Patrick's College, Manly, should be
made a national seminary. This was a question which
raised implicitly the whole matter of the encouragement
or otherwise of an Australian-born priesthood. The Roman
answer was against a national seminary, but directed that
provincial and diocesan seminaries should be established
forthwith to build up an Australian-born clergy. The principle of a native clergy had been firmly asserted, but the
bishops' localism had been recognised too.

Archbishop Mannix responded immediately, acquiring a

property at Werribee which was opened as Corpus Christi College in March 1923. Other dioceses were much slower; Queensland opened the Pius XII Seminary at Banyo in 1941; then South Australia and Western Australia in the following year.

With the Roman decision, and with both Manly and Werribee producing priests, a change in the nature of the hierarchy was inevitable. Up to 1930 there had been four Australian-born bishops, W. B. Kelly of Geraldton, J. H. Norton of Port Augusta, P. Dwyer of Maitland, and J. Dwyer of Wagga Wagga. All these men had, however, received their final training as priests in Ireland. The Dwyers, for instance, had begun their training at St Charles's Seminary at Bathurst, and then gone on to Clonliffe College in Ireland. The change did not come until 1930, when Monsignor Terence McGuire was made Bishop of Townsville and Father James O'Collins was made Bishop of Geraldton. It would have been hard to find dioceses more remote from the centres of church affairs. Nevertheless, the Irish monopoly of the hierarchy had been broken. Bishops McGuire and O'Collins were the first products of Manly to become bishops in Australia—though, and this was to become typical, Bishop O'Collins had pursued the last four years of his clerical studies in Rome. As Monsignor McGuire had been in the vanguard of the Manly Union agitation, his appointment was regarded as marking a great and significant victory in the campaign.

Other appointments of Australian-born bishops followed smoothly. In 1931 Patrick Farrelly was made coadjutor Bishop of Lismore, and Thomas Fox, Bishop of Broken Hill. In 1932 Romuald Hayes was made Bishop of Rockhampton. Again, these were appointments to minor dioceses, as was that of Norman Thomas Gilroy to the diocese of Port Augusta in 1934. But in February 1937 Manly had its first Archbishop, Justin Simonds, who was appointed to Hobart. As the first Australian-born Archbishop, he received, under the terms of Archbishop Polding's will, Polding's episcopal ring. (He became coadjutor to Dr Mannix in 1942.) This was closely followed, in July 1937, by the appointment of Bishop Gilroy to the coadjutorship of Sydney. By this time, Archbishop Kelly had virtually retired, living mostly at the Archbishop's residence at Manly, his great triumph having been the International Eucharistic Congress in Sydney in 1928. With Archbishop Gilroy's succession to Sydney in March 1940, Australianism had effectively arrived. The long archepiscopates of Drs Mannix and Duhig, ending in the 1960s, were the protraction of an earlier phase. The Irish rearguard action had been stiff, and prolonged. Even in 1939 a senior Irish priest in Australia was writing home: 'Rome has spoken—native clergy is the cry—so we must submit.'

Archbishop Gilroy was in every sense an Australian Catholic of his generation. Born in a Sydney working-class suburb in 1896, he had been educated in the Catholic school system. He had joined the Public Service—the Post Office—and he had been, as a young telegraph operator on a troopship, present at Gallipoli. He had entered St Columba's College, Springwood, in 1917, went to Propaganda College in Rome in 1919, was ordained in 1923, and returned to Australia to be one of the secretaries to the Apostolic Delegation until 1930. This strong Roman background was to become typical: the current situation is one in which about two-thirds of the Australian hierarchy have received part of their clerical education in Propaganda College. In 1931 Dr Gilroy became secretary to the Bishop of Lismore, and in December 1934 he was made Bishop of Port Augusta; then followed the coadjutorship of Sydney in 1937. He was made Archbishop in 1940, and, in 1946, he was created Cardinal.

But this is to take the Manly movement ahead, to its logical conclusion. To return to the 1920s and 1930s. The pro-Australian movement among the clergy was vigorous and assertive enough, but culturally and intellectually it tended to be—with a few exceptions—both shallow and narrow. Its major literary figure was Father P. J. Hartigan ('John O'Brien') whose verse collection, *Around the Boree Log,* was published in 1921, and achieved immediate popularity. Its historian was Dr Eris O'Brien whose pioneering works on the early days of Australian Catholicism began appearing in 1922. As to the working out of the practical application of Catholic principles to Australian life, the Manly movement had sufficient vigour to revive, in 1924, the *Australasian Catholic Record*. Cardinal Moran had founded this quarterly in 1895, but it had lapsed in 1913 for want of support. The revived *Record* published much that was pointedly Australian, serious-minded and of immediate or enduring worth. But the problem was that interest and creative productivity were confined to a very few priests. A writer in *Manly,* in 1923, asked: 'Are the clergy unintellectual?' His answer was 'yes', and he claimed that most of the clergy would agree with him. He blamed seminary training. This explanation is too simple: a practical church facing practical problems demanded practical priests. But his estimate was valid. Most clergy were simply not interested in intellectual affairs.

The comparative absence between 1925 and, say, 1954 of any spectacular collisions between Catholicism and the rest of the community gives to this period a deceptive air of tranquil progress in the affairs of the church. On the surface all seemed well. However, some observers believed that this tranquillity masked stagnation.

In 1933 Father Cusack was again outspoken, this time in suggesting that the gravest danger to Australian Catholicism was its crowded churches. He contended that the vigour of what church life there was distracted attention from what was really a situation of serious decline. Although Father Cusack did not quote them, national statistics supported his conclusion. In 1901 Catholics comprised 22.6 per cent of the Australian population; in 1910, 19.4 per cent; in 1935, 17.5 per cent. Actual numbers of Catholics had of course increased, but the vision of a Catholic Australia was growing more dim, not brighter.

The decline may be explained partly in terms of the non-Catholic complexion of immigration in the 1920s, but there was much more to it than that. The assertion that the church was losing headway in Australia had been central to the Manly Union case. By the mid-1920s, and throughout the 1930s, leakage from the church was a subject of major concern among them. Who were falling away? Intellectuals particularly, also workers, to whom communism appealed, and also Catholics in remote areas—as Bishop Killian of Port Augusta reported with alarm in 1925. Why was there this leakage? Naturally the Manly answer was a predominantly clerical one: because Catholic priests were not going into the world to convert it, because the Australian church was neglecting its duty to pursue its universal role.

Father Cusack's argument was based on personal experience of parish life. When, as a newly ordained priest, he had begun parish work in the city of Sydney in 1911, the number of careless Catholics he found was far beyond his gravest thoughts: three in five Catholics in his parish attended Mass. He found a country parish worse. And in 1933, in suburban Eastwood, out of 1,150 Catholics about half did not attend Mass. He had conducted a survey among his clerical colleagues which indicated that in Sydney diocese, in 1933, just over half the Catholic population attended Mass in any way regularly. In terms of a Catholic's religious obligations under pain of serious sin, Father Cusack's figures revealed a disturbing situation. However, their comparison with present attendance rates (60-70 per cent) casts a less glaring light on the 1920s and 1930s; there is ample scope at any time to point out the great discrepancy that may exist between Catholic principles and the behaviour of a substantial proportion of Catholics.

Nor was Father Cusack's allegation that the church was not going into the world factually correct. In 1925 a meeting of bishops was held at Wagga Wagga to discuss the urgent need for a fund to maintain and propagate the faith among Catholics in isolated districts, among immigrants, among Aborigines. The stumbling block was money. The tightening of the Australian economy in the mid-1920s seriously constricted the work of the church. By 1925 Sydney archdiocese was finding, for virtually the first time, that it could not implement plans, such as that to build a residence for the coadjutor, because collections were bringing in only half of what had been expected. Missions in particular suffered. Of importance was the 1925 decision of the meeting of bishops to encourage the Holy Name Society as a national organisation. This Society, originally prompted by the Council of Lyons in 1274, and a special mission of the Dominican Order, had its Australian foundation in Adelaide in 1921, where it was introduced by the Irish Dominican, Father W. V. McEvoy, O.P. Its aim was to foster religious devotion and practice among men by reverence for the Name of Christ, by control of speech, and by regular and corporate attendance at the sacraments. Following the 1925 decision of the bishops, the Holy Name Society rapidly became a feature of parish life throughout the whole country. Its aspirations were basically pastoral and sacramental rather than directly doctrinal and social, but it was a powerful factor in fostering parish unity, and in bringing about a closer relationship of understanding between priests and Catholic men.

Further facts which told against Father Cusack's contention were the beginnings of lay action, with the establishment (by Frank Sheed) in 1925 of a Catholic Evidence Guild, which, on the English model, undertook public platform expositions of Catholicism; and also, from 1928, the beginning of Catholic radio broadcasting. The Sydney radio station 2SM (the initials standing for St Mary's) was founded in 1931. Its most popular programme was a Question Box conducted by Dr Leslie Rumble, M.S.C., a feature now nearly forty years old. In the days before television, this programme was enormously successful, being flooded with queries, and holding a wide audience.

Meanwhile, in the 1920s and 1930s, the broad river of professional politics flowed on, bearing many Catholics, but none swimming against the prevailing currents. The Manly Australianism had been non-political or, more exactly, cynical about politics. In large part this was a reaction against the intense political interests of the Irish, a swing towards a strong emphasis on pastoral problems. It was also a reflection of the fate of, and public response to, Catholic political activity. In the 1930s the prevalent Manly attitude was summed up in such comments as: 'Bitter tirades won't alter the political situation, and it certainly will affect the prospects of the church most disastrously', and: 'None of the collections of twaddle which make up the platforms of the different parties in Australia are built on a Christian philosophy, and we can only do our best to support whatever is good in any of them.' This reaction is explicable also in terms of the political situation at that time. As the Depression deepened, economic problems dwarfed the political. Between the wars, little occurred to disturb the remarkably stable alliance between Catholics and the Labor

Party—indeed the economic pressures were such as to strengthen the alliance. The Labor government, led by the Catholic James Scullin, 1929-31, did as much for Catholic policies as the non-Labor government led by the Catholic Joseph Lyons, 1931-9—that is, nothing. For most Catholics, as Catholics, politics was just not an issue. They voted according to their economic status—that is, mostly Labor.

However, the Australianism evident among the clergy after the formation of the Manly Union had also appeared among the laity in a small way in the 1920s, but in the 1930s it was becoming a vigorous, growing movement. By the early 1920s Catholic university students throughout Australia had firmly launched their own organisations. Dr Mannix's encouragement was one factor which made this movement particularly strong in Melbourne, but it was vigorous elsewhere too, for instance in Perth, under Monsignor J. T. McMahon's guidance. Suspicion among the hierarchy of university Catholics was strongest in Sydney. One cause was the strongly secularist tone of Sydney University; another was the name which university students chose for their organisations—Newman Societies—first formed in Melbourne in 1910. Some Irish priests looked askance at this, as another instance of anti-Irishism, for Cardinal Newman, as an English intellectual, was not among their heroes. In 1915 Archbishop Kelly received anxious letters from the Irish College in Rome suggesting that Moran Societies would be a much more appropriate name for such university organisations.

An English orientation is apparent also in the name of a society formed in Melbourne in 1931 by a group of Melbourne Catholic university students and graduates, led by the lawyer F. K. Maher: the Campion Society was named after the English Jesuit martyr of the sixteenth century. And this society, founded for the purpose of providing Catholic adult education, also drew heavily on English Catholic social thought, especially that of Hilaire Belloc and G. K. Chesterton. In this, the Campion Society had forerunners in the group which published the monthly review *Australia* between 1917 and 1920.

The birth of Newman Societies and the Campion movement pointed to the changing socio-economic composition of the Catholic community: the movement of a growing number of Catholics into the universities, the professions and educated intellectual life generally. However—and a social survey of Melbourne suburbs, published in 1967, shows this still to be true—Catholics, in their occupations and place of living, remained towards the bottom of the socio-economic scale. The Campion Society, which spread from Melbourne to other states in the early 1930s, was directed towards this situation; its roots and concern were in and with the working classes. Its intellectual setting was the response of the church overseas to social problems and economic depression.

Central to this response was Pope Pius XI's encyclical *Quadragesimo Anno,* on the reconstruction and perfection of the social order, published in pamphlet form in Australia in July 1931. There had already been some Australian hierarchical comment on related subjects. In 1930 Archbishop Sheehan published his views on the relationship between socialism and labour, in which he maintained: 'Marxism is simply not on the horizon of practical politics in this country.' Reassessing his position in 1932, he was less sure. Although the Labor Party programme was so far not opposed to Catholic social principle, he believed the possibility existed that it might become so, particularly as the Party seemed unable to shake off communists.

However, the keynote of the new movement that was developing around the Campion societies was, at this stage, not so much anti-communist as anti-capitalist. A remark made by Archbishop Mannix in 1931 expresses this outlook precisely: 'The greatest force in spreading Communism at the present time is the failure of Capitalism.' Mannix made no secret of his feelings about capitalism, nor of his opinion that the continuance of his programme of church and school building, by providing employment, was an assistance to the economy. The bishops of New South Wales, in their Joint Pastoral of May 1931, took a less pointed stand, condemning not capitalism, but its evils, and proffering destitute Catholics condolence in recalling that 'for half a century you have been subjected to a callous financial persecution by the secular State'.

In 1934, in Melbourne at the National Eucharistic

Congress, there was a conference of people, mostly students and graduates, associated with the Newman and Campion movements. Dr Mannix made clear to this meeting his openness to any scheme it might devise to promote a Christian social order:

> His Holiness the Pope himself has been sending a clarion call to the whole world, not directed to the Bishops and priests, but to the laity . . . You are the leaders of the people . . . any ideas that you may initiate to make things better than they are at present will receive a cordial welcome, and will be assured of the utmost consideration. And I can assure you that I shall leave nothing undone to give effect to any feasible proposal.

This was more than hierarchical tolerance. It was a clear invitation, to which the conference responded by deciding to consolidate the movement it represented, on the basis of 'Catholic Action'.

Catholic Action was the name given by Pope Pius XI to his campaign, given form and organisation in the planning of the Abbé Cardijn, to deal with the problems of the church in the modern world. Generally, it amounted to the organisational involvement of the laity in the apostolic work of the church, under the guidance of the bishops, particularly in those areas of life with which the clergy had lost contact: 'the great scandal of our time is that the Church has lost the working class', said the Pope to the Abbé Cardijn in 1925. How would it regain that class? As the Pope put it in *Quadragesimo Anno*: 'Undoubtedly the first and immediate apostles of the workingmen must themselves be workingmen.' The laity were to be involved in the apostolic work of the church in an intimate, direct way.

Excepting Archbishop Mannix, the Australian hierarchy's understanding of Catholic Action in 1934 reveals little of the special social emphasis given to it by the Pope. At the 1934 Eucharistic Congress, Bishop Barry of Goulburn spoke on Catholic Action for men. His understanding of it was very broad—the organisation of Catholic football clubs, sewing for the poor, taking up collections for the church or Catholic schools—but the particular emphasis he gave his address was spiritual and devotional. The extension of the Holy Name Society was what Bishop Barry pleaded for as Catholic Action.

This spiritual understanding of Catholic Action is even more evident in Archbishop Kelly's Pastoral of August 1934 on Catholic Action in the Archdiocese of Sydney:

> We may acquit ourselves of the duty of 'Catholic Action' by practices of Catholic devotion under the special invocation of the Queen of all Saints . . . First we must pray; secondly, parents must instruct their children in the fear and love of God, in prayer and in obedience; thirdly, the Clergy and the Teacher must assist in Church and in School; fourthly, social organisations approved by the Church, are to be formed for both the young and adults; fifthly, good reading matter is to be provided and the contrary precluded; sixthly, piety is to be fostered in every home, and family prayer regularly kept up; seventhly, the churches are to be adorned . . .

When, in 1925, the Abbé Cardijn had secured, with difficulty, an audience with the Pope, Pius XI had asked, 'What do you want?' Cardijn replied, 'Most Holy Father, I want to kill myself in order to save the working class.' 'At last!' the Pope exclaimed. 'At last someone has come to talk to me about saving the rank and file.' It was in keeping with this spirit, and in line with this social emphasis, that the Melbourne movement of university students and workers developed in the 1930s, opening contacts with Europe and America, particularly under the influence of Hilaire Belloc's thinking, but always conscious of both the Australian situation and the world Catholic context.

This movement found its focus and expression in the publication, from January 1936, of the monthly *Catholic Worker*. Those who assembled to send out the first issue typified the composition of the movement: 'A couple of undergraduates, a brewery worker, a couple of teachers, two grocers, half-a-dozen factory hands, a Corpus Christi student . . . Packing completed, we said a decade of the Rosary for the success of the paper, and then drank its health.' They had £7 6s in the bank, and the first bill was for over £20. But the paper was an immediate success, reaching, by February 1941, a national circulation of 55,000. Its first editor was a law student, B. A. Santamaria.

What had been born in Melbourne in the 1930s was a new Catholic lay movement of dynamic enthusiasm, intellectual and with a deep, indeed passionate, social commitment. It was, to some extent, part of a general social movement; outside the church, other young intellectual idealists were being swept towards communism. The mission of the *Catholic Worker* was to help build 'a new Christian social order based on Catholic social teaching'. The major problems it saw were, in general, the development of the Servile State (Belloc's phrase to describe the State's trend towards totalitarian enslavement of individual minds and lives), in particular the decline of the family, depopulation, the destruction of rural life and a proper agricultural economy, the growth of oppressive capitalism, and communism. Its proposed remedy was the reorganisation of economic society so as to create a co-operative commonwealth, based on a wide distribution of property among all the people, through co-operative ownership, and shareholding, by workers. The possession of property was held to be the guarantee of democratic freedom—and in this, capitalism was no less an enemy than communism: neither system allowed workers the possession of property. But as capitalism prevailed in Australia, it was the major real enemy.

In 1937 the Fourth Plenary Council of the Archbishops and Bishops of Australia, probably prompted by Dr Mannix, approved the establishment of a National Secretariat of Catholic Action, with F. K. Maher and B. A. Santamaria to conduct it. A committee of bishops was appointed to advise and assist them. However, the initiative for this decision came from the leaders of the Campion movement, not from the hierarchy. If, formally, there was now organised collaboration between laity and hierarchy on Catholic Action, this was not particularly effective outside Melbourne. Archbishop Kelly's Pastoral on Catholic Action in December 1937 showed that his conception of Catholic Action remained firmly anchored to individual and family piety: 'Pictures of Our Saviour, of His Crucifixion, of His Sacred Heart, together with representations of the Mother of God and of our Patron Saints, are to cheer and adorn every room.' And Archbishop Kelly left no room for lay initiative: 'Our Pastors will instruct and direct us according to the orders issued by our Holy Father . . .' By the late 1930s Dr P. J. Ryan, M.S.C., was becoming increasingly prominent in Sydney affairs with his promotion of a Christian solution to social problems, on lines similar to the Melbourne movement: he stepped this up, from 1943-4, into a vigorous anti-communist campaign. Some Manly priests became enthusiasts for the Catholic rural movement ('The City slays Life'). However, the lay ferment, so striking in Melbourne, had less vitality elsewhere.

Following its establishment, the National Secretariat of Catholic Action initiated a general social studies movement, and set up several Catholic Action organisations—the Young Christian Workers, the Young Christian Students' Movement, the National Catholic Girls' Movement, and the National Catholic Rural Movement. All these organisations promptly took root and flourished, particularly in Victoria.

Meanwhile, the Spanish Civil War was working a change in the Catholic social movement's attitude towards communism. In 1936 the *Catholic Worker* did not regard communism as a real enemy: 'Communism is *not* our great adversary. The exalted position of Public Enemy No. 1 is reserved for Capitalism . . . because today it dominates the world.' However, the Spanish situation brought a confrontation between Catholicism and communism. Australian Catholic opinion was largely pro-Franco. It interpreted the Spanish conflict in very simple anti-communist terms, just as it saw fascism generally (particularly Mussolini's variety) in very simple anti-communist terms. The world view of the Sydney *Catholic Press* in the 1930s stressed communism as the great menace to civilisation, and tended to ignore or excuse the less attractive characteristics of communism's fascist enemies. Not that there was anything unusual in this—it was an attitude shared by large and influential sections of non-Catholic opinion—but, particularly when the Spanish Civil War crystallised the issues, it drew down on the church the wrath of communists, who accused Catholicism of pro-fascist commitment. The Spanish war and local Catholic-communist confrontation awoke the *Catholic Worker* group to a concern about the power of communism overseas. It was a short step to concern about communist activities in Australia. By 1940 B. A. Santamaria was discussing with Archbishop Mannix communist ambitions to take over the Australian Labor Party. The Archbishop promised support and financial help to foil such ambitions.

By this time, the ties between the Catholic Action Secretariat and the Australian hierarchy had become much closer and more effective. One expression of this harmonious co-operation was the institution, in 1940, of an annual Social Justice Sunday with a related episcopal statement. These Social Justice Statements, some of them written by Mr Santamaria himself, continued, in another form, the Catholic tradition of searching criticism of existing Australian society. The 1943 statement, *Pattern for Peace,* was presented to the Federal government as a programme of social reconstruction, stressing decentralisation, self-government of industry, development of agriculture and rural life, and the building up of population. That these statements had a real audience is indicated by the circulation of the 1948 statement on *Socialisation*—nearly a quarter of a million. That they did not deal in comfortable platitudes was consistently apparent, as in 1951: 'The great issue which faces the Australian people today is whether Australia will survive as a nation of European origin and of Christian culture beyond what in the view of history would be but a few years.'

However, even in presenting the *Pattern for Peace* in 1943, the hierarchy and Catholic Action leaders were conscious that any such plan of social reconstruction was threatened by the growth of communist infiltration in the trade union movement. The Communist Party, after a brief period of being an illegal organisation in 1940-1, had embarked on a successful policy of introducing its members and sympathisers into controlling positions in unions. In 1945, to combat this, Mr Santamaria asked the bishops of Australia for moral and financial support, which they gave at their meeting in Sydney in September. A Catholic Social Study Movement—from which the term 'The Movement' derives—was formed as a loose national alliance of Catholic actionists, particularly unionists, with the object of fighting communism in the union movement. It sought for tactical reasons to avoid publicity, a policy which later gave rise to charges of conspiratorial secrecy.

The thinking behind The Movement is clearly expressed in the 1947 Social Justice statement, *Peace in Industry*:

> The imminent danger facing this country is that the Communist party will use the power which it has gained over a large part of the trade union movement to overthrow the machinery of Government, to seize political power for itself, and to achieve the ends of Communism—the destruction of political, social and religious freedom.

The Labor Party itself was aware of the communist danger, and in New South Wales in 1945, and Victoria in 1946, 'Industrial Groups' were set up to win back control of the trade union movement from the communists. Catholics, particularly those of The Movement, became prominent, indeed dominant, in these groups.

The industrial warfare of 1945-9, between communist-controlled unions and the government, was paralleled within the union movement by a struggle for control between communists and industrial groupers. By 1954 the groupers had achieved remarkable success in winning control of unions from communists. And because the Australian Labor Party reflected the nature of the industrial movement, groupers were becoming numerous and prominent within ALP counsels also.

On 5 October 1954 Dr H. V. Evatt, parliamentary leader of the Federal Labor Party, publicly charged a group of Labor Party members in Victoria with being 'disloyal to the Labour movement and to Labour leadership'. 'It seems certain,' he declared, 'that the activities of this small group are largely directed from outside the Labour movement.' It was obvious, and it rapidly became explicit, that Dr Evatt's references were to the industrial groups, to the Catholic Action movement within the labour movement, to Mr Santamaria and to Archbishop Mannix. His charges amounted to the claim that the Catholic church, its bishops and laity, were plotting to take over control of the ALP, and ultimately the Australian government, using the industrial groups as a cover for secret infiltration of Catholic Action elements into the party.

Dr Evatt's denunciation detonated a series of sectarian and political explosions of a most damaging and destructive kind. Much of the history of these events lies outside the scope of this book: treatment here is restricted to their relationship to Catholic affairs. Briefly, what occurred between 1954 and 1957 was a period of confusion, expulsions and splits within the ALP. Groupers, and supporters of The Movement, were ejected from the ALP, or left it, at the cost of disruption of the labour movement, the downfall of several state Labor governments, and the continued exclusion of the ALP from Federal power; it has not held office since. Those whom the ALP had purged formed splinter anti-communist Labor Parties which eventually consolidated into the Democratic Labor Party. This party, distinguishing itself from the ALP mainly on its vigorous anti-communist focus, could not command sufficient support to secure representation of its own in parliamentary lower houses, but it has had sufficient to keep the Federal ALP out of office, and to elect a small group of Federal Senators who have held, from time to time, the balance of power in that parliamentary chamber.

That such far-reaching repercussions should flow from Dr Evatt's remarks in 1954 requires some explanatory comment: again the confining of treatment here to the Catholic element within a much wider political situation must be stressed.

By 1954 its success through the activity of industrial groups had brought about a change of temper and outlook within The Movement. It had started out with the simple intention of destroying communism within the unions. Involvement in this task naturally made it sensitive to all signs of leftward inclinations, and it gradually came to look askance at the attitudes it discerned in the existing ALP leadership. In 1947-8 there had been the attempt by the Labor Prime Minister, Ben Chifley, to nationalise the banks; in 1951 the Liberal government's efforts to secure by referendum the banning of the Communist Party failed, with Dr Evatt vigorously prominent, and allied with communists, in the anti-banning campaign; and then, in 1954, Dr Evatt's role in the Royal Commission which investigated Vladimir Petrov's allegations about Russian espionage in Australia, furnished his critics with further evidence of left-wing sympathies. Furthermore, there had developed within The

Movement by this time, notably since the communist seizure of power in China in 1949, a growing preoccupation with the external as well as the internal threat of communism to Australia. Movement members became more and more concerned about Australia's foreign and defence policies —and increasingly dissatisfied with those of the ALP, which seemed to them dangerously soft towards communism.

By the time of Dr Evatt's denunciation, The Movement was convinced that both he and ALP policies were gravely inadequate to meet the menace of communism. Coming just before the ALP elected a leader, Dr Evatt's charges invite interpretation as a device to destroy, by the use of sectarianism, his strongest critics, who wished to eject him; he was free with denunciations of 'clerical fascism' and the like. Nevertheless, the facts were that The Movement was defeated, and Dr Evatt re-elected, in a context which still retained a strong Catholic flavour.

The Catholic social militants, The Movement members, were only one section, the younger section, of Catholic ALP membership and support. Since the 1920s about half of the Labor Party's Federal and state parliamentary strength had been Catholic. Over half the Scullin cabinet of 1929 were Catholics. In 1951 forty-five of the eighty-one members of Federal Labor caucus were Catholics. The New South Wales Premier, J. T. Lang, expressed the attitude of many of these Catholic politicians when he remarked: 'I refuse to accept the idea that a politician's Church was entitled to come between him and his duty to the people.'

As in all their social relations, Catholics' attitudes to public affairs and political activity have been divided between the desire for independence and the wish to conform. But because of Catholicism's origins in social and economic inferiority, the wish to conform strongly predominated. From the penal beginnings, and especially after the flood of free immigration began in the 1850s, the Irish Catholic 'lower orders' set out to succeed in the society they had joined, to secure money and rank, public and social recognition. Many of them did succeed, sometimes at the cost of maintaining that their Catholicism was an individual foible, not a social obligation. In terms strictly of faith, the casualty rate was low. Because of the respectability

security and comparative protection from bigotry which they offered, certain areas of the Public Service became the earliest focal point for the ambitions of poorer Catholics, a trend which became evident in the later years of the nineteenth century. The new Labor Party of the 1890s filled a similar role, opening, for the first time, an avenue by which Catholic workers could aspire to the power and prestige of politics.

In politics, Catholics workers were outsiders, in that they were workers, and in that they were Catholics. As workers they had found something in common with other workers—the labour movement: they tended to stress what was in common and minimise what was different—their Catholicism. Most of those who entered politics had little education, and were unaware of any impingement of their religion on public affairs—or if they were they sought to minimise it in view of the hostility assertion would provoke. They had, in the main, neither the intellectual equipment nor the disposition to search for and consider whatever Catholic principles might apply to their political position. The alignment between Catholics and Labor Party was natural on both a human and a socio-economic level. Clearly, advantageous practical gains seemed more important than complex disputable principles, and in any case Catholics were prisoners of the political situation: the non-Labor parties were much more hostile to them than Labor. So, in a sense, on a practical level, all the possible reflection, all the theoretical niceties, were irrelevant. Thus, the Catholic tradition in the Labor Party had become, by the 1920s, firmly unreflective, and non-theoretical; what mattered was not the party objective (socialisation after 1921), nor the ideals of individual members (say, Dr Evatt), but the Party's immediate programme of practical policies and its basic Australian common sense.

To Catholic Labor politicians and their supporters, of this traditional frame of mind, The Movement's charges that the ALP was soft on communism seemed absurd, basically unreal and obsessive. As to The Movement's positive programme of implementing Catholic social principles, the Catholic Labor traditionalists regarded this as dangerous fanaticism, the advocacy of impractical formulae alien to

the *ad hoc* temper of Australian politics. Indeed, if anything was potentially revolutionary, the traditionalists believed, it was The Movement's policies, which envisaged a radical reconstruction of Australian economic life, an endeavour which offended their gradualism and their sense of practical politics. And, of course, the traditionalists, old in the ways of machine politics, regarded The Movement as a direct threat to their personal positions and power.

The idealists and enthusiasts of The Movement found the traditional Catholic Labor men contemptible, and made no secret of this opinion, to the further alienation of those they criticised. The Movement's view was that Catholics in the labour movement were obliged to avow and act on Catholic social principles. If they did not—perhaps even if they differed from The Movement's interpretation of such principles—their integrity and motivation were placed in question. Clearly, for a range of reasons, Catholic opinion on the Labor Party was so deeply divided as to permit little chance of avoiding a bitter breach.

In that breach, the prominence of Mr Santamaria requires some comment. Born in 1915 of Italian migrant parents, Mr Santamaria studied Law at the University of Melbourne, and was admitted to the Victorian bar in 1937. He, and the group of people associated with him, represented two new phenomena in Australian Catholic lay life — non-Irishism, and dedicated social enthusiasm—and they became allied with the foremost living divisive personality, Archbishop Mannix.

Mr Santamaria's non-Irishism was not anti-Irishism. He and the group he led were merely different, and had qualities of enthusiasm, subtlety and intellectuality not particularly notable in lay life previously. Many in The Movement had European rather than Irish origins; those with Irish origins thought in Australian terms.

But most important in distinguishing Mr Santamaria and his followers from the traditional laity was their enthusiasm. Enthusiasm, as a socio-religious phenomenon, has attracted a great deal of study, for example, by Ronald Knox in *Enthusiasm*, and in the classic work of Ernest Troeltsch, *The Social Teaching of the Christian Churches*. Using the term 'sect' in the sociological sense of, for example, Troeltsch,

what Mr Santamaria and The Movement formed was a sect—
that is, a group of dedicated men who were determined to put
a Catholic social programme into political action: they were
setting out to reform the existing social order according to
a doctrine, or set of principles. Little wonder that they
found themselves at war with that existing social order.
For, those who were identified with, or comfortable within,
or tolerably reconciled to that existing social order were
profoundly irritated by those who sought to disturb or
destroy that order, and create a new world of perfection.
What The Movement believed was a constructive effort to
better society seemed to its opponents a destructive attempt
to destroy what had already been built, in the interests of
a fanatical crusade to achieve some ridiculous utopia.

It is significant that most contemporary sociological efforts
to describe typical relationships between religion and society
start from a basic distinction between 'church' and 'sect'
tendencies within Christianity. The 'church' represents the
conservative tendency which becomes, or seeks to become,
an integral part of the existing social order. It accepts, or
makes the best of, the world as it is. The 'sect' expresses
the revolutionary tendency which rejects the world as corrupt, it having departed too far from the teachings of Christ.
The 'sect' seeks to rebuild society on the basis of the un-
diluted, uncompromising Christian formula; it attempts to
make Christian principles actual in everyday life.

Some members of The Movement went so far in their
repudiation of the existing, corrupt world, and the modern
city (Babylon, they called it), as to follow Ray Triado into
the bush wilderness of the Australian Alps. There they
attempted—and failed—to set up a primitive agricultural
community of a kind so glowingly depicted in much of
The Movement's propaganda. In a pamphlet published in
1947, *Australian Dream,* by D. G. M. Jackson, there is
set out in very considerable detail—down to wayside cruci-
fixes, sane liquor laws, and Angelus bells—an imaginative
picture of what Australia might be if it was reconstructed
according to Catholic social policy. Dream or nightmare,
it is a vision of complete transformation, transfiguration. If
The Movement is interpreted in such terms of sect—a party
of idealists dedicated to transforming the world according to

their principles—the deeply divisive effect it had on Catholicism is readily understandable; the bitter clash between church and sect is as old as Christianity itself.

Mr Santamaria's personal obtrusion as a storm centre is explicable in terms of his remarkable qualities of leadership. He was the key figure, the basic decision maker, with astonishing tactical ability and tireless energy. Nevertheless his prominence was to some extent a product of the anonymity of The Movement and its avoidance of publicity. When public attention focused on this hitherto unknown force, Mr Santamaria came to personify a movement which could not otherwise be readily identified by the popular mind.

Important, too, was The Movement's close relations with Dr Mannix. The Archbishop had been a controversial figure since his arrival in Australia. He epitomised an older aggressive Catholicism which had generated a hostile reaction among non-Catholics—and also from some Catholics. The alliance between The Movement and Dr Mannix thus tapped old wellsprings of distrust and dislike: to many of an older generation, here was Mannix on the march again. While still an undergraduate, Mr Santamaria began an association and friendship with Archbishop Mannix which lasted until the Archbishop's death. Though their temperaments were different, as were their cultural backgrounds, they were two men of the same socio-religious mould; both were prepared, in terms of their understanding of Catholicism, to challenge and confront the world.

And so it was that The Movement, Mr Santamaria and Dr Mannix aroused, on one side, dedicated loyalty, devotion, hero-worship, and on the other, anger and detestation, enmity.

What did all this add up to, in its effects on the Catholic community? The long-standing Catholic political commitment to the Labor Party had been challenged from within Labor itself, and was now shattered. What remained was still a very substantial Catholic commitment, but the alignment as such was sundered: a large and vigorous minority of Catholic opinion repudiated Labor and turned to other political outlets, mainly the Democratic Labor Party.

When this rift occurred, it revealed that, at a fundamental level, it was overdue. The social and economic harmonies, which were the basis of the Catholic-Labor alignment initially, no longer existed in anything like the same degree. The first half of the twentieth century had brought great changes in Australia, and in the position of Australian Catholics. The Catholic population had ceased to be what it was before, a group at the bottom of the socio-economic ladder. Now they occupied all rungs on that ladder, if few in numbers at the top. They had become strong in those safe professions where status and reasonable income were virtually assured, such as medicine and law. For Australians as a whole, affluence, particularly after 1945, took them away from Labor, and this was particularly true of Catholics. Even without the vigorous precipitations of the years following 1954, it seems that Labor and an increasing section of the Catholic vote would have gradually parted company on the same grounds as they had come together, economic and social. However, the breach when it came was sudden and painful, creating chaos and confusion and great bitterness between Catholics of differing viewpoints and allegiances. Certainly it came with its meaning and consequences little pondered, and it alienated from Labor, on grounds of principle and conscience, many Catholics who were still at one with it on socio-economic grounds. It did much damage within the Catholic community, especially in the injection of venom, and the fostering of bitter divisions.

Nevertheless, the split with Labor, and internecine conflict within the church, was not without redeeming benefit. Lamentable and deeply wounding as civil wars are, they do raise and clarify fundamental matters at issue, and force participants to ponder questions of identity, meaning, and destiny. The split with Labor and the divisions among Catholics took place on the question of communist danger and influence. This was an ideological issue raised fair and square in a political world ideologically barren, and one which also focused attention on developments in Asia, which Australia needed to heed. More, the split, and the questions it raised, induced a vigorous and searching intellectual ferment among Catholics, and between Catholics and non-Catholics, on a wide variety of political, social and religious topics. Far from plunging Australia back into a new age of bigotry, the sectarian explosion begun in 1954 seems to have somewhat cleared the air.

Perhaps even more importantly, the end of the slavish attachment to Labor changed the status of the political activities and votes of Catholics from those of prisoners to those of desirable, sought-after supporters. The desertion of a sufficiently large proportion of the Catholic vote to support the continued existence of a third party, exclude Labor from office, and maintain a Liberal-Country Party government, has demonstrated that Catholic opinion is a vital political factor, not to be ignored as it was formerly. And the issue of most vital concern to Catholics is education. It is significant that Liberal governments—beneficiaries of the end of the old Catholic-Labor order—have made increasing grants available to Catholic schools; the decision of state governments late in 1967 to give direct aid to pupils in independent schools, a decision which conceded a principle of vital importance to Catholics, is in this context.

To return to the events which followed Dr Evatt's denunciation of The Movement: The bishops' Joint Pastoral of 1955 commended in glowing terms the anti-communist work of the industrial groups in trade unions. But in the years immediately following, a sharp and passionate division of Catholic opinion at all levels, hierarchical, clerical and lay, became evident. The division had a rough geographical form, between opinions dominant in Sydney and New South Wales on the one hand, and those dominant in Melbourne and Victoria on the other. The Sydney view amounted to the belief that a severance between Catholics and the ALP would be a bad thing: Catholicism would be best served by retaining the alignment, and avoiding all the damaging furore of a withdrawal. Their opinion was that The Movement's estimate of the reality of the communist danger was gravely exaggerated, panic-mongering. In any case, the way to fight communism was not to abandon the ALP to its left wing, but to stay in the party and retain whatever influence in it Catholics already had. The Sydney opinion was that the DLP, with its strong Catholic complexion, verged on being a church party, representing a stupid and deleterious isolation of the Catholic body from the rest of the Australian community. The Melbourne view was that the ALP was past redemption, that it had gone so far towards communism that to remain in it was to abandon Catholic principle, and that its foreign policy was such as to be a menace to Australia as a whole. No Catholic could, in conscience, remain associated with it. The ALP must therefore be opposed from outside, until it came to its senses. As to the DLP, this was not Catholic in any confessional sense. It was not seeking minority concessions, or even fighting for religious principles so much as championing the common good—firm anti-communism for Australia.

These conflicting arguments were reflected in a division within the hierarchy, in which leading members of the hierarchy in Victoria, Tasmania and Western Australia, led by Dr Mannix, favoured the policy represented by the DLP, whereas leading members of the hierarchy in New South Wales, South Australia and Queensland took an opposing view. These differences, and the whole pattern of developments since 1954, raised the question of the nature and aims of Catholic Action in Australia; they raised the general question of the relation between religion and politics, and the particular question of the nature of The Movement—was it an independent lay movement, or was it Catholic Action in the strict sense, that is, under full episcopal control?

In 1957 these questions were submitted to Rome. The decision given was, essentially, a compromise, with elements to satisfy both views. The Movement was to confine itself to the spiritual and moral formation of the laity, under the authority of the bishops. Rome stated that a confessional political party was not desirable in Australia. At the same time it was made clear that the laity was not only free to act, but obliged to do so, in the trade union and political fields, in order to promote Catholic social principles and combat communism. As a result of this decision, The Movement groups were reconstructed for strictly adult education purposes, within each diocese, and subject to the local bishop. And in December 1957 the leaders of The Movement created a purely civic organisation, the National

Civic Council, to continue the work that they had been doing.

This Roman decision clarified the situation, and reduced friction, in that each bishop could, to a considerable extent, determine the form the lay apostolate took in his own diocese. It did not terminate the division of opinion. In the middle of 1960 the two views of the political situation clashed publicly in statements from Auxiliary Bishop Fox and Archbishop Mannix in Melbourne, and Dr Rumble, a church spokesman in Sydney, over the question of whether or not Catholics could, in good conscience, vote for the ALP. Melbourne said no, Sydney said yes.

Such a fundamental and deeply felt split in Catholic opinion could not but leave a legacy of acrimony, which still exists, though greatly tempered and now not in the forefront of Catholic affairs. The heat of the issue diminished with the death, in November 1963, of Archbishop Mannix, whose outspoken intransigence, and support for Mr Santamaria, were central features in the protracted controversy. He was succeeded by Archbishop Simonds, who did not share Dr Mannix's enthusiasm for The Movement. Illness prevented Archbishop Simonds from pursuing any vigorous policy; he died in 1967.

While the spectacular dispute over The Movement was proceeding, the composition of the Catholic community was rapidly changing. The post-war assisted immigration scheme which brought two-and-a-half million migrants to Australia brought an enormous addition—about half this total—to the ranks of Catholicism, mainly from southern Europe. In 1933 the proportion of Catholics in Australia was 17.5 per cent. In 1947 it was 20.7 per cent. At present it is about 26 per cent. This migrant influx, while greatly diversifying the Catholic body, brought enormous problems —those of including Catholics of other cultural traditions, languages and habits within the existing Catholic structure. The impact of the migrants was felt mainly at the basic levels of the provision of adequate and appropriate pastoral ministry, where various forms of chaplaincy were sometimes used, and the provision of Catholic education. So it is that, with migrants and natural increase, there is a strong sense in which the Australian church is still a missionary one, still straining resources to meet the basic demands of the practice of the faith—a situation which continues and reinforces the traditional tendency for the practical virtues to take precedence over the reflective and intellectual.

However, with the changing nature of the Australian-born Catholic community, lay intellectual life has grown to be an element of considerable importance within the church. Up to the Second World War the contribution of Catholics to Australian intellectual and cultural life was substantially less than their numbers warranted. They had avoided the more hazardous areas of intellectual, artistic and creative activity. Even in the areas where they were present, the hostility of their environment fostered withdrawal; their habits were cautious and indrawn, their dispositions unimaginative, unadventurous. Only recently has a prosperous economy diminished the obsession with security and caution characteristic of a socially emergent Catholicism. The present generation is the first to be able to afford the luxury of intellectual jam with its religious bread and butter.

The beginnings of current lay intellectual life may be traced back to the 1950s. Again Melbourne led the way. In 1950 a Mannix scholarship was established to send Catholic university students overseas for further study. In 1955 the booklet *The Incarnation and the University* signalled a growing concern, which spread from the University of Melbourne, with Catholic intellectual formation. In 1958 the Newman movement in Sydney launched the annual review *Manna*. Melbourne already had, from the 1940s, the two Jesuit produced journals *Twentieth Century* and *Social Survey*, and was soon to found the lay review *Prospect*.

Lay intellectual life of a vital and widespread kind was a very new development in Australia, a departure from the dominant Catholic tradition. Its newness and general lack of contact with centres of Catholic learning brought problems. Some of the new Catholic intellectuals, finding themselves more in harmony with the secular tradition than what they knew of the Catholic, tended towards the pursuit of conformity, deference towards secular intellectual life and its institutions. This tendency sought to reduce Catholicism to its least self, an entity which whilst still surviving separately, yet merged most happily with its

secular environment. The most distinct facet of this conformist movement has been a philosophic ferment, strongly
critical of traditional and particularly Thomist modes of
thought, which were pillorised as arrogant, divisive and
stultifying. This has provoked a reaction, which has insisted
on conformity to traditional intellectual patterns. Such
insistence, while harsh and sterile in some narrow areas,
has been more generally firm, formative and undramatic,
rather than assertive: it has been strong in many religious
orders and societies, and derives in substantial part from
those educated in Rome's Angelicum University.

However, this intellectual ferment has very shallow roots;
there has been little real contact between intellectuals and
ordinary Catholics. The church in Australia has, at present,
two forms of lay leadership which have virtually separate
existences: the intellectuals, and those Catholics, prominent
in non-intellectual pursuits, who are loyal and energetic
workers in the day-to-day affairs of the church.

The problem which currently exercises most Catholics,
and that very deeply, is the problem of Catholic education.
Inundated by the post-war flood of children, understaffed,
beset by the accelerating expenses of expanding educational
requirements, the system has shown grave strain. The
response of the hierarchy has been, on the whole, an attempt
to maintain the system *in toto*; the means has been the
rationalising of the system to produce greater efficiency,
and diversion of almost the whole of church revenue into
educational funds. However, the character of the system
is changing rapidly. Until recently—the last five or ten
years—the system has been almost exclusively the preserve
of the religious, mainly brothers and nuns. Now, in some
dioceses, about half the teachers are lay persons. The
implications of such fundamental changes have been little
considered. The emergency demands of a crisis situation,
and the constant hope that it will be solved in the very
near future by increasing government aid, have produced
an education policy distinguished—at least until recently—
by its short term nature, its day-to-day expediency, its
ad hoc decisions, rather than by any consistent and thoughtful planning.

The context of these recent developments has been the

beginnings of what appears to be a vital new wave of unprecedented lay concern with, and participation in, the counsels of the church. The immediate effect of the Vatican Council of 1962-5 on the Australian Catholic scene was to turn the focus of interest and concern away from its previous absorption with politics and society towards a much greater emphasis on liturgy and theology—and ecumenism. The liturgical movement, spearheaded earlier by the Living Parish organisation, had a direct impact on the religious lives of all Australian Catholics, particularly through changes in the Mass. Theological discussion is within narrower confines, but vigorous nevertheless, although as yet largely derivative from European sources. Ecumenism has greatly improved relations with non-Catholic churches, and co-operation in common Christian tasks is increasingly prevalent.

But, most important of all, among the obvious effects of the Council (putting aside its paramount, reviving spiritual effects) has been a change in the internal structure of the church. The Council introduced into the church a new era of lay participation in policy and decision making; a new era in which, between clergy and laity, there was 'a diversity of ministry, but a oneness of mission'; in which 'the laity share in the priestly, prophetic and royal office of Christ'. Such has been the nature of clerical-lay relations in Australia, typified by the priest as authoritative leader, decision-maker and spokesman, the layman as silent follower, that the new era has opened not without signs of impatience and tension. Tempering and balancing this, there exists also within Australian Catholicism at all levels a new, more tolerant, more understanding though more questioning energy, indeed a new spirituality, derived at least in part from the Vatican Council. The form this new energy will take is still obscure. Catholics are still unsure of their identity, of who they are. They are Catholics. They are Australians. But the integration of these identities lies, it would seem, beyond the purview of the present.

A Note on Sources

Much of this book is based directly on archival material, but its extent and variety, the demands of space, and the absence of organisation and cataloguing in some of the archives consulted, make it impossible to do more than to indicate to scholars, in broad terms, the location, range and general nature of the primary documentation over which research has been conducted.

The archives, mainly correspondence, held by the following have been consulted, within the various limits of access laid down by the appropriate ecclesiastical authorities: (1) St Mary's Cathedral, Sydney. The basic collection for any study of the Catholic Church in Australia, vast in dimensions, and very wide in historical scope; (2) The Irish College, Rome, particularly the extensive Australian correspondence of Cardinal Cullen and Monsignor Kirby, 1838-1895, in all approximately 1,200 letters; (3) All Hallows College, Dublin. The Australian correspondence, 1844-, amounts to about 800 letters; (4) Dublin Archdiocese. Australian correspondence from the 1840s to the 1860s was studied, but the archive is currently closed after that period, to permit classification; (5) Archives of the Primate of Ireland, Armagh. Correspondence from Cardinal Moran to Cardinal Logue, 1880s to 1890s; (6) Some minor items are in St Patrick's College, Maynooth, and the Diocese of Limerick.

The files of the following newspapers were consulted: *Catholic Press* and *Freeman's Journal* (Sydney); *Advocate* and *Tribune* (Melbourne). Extensive use was made of newspaper clippings held by St Mary's Cathedral archives.

Reference was made to a wide range of Pastoral Letters and pamphlets, notably those held in St Mary's Cathedral archives, and at St Patrick's College, Manly.

The following theses and papers were consulted:
Brown, Robert J., 'The Catholic Federation of New South Wales 1912-1923. With particular reference to the Democratic Party 1919-1925'; Government III Thesis, University of Sydney, 1954.

Burns, Ian H., 'The Founding of the Hierarchy in Australia 1804-1854', A Dissertation presented for the Degree of Doctor of Canon Law to the Pontifical Scientific Missionary Institute of the Pontifical University of Propaganda Fide, Rome, 1954.

Lyons, M., 'Catholics and Conscription—A Study of Attitudes, N.S.W. 1916-1917', Arts IV Thesis in History, University of New South Wales 1966.

Malony, John N., 'The Australian Hierarchy and the Holy See 1840-1880', Paper presented to Section E History, ANZAAS Congress, Melbourne, 1967 (roneoed).

Marshall, M. B., 'Some Aspects of the Australian Protestant Defence Association 1901-1904', Government III Honours Thesis, University of Sydney, 1961.

'Some Aspects of the candidature of Cardinal Moran for the Federal Convention in March 1897, with particular reference to the attitudes of the Catholic and Protestant Presses to this issue', Government II Distinction Thesis, University of Sydney, 1960.

Payten, Margaret, 'William Augustine Duncan 1811-1885', M.A. Thesis, University of New South Wales, 1965.

Phillips, Patricia K., 'John McEncroe', M.A. Thesis, University of Sydney 1965.

Shanahan, Mary M., 'Henry Gregory and the Abbey-Diocese of Sydney 1835-1861', M.A. Thesis, University of Sydney, 1965.

Guide to Further Reading

GENERAL

Austin, A. G., *Australian Education, 1788-1900: Church, State and Public Education in Colonial Australia*, Sir Isaac Pitman & Sons, Melbourne, 1961.

Australian Dictionary of Biography, 2 vols, Melbourne University Press, 1967. (Contains brief biographies of leading personalities.)

Birt, H. N. (O.S.B.), *Benedictine Pioneers in Australia*, 2 vols, Herbert & Daniel, London, 1911. (A detailed account from the beginnings up to Archbishop Vaughan's death in 1883, from a Benedictine viewpoint.)

Byrne, Mons. F., *History of the Catholic Church in South Australia*, J. P. Hansen, Adelaide, 1914. (From the beginnings to 1872.)

Cleary, P. S., *Australia's Debt to the Irish Nation Builders*, Angus & Robertson, Sydney, 1933.

Cullen, Rev. J. H., *The Catholic Church in Tasmania*, Hobart, 1948.

Daniel-Rops, H., *History of the Church of Christ* (trans. from the French by John Warrington), especially:
Vol. 8: *The Church in an Age of Revolution, 1789-1870*, Dent, London, 1965;
Vol. 9: *A Fight for God, 1870-1939*, Dent, London, 1966. (Give the general European background.)

Fogarty, Brother Ronald, *Catholic Education in Australia, 1806-1950*, 2 vols, Melbourne University Press, 1959. (A comprehensive, detailed study.)

Hogan, J. F., *The Irish in Australia*, George Robertson & Co., Melbourne & Sydney, 1888.

Inglis, K. R., 'Catholic Historiography in Australia', *Historical Studies, Australia and New Zealand,* Vol. 8, No. 31, November 1958. (Critically discusses Catholic historical writing generally.)

Latourette, K. S., *Christianity in a Revolutionary Age,* Vol. 3: *The Nineteenth Century Outside Europe,* Eyre & Spottiswoode, London, 1961; Vol. 5: *The Twentieth Century Outside Europe,* Eyre & Spottiswoode, London, 1963.

Luscombe, T. R., *Builders and Crusaders,* Lansdowne Press, Melbourne, 1967. (Essays on some prominent figures in Australian Catholic history.)

Mac Caffrey, J., *History of the Catholic Church in the Nineteenth Century,* 2 vols, M. H. Gill & Son, Dublin, 1909. (Particularly useful for Irish background.)

McCarthy, P., 'The Foundations of Catholicism in Western Australia: 1829-1911', *University Studies in Western Australian History,* Vol. 2, No. 4, July 1956.

McMahon, Rev. John F., *One Hundred Years. Five Great Church Leaders,* Perth, 1946. (A biographical approach to Western Australian Catholic history, 1846-1946.)

Moran, Cardinal P. F., *History of the Catholic Church in Australasia,* Oceanic Publishing Co., Sydney, n.d. [1896]. (An enormous, detailed compilation from the beginnings to 1896.)

Murtagh, James G., *Australia: The Catholic Chapter,* Angus & Robertson, Sydney, 1959. (Emphasises the Church's relations with Australian society.)

New Catholic Encyclopedia, McGraw Hill, New York, 1966. (Australian historical articles, particularly by Father Murtagh.)

O'Farrell, P. J., 'The Writing of History', *Manna,* No. 3, 1960. (Comments on K. R. Inglis's article above.)

Reading of particular relevance to each chapter division is as follows:

CHAPTER 1   FOUNDATIONS 1788-1835

Clark, C. M. H., *A History of Australia*, Vol. 1: *From the Earliest Times to the Age of Macquarie*, Melbourne University Press, 1962.

Historical Records of Australia.

Journal of the Australian Catholic Historical Society. (Vol. 2, Part 2, 1967, contains a list of eighty-eight papers presented to the Society, and held at Sancta Sophia College.) Particularly:

    Duffy, Mons. C. J., '100 Years in Education', Vol. 2,
    ——Part 1, 1966. (ed.). 'Catholic Religious and Social Life in the Macquarie Era', Vol. 2, Part 1, 1966.

    ——'The Leaving of the Consecrated Host by Father Jeremiah O'Flynn', Vol. 2, Part 2, 1967.

    Eddy, Rev. John (S.J.), 'John Joseph Therry—Pioneer Priest', Vol. 1, Part 3, 1967.

    Scarlett, E. J. L., 'The Fitzpatrick Family 1810-1904', Vol. 2, Part 1, 1966.

    Waldersee, J., 'Father Daniel Power', Vol. 2, Part 2, 1967.

Kenny, J., *A History of the Commencement and Progress of Catholicity in Australia*, Sydney, 1886. (Up to 1840.)

O'Brien, Eris M., *The Dawn of Catholicism in Australia*, 2 vols, Angus & Robertson, Sydney, 1928.

——*The Foundation of Australia*, Angus & Robertson, Sydney, 1950.

——*The Foundation of Catholicism in Australia: Life and Letters of Archpriest John Joseph Therry*, Angus & Robertson, Sydney, 1922.

O'Hanlon, Sister M. Assumpta (O.P.), *Dominican Pioneers in New South Wales*, Australasian Publishing Co., Sydney, 1949.

Robson, L. L., *The Convict Settlers of Australia*, Melbourne University Press, 1965.

Shaw, A. G. L., *Convicts and the Colonies*, Faber and Faber, London, 1965.

CHAPTER 2   THE BENEDICTINE DREAM 1835-1865

Australian Catholic Record. (Contains a large number of historical articles on this period, for example Monsignor J. J. McGovern's series on Archbishop Polding, particularly in the New Series, from 1924.)

Barrett, John, *That Better Country: The Religious Aspect of Life in Eastern Australia, 1835-1850,* Melbourne University Press, 1966.

Cable, K. J., 'Protestant Problems in New South Wales in the Mid-Nineteenth Century', *Journal of Religious History,* Vol. 3, No. 2, December 1964.

Coughlan, Neil, 'The Coming of the Irish to Victoria', *Historical Studies, Australia and New Zealand,* Vol. 12, No. 45, October 1965.

Duffy, Sir Charles Gavan, *My Life in Two Hemispheres,* 2 vols, T. Fisher Unwin, London, 1898.

Gregory, J. S., 'Church and State, and Education in Victoria to 1872', *Melbourne Studies in Education, 1958-1959* (ed. Dr E. L. French), Melbourne University Press, 1960.

Grose, K., '1847: The Educational Compromise of the Lord Bishop of Australia', *Journal of Religious History,* Vol. 1, No. 4, December 1961.

Marks, S. R., 'Mission Policy in Western Australia, 1846-1959', *University Studies in Western Australian History,* Vol. 3, No. 4, 1960.

Roe, Michael, *Quest for Authority in Eastern Australia, 1835-1851,* Melbourne University Press/Australian National University Press, Melbourne, 1965.

Shanahan, Mother M., 'Bishop Davis: 1848-1854', *Manna,* No. 6, 1963.

Suttor, T. L., *Hierarchy and Democracy in Australia, 1788-1870,* Melbourne University Press, 1965.

Thorp, Rev. Osmund (C.P.), *First Catholic Mission to the Australian Aborigines,* Pellegrini & Co., Sydney, 1950.

Ullathorne, Archbishop, *From Cabin Boy to Archbishop: The Autobiography of Archbishop Ullathorne,* with an introduction by Shane Leslie, Burns & Oates, London, 1941.

Walker, R. B., 'The Abolition of State Aid to Religion in New South Wales', *Historical Studies, Australia and New Zealand,* Vol. 10, No. 38, May 1962.

CHAPTER 3   THE EDUCATION QUESTION 1865-1884

Dow, Gwyneth M., *George Higinbotham: Church and State,* Sir Isaac Pitman & Sons, Melbourne, 1964.

Martin, A. W., 'Henry Parkes: Man and Politician', *Melbourne Studies in Education, 1960-1961* (ed. Dr E. L. French), Melbourne University Press, 1962.

——'Faction Politics and the Education Question in New South Wales', *Melbourne Studies in Education, 1960-1961.*

O'Neill, Rev. G., *Life of the Reverend Julian Tenison Woods, 1832-1889,* Pelligrini, Sydney, 1929.

——*Life of Mother Mary of The Cross,* Pelligrini, Sydney, 1931.

Pledger, P. J., 'The Common School Boards, 1862-1872', *Melbourne Studies in Education, 1959-1960,* Melbourne University Press, 1961.

Thorp, Rev. Osmund (C.P.), *Mary McKillop,* Burns & Oates, London, 1957.

CHAPTER 4   THE REIGN OF CARDINAL MORAN 1884-1911

Bollen, J. D., 'The Temperance Movement and the Liberal Party in New South Wales Politics, 1900-1904', *Journal of Religious History,* Vol. 1, No. 3, June 1961.

Cahill, A. E., 'Cardinal Moran and the Chinese', *Manna,* No. 6, 1963.

——'Catholics and Politics in New South Wales', *Journal of Religious History,* Vol. 4, No. 1, June 1966.

——'Catholicism and Socialism: the 1905 Controversy in Australia', *Journal of Religious History,* Vol. 1, No. 2, December 1960.

Carr, Most Rev. Thomas Joseph, *Lectures and Replies,* Australian Catholic Truth Society, Melbourne, 1907.

Corish, Patrick J., 'Political Problems 1860-1878', in a *History of Irish Catholicism,* Vol. 5, Gill & Son, Dublin, 1967. General editor, Patrick J. Corish. (For Irish background.)

Ford, Patrick, *Cardinal Moran and the A.L.P.*, Melbourne University Press, 1966.

Hamilton, Celia, 'Irish Catholics of New South Wales and the Labor Party, 1890-1910', *Historical Studies, Australia and New Zealand*, Vol. 8, No. 31, November 1958.

Healy, Most Rev. John, *Papers and Addresses*, Catholic Truth Society of Ireland, Dublin, 1909.

Leslie, Shane, *Cardinal Gasquet*, Burns & Oates, London, 1953.

Mac Suibhne, Peador, *Cardinal Cullen and his Contemporaries*, 3 vols, Leinster Leader Ltd, Massachusetts, 1961, 1962, 1965.

McClelland, V. A., *Cardinal Manning: His Public Life and Influence, 1865-1892*, London, 1962.

McDonald, Walter, *Reminiscences of a Maynooth Professor*, Jonathan Cape, London, 1925. (Paperback edition, edited, with a Memoir by Denis Gwynn, Mercier Press, Cork, 1967.)

Mahon, Brother J. M., 'Cardinal Moran's Candidature', *Manna*, No. 6, 1963.

Mansfield, Bruce, *Australian Democrat: The Career of Edward William O'Sullivan, 1846-1910*, Sydney University Press, 1965.

Norman, E. R., *The Catholic Church and Ireland in the Age of Rebellion, 1859-1873*, Longmans Green, London, 1965.

O'Brien, Eris, 'Cardinal Moran's Part in Public Affairs', *Royal Australian Historical Society Journal and Proceedings*, Vol. 28, Part 1, 1942.

'O'Brien, John' (Rev. P. J. Hartigan), *On Darlinghurst Hill*, Ure Smith, Sydney, 1952.

O'Farrell, P. J., 'The History of the New South Wales Labour Movement, 1880-1910: A Religious Interpretation', *Journal of Religious History*, Vol. 2, No. 2, December 1962.

---'McCabe and Sectarianism', *Manna*, No. 6, 1963.

--- ' "Socialism", a 1905 Pamphlet', *Twentieth Century*, Vol. 16, No. 3, Autumn 1962.

Pearl, Cyril, *Wild Men of Sydney*, W. H. Allen, London, 1958.

Suttor, T. L., 'The Criticism of Religious Certitude in Australia, 1875-1900', *Journal of Religious History*, Vol. 1, No. 1, June 1960.

Walsh, P. J., *William J. Walsh*, Longmans Green, London, 1928.

CHAPTER 5 DR MANNIX 1911-1925

Brennan, Nial, *Dr Mannix*, Rigby Limited, Adelaide, 1964.

Brady, E. J., *Doctor Mannix*, Library of National Biography, Melbourne, 1934.

Duhig, Archbishop James, *Crowded Years*, Angus & Robertson, Sydney, 1947.

——*Occasional Addresses*, Angus & Robertson, Sydney, 1934.

Greening, W. A., 'The Mannix Thesis in Catholic Secondary Education in Victoria', *Melbourne Studies in Education 1961-1962*, Melbourne University Press, 1963.

Hamilton, Celia, 'Catholic Interests and the Labor Party: Organised Catholic Action in Victoria and New South Wales, 1910-1916', *Historical Studies, Australia and New Zealand*, Vol. 9, No. 33, November 1959.

Moran, Herbert M., *Viewless Winds*, Peter Davies, London, 1939.

Murphy, Frank, *Daniel Mannix*, Advocate Press, Melbourne, 1948.

Scott, Ernest, *Australia During the War*, Vol. 11, Official History of Australia in World War I, Angus & Robertson, Sydney, 1943.

CHAPTER 6 PROBLEMS OF IDENTITY AND POLITICS 1925-1967

Australasian Catholic Record, 1924-

Knopfelmacher, Frank, *Intellectuals and Politics*, Thomas Nelson, Melbourne, 1968.

Mayer, Henry (ed.), *Catholics and Free Society*, F. W. Cheshire, Melbourne, 1961.

Manly, 1916-42. (This periodical contains articles of value, especially for the 1920s.)

O'Farrell, P. J., 'The Australian Labour Split', *Landfall*, Vol. 12, No. 2, June 1958.

——'The Church in Australia', *Dublin Review,* Summer 1966.

Santamaria, B. A., *The Price of Freedom,* Campion Press, Melbourne, 1965.

Truman, Tom, *Catholic Action and Politics,* revised and enlarged edition, Georgian House, Melbourne, 1960.

Webb, Leicester, 'Churches and the Australian Community', *Melbourne Studies in Education, 1958-1959,* Melbourne University Press, 1960.

Index

289